Medical Law and Ethics

Medical Law and Ethics

Leanne Bell

PEARSON

Harlow, England • London • New York • Boston • San Francisco • Toronto • Sydney
Auckland • Singapore • Hong Kong • Tokyo • Seoul • Taipei • New Delhi
Cape Town • São Paulo • Mexico City • Madrid • Amsterdam • Munich • Paris • Milan

Pearson Education Limited
Edinburgh Gate
Harlow
Essex CM20 2JE
England

and Associated Companies throughout the world

Visit us on the World Wide Web at:
www.pearson.com/uk

First published in 2013

© Pearson Education Limited 2013

ISBN 978-1-4082-4131-8

British Library Cataloguing-in-Publication Data
A catalogue record for this book is available from the British Library

Library of Congress Cataloging-in-Publication Data
A catalog record for this book is available from the Library of Congress

10 9 8 7 6 5 4 3 2 1
16 15 14 13 12

Typeset in 10/14pt ITC Giovanni Std by 35
Printed and bound by Henry Ling Ltd., at the Dorset Press, Dorchester, Dorset

Dedication
For Darren, for always

Contents

Join over 5,000 law students succeeding with MyLawChamber

Visit **www.mylawchamber.co.uk/bell** to access a wealth of tools to help you develop and test your knowledge of medical law, strengthening your understanding so you can excel.

- Interactive multiple-choice questions to test your understanding of each topic
- Practice exam questions with guidance to hone your exam technique
- Weblinks to help you read more widely around the subject and really impress your lecturers
- Legal newsfeed to help you read more widely, stay right up to date with the law and impress examiners
- Audio legal updates to help you stay up to date with the law and impress examiners

Guided tour

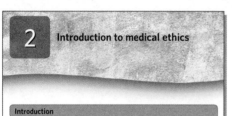

Introduction

Every legal provision drafted, every case decided and every piece of guidance issued regarding the legality of a particular act of a medical professional requires the author to grapple with ethical questions that go to the very heart of human existence. As Dr David Jenkins has remarked, put simply, 'ethics is about being human'.[1] Given that medicine is about treating human beings at the most vulnerable and fundamental points in their lives, the simple fact is that medical law and medical ethics are inevitably and inextricably linked. Yet there is no escaping the fact that as disciplines, law and ethics are very different. While the law requires clarity, overall good for the many rather than for every individual and some idea of a common and shared standard from

Chapter introductions briefly outline the key themes and issues to be covered in the following chapter and help you focus your learning.

KEY CASE

Fairchild v Glenhaven[10]

The claimants in this case had all developed the fatal lung disease mesothelioma. The condition was caused by inhalation of asbestos fibres and each claimant could prove that they had been negligently exposed to such fibres in the course of their employment. However, they had all worked for several employers over the years, all of whom had negligently exposed them to this material and it was not possible to establish which defendant had been responsible for the single fibre that entered the lungs and caused the disease in each of them. The House of Lords held that it could not be argued that each employer materially contributed to the damage because only one fibre could have caused the condition, but said that each employer had materially increased the risk of the claimants developing the disease and therefore it would hold the defendant liable.

Key case boxes highlight the facts and the key legal principles of leading cases you need to be aware of in your study of medical law.

ETHICS QUESTION

There is no doubt that the pre-action protocol and the civil procedure rules post-Woolf have sped up the clinical negligence process and have streamlined the system, with time and cost benefits to all concerned. However, forcing parties to agree on medical evidence, factual details and other elements of the case may not be the best way of achieving justice. For example, in *Hubbard* (referred to earlier), the claimant was concerned that because he did not have legal representation (which, of course, he is not required to have), his medical expert would feel intimidated when meeting with the defendant's medical expert and their legal team and would end up agreeing with them on issues rather than standing her ground. Is widening access by making the system cheaper and quicker so important that it justifies the fact that the court does not get to analyse each case in as much detail? Is poorer justice for many better than superior justice for a few?

Ethics questions raise controversial issues surrounding particular areas of medical law throughout the text, encouraging you to consider your opinion and develop your critical thinking skills.

Summary

The real problem with critically analysing the law in relation to surrogacy is that there is very little law to evaluate. The approach taken has very much been one of turning a blind eye and not criminalising the conduct of those involved, but not providing legal protection or encouragement in the process. The problem with this approach (and one that is echoed in Chapter 10 when we discuss the middle-ground approach taken to abortion) is that in attempting to please everyone it actually pleases no one. It allows people to embark on surrogacy arrangements without the necessary legal protections and leaves them in a legal lacuna that can have devastating practical and emotional consequences in the albeit relatively small number of cases where things go wrong and the agreement breaks down. The absence of proper statutory regulation leads to judges having to be very creative when it comes to dealing with the real situations and children before them, so they are forced to take sensitive and practical steps such as retrospectively authorising illegal payments and separating strict legal parenthood from custody arrangements. Jackson is highly critical of this lack of guidance and statute and comments of judges such as Macfarlane J and Hedley J:[32] 'Their sensitive and non-judgmental attempts to safeguard the interests of children and their parents with wholly inadequate legal tools should be required reading for ministers.'[33]

Chapter summaries at the end of each chapter help you to identify, recap and pull together the key points following your reading.

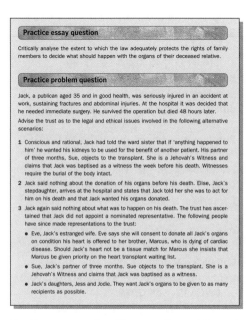

Self-test questions

1 What is the difference between 'euthanasia' and 'assisted suicide'?
2 In what circumstances may a doctor withdraw life-prolonging treatment from a patient who lacks capacity?
3 What was the legal effect of the decision in *Purdy v DPP*?
4 Does the practice of euthanasia infringe a person's human rights under the Convention?
5 What criminal charge will a person face if they assist somebody to commit suicide?
6 What is meant by the doctrine of double effect?

Self-test questions at the end of every chapter help you to check you have fully understood the topics you have read.

Practice essay question

Critically analyse the extent to which the law adequately protects the rights of family members to decide what should happen with the organs of their deceased relative.

Practice problem question

Jack, a publican aged 35 and in good health, was seriously injured in an accident at work, sustaining fractures and abdominal injuries. At the hospital it was decided that he needed immediate surgery. He survived the operation but died 48 hours later.

Advise the trust as to the legal and ethical issues involved in the following alternative scenarios:

1 Conscious and rational, Jack had told the ward sister that if 'anything happened to him' he wanted his kidneys to be used for the benefit of another patient. His partner of three months, Sue, objects to the transplant. She is a Jehovah's Witness and claims that Jack was baptised as a witness the week before his death. Witnesses require the burial of the body intact.
2 Jack said nothing about the donation of his organs before his death. Elise, Jack's stepdaughter, arrives at the hospital and states that Jack told her she was to act for him on his death and that Jack wanted his organs donated.
3 Jack again said nothing about what was to happen on his death. The trust has ascertained that Jack did not appoint a nominated representative. The following people have since made representations to the trust:

  ● Eve, Jack's estranged wife. Eve says she will consent to donate all Jack's organs on condition his heart is offered to her brother, Marcus, who is dying of cardiac disease. Should Jack's heart not be a tissue match for Marcus she insists that Marcus be given priority on the heart transplant waiting list.
  ● Sue, Jack's partner of three months. Sue objects to the transplant. She is a Jehovah's Witness and claims that Jack was baptised as a witness.
  ● Jack's daughters, Jess and Jodie. They want Jack's organs to be given to as many recipients as possible.

Practice essay and problem questions at the end of chapters help you to test your knowledge and practice applying the law to exam style questions.

Table of cases

Table of statutes

Table of statutory instruments

Table of European Union legislation

Table of international treaties and conventions

Preface

My intention in writing this book was to combine a clear and accessible explanation of the often complex and challenging legal rules governing medical care in England and Wales with a stimulating examination of the social, political and ethical arguments such care provokes. Medical law has fascinated me since I first studied it as an undergraduate and my hope is that I have managed to communicate effectively the passion that I feel for a legal subject that, more than any other, impacts on all of us at some stage of our lives, both directly and in relation to those we care about. The brutal reality is that our healthcare workers are dealing with matters of life and death, caring for people when they are at their most vulnerable, in a society where respect for their profession has decreased (not least due to scandals such as Harold Shipman and the various organ retention cases during the 1990s), demands have increased and both funding and regulation are increasingly complex and difficult challenges. Against all of that, scientific advances are making new treatments and procedures available that present new ethical dilemmas (such as whether we should create embryos made from both human and animal material in order to further medical research, or whether abortion should be permitted up to 24 weeks when babies as young as 22-weeks' gestation have surivived). As ever, the law must somehow tread a path that effectively regulates the medical profession, the provision of healthcare and the carrying out of medical research while upholding and respecting the rights and views of the millions of people who make use of those services every year. It is the pursuit of this elusive path that I hope this book draws out and it was my aim to make it relevant and useful for not only students of medical law but also those studying medical sciences, people working in healthcare and anyone who wants a deeper understanding of these fascinating issues.

There are many people to whom I am indebted in the production of this book. The medical law team here at Northumbria University (Michelle Robson, Helen Kingston and Kristina Swift), who made the early years of teaching the subject so much easier by providing guidance, advice, discussion and access to their extensive knowledge of the subject, are owed a huge debt of gratitude. Other colleagues have offered their support and assistance and in various ways have taught me how to communicate better as a teacher and a writer, but one who must be singled out for special mention is Alan Davenport, who was never in any doubt that the book would materialise (even when I was not nearly so sure!) and showed me how to be a good teacher and a good friend.

The team at Pearson and, in particular, Owen Knight, who has looked at many, many drafts with good grace and given extensive advice and support, have been fantastic to work with and have spent at least as many hours as I, if not more, making the finished product as good as it could be . . . thanks for all your work!

I am also indebted to a special little boy called Matthew, who exposed me to the reality of receiving medical care in the NHS for several years and challenged all my preconceptions about the rights and wrongs of medical care and medical ethics – he was a wonderful, courageous and insightful person and my understanding of the dilemmas facing the healthcare system, my teaching, my writing and ultimately this book are all the better for having known him.

Finally, I must thank my children, Liv, Sam and Riley (for being a source of constant inspiration to me and for deepening my understanding and appreciation of many of the complex ethical and moral issues covered in the book so much more than any course, book, lecture or study could ever hope to) and my husband Darren (for being a proofreader, soundboard, supporter, constructive critic, childcare provider and in short, making the book possible) – I couldn't have done it without you.

Leanne Bell
February 2012

1 Structure of healthcare in England and Wales

Introduction

The healthcare system in England and Wales has an extremely complex structure and this becomes increasingly so with every reform and review that takes place. We have a mixture of state-funded care (largely delivered through the National Heath Service (NHS)), privately funded care and, now, international provision of care within the EU and beyond.[1] In addition to the fact that the system as a whole is large and complex, there are continuous efforts by each successive government to reform it, based on various policy and economic issues. At the time of writing, the coalition government is attempting sweeping reforms of the NHS, including the proposal that GPs be tasked with commissioning services and managing budgets. This has been met with much criticism and is currently being reviewed.[2]

In this chapter, the NHS will be described and its structure as it currently stands will be set out. The legal framework within which state-funded care sits will also be examined, before we briefly consider the differences between state-funded and private care and some methods of redress available to patients when things go wrong. The aims of the chapter are to:

- set out the structure of the NHS and the legal rules governing provision of care
- explain who and what the various bodies are that operate within the system and their overall remit and function
- contrast the state system with private healthcare, especially in terms of methods of redress where care has been substandard.

---

[1] See for example *R (on the application of Watts)* v *Bedford PCT* [2006] 3 WLR 213 where a trust may be required to pay for treatment obtained by the patient in another country because the waiting time here is unreasonably long.

[2] See the 5th Report of the Select Committee on Health, HC 796-1, 796-2 and 796-3.

The NHS

In 1942 Sir William Beveridge laid his influential report (known from then on as the Beveridge Report) before Parliament. It was a revolutionary document proposing drastic social change in England and Wales. As he stated in the report:

> Now, when the war is abolishing landmarks of every kind, is the opportunity for using experience in a clear field. A revolutionary moment in the world's history is a time for revolutions, not for patching.[3]

The report laid the foundations for the modern welfare state as we know it and greatly influenced the National Health Service Act 1946, which created a comprehensive health service that was to be free at the point of need and funded by taxation. The NHS actually came into being as a result of the Act on 5 July 1948 and from that point on, it has been the responsibility of the Minister for Health to make sure that England and Wales has a comprehensive health service. As an organisation, the NHS has largely become something that we take for granted these days, but it is important to appreciate what a revolutionary and amazing thing it was when it was created. The idea that all citizens could have free access to good quality healthcare, wherever they lived and whatever their class or economic means, was nothing short of life changing for those living in England and Wales at the time. The NHS is something that has very much become part of our national consciousness and, as such, is constantly at the heart of political and economic debates about how best to continue to run and fund it. The following figures help put this into context.

SOME STATISTICS

- The NHS employs over 1.5 million people – only the Chinese People's Liberation Army, the Wal-Mart supermarket chain and the Indian Railways directly employ more people.
- On average, the NHS deals with one million patients every 36 hours – that is almost eight people per second.
- Each GP sees on average 140 patients per week.
- When launched in 1948, the NHS budget was £437 million (about £9 billion at today's value). In 2008 its budget was £90 billion. Given that the NHS is funded primarily by taxation, that equates to £1500 from every man, woman and child in the UK.[4]

---

[3] PREM 4/89/2, pp. 41–2 (November 1942).
[4] See 'Governing the NHS', 2008, available at http://www.kingsfund.org.uk/publications/governing_the.html.

Structure

In terms of structure, the Department for Health is the body that is in overall charge of the NHS. The Secretary of State for Health is a cabinet minister and reports directly to the Prime Minister. There are then 10 strategic health authorities (SHAs) that oversee the NHS trusts in their own areas.[5] The devolved administrations in Scotland, Wales and Northern Ireland run their own local NHS services separately.

The NHS is run according to several 'core principles' that are set out on its website.[6] These are:

- The NHS will provide a universal service for all based on clinical need, not ability to pay.
- The NHS will provide a range of comprehensive services.
- The NHS will shape its services around the needs and preferences of individual patients, their families and their carers.
- The NHS will respond differently to the needs of different populations.
- The NHS will work continually to improve quality of services and to minimise errors.
- The NHS will support and value its staff.
- Public funds for healthcare will be devoted solely to NHS patients.
- The NHS will work with other bodies to ensure a seamless service for patients.
- The NHS will help to keep people healthy and work to reduce health inequalities.
- The NHS will respect the confidentiality of individual patients and provide open access to information about services, treatment and performance.

While these core principles are to be commended and have laudable aims, this book is an examination of medical law and as the chapters ahead will demonstrate, it is not difficult to see examples in which these core principles are seemingly not being adhered to, whether due to lack of funds or apparent poor systems and management. Thinking as lawyers, such grand principles should never be taken at face value, so set out in the following are the core principles again, with some comments about where perhaps the NHS needs to improve its delivery:

- The NHS will provide a universal service for all based on clinical need, not ability to pay.
  The NHS already fails to provide certain drugs or treatments where it feels that the money can be better spent elsewhere. For example, the drug Herceptin, which is used to treat certain types of breast cancer, was denied to many patients on the

---

[5] SHAs are to be abolished under the Health and Social Care Act 2012, which received Royal Assent on 12 March 2012.

[6] http://www.nhs.uk/NHSEngland/thenhs/about/Pages/nhscoreprinciples.aspx, accessed 11 July 2011.

basis of cost and one of these patients, Mrs Rogers, brought a judicial review when she ran out of private funds to pay for the drug and was left with the possibility of having to stop treatment. For a further detailed discussion of such issues see the NHS v Private Healthcare section in this chapter.

- The NHS will provide a range of comprehensive services.
  Not all NHS trusts provide the same range of services. For example, the National Institute for Clinical Excellence (NICE) recommends that each trust should offer infertile couples three free cycles of in-vitro fertilisation (IVF) before requiring them to pay. However, many trusts provide fewer or even no free cycles, arguing that they cannot afford to do so (see Chapter 7 for more details). Other services, such as gender reassignment surgery, have also not been provided in some trusts over the years on costs arguments.

- The NHS will shape its services around the needs and preferences of individual patients, their families and their carers.
  The sheer number of patients and services may make this unrealistic today.

- The NHS will respond differently to the needs of different populations.
  When the NHS was first established, this may have seemed achievable but the organisation now provides healthcare for over 60 million people. Economies of scale are inevitable so, for example, many maternity units will provide one course of ante-natal classes, rather than a programme of specific classes tailored for young mothers, single parents etc.

- The NHS will work continually to improve quality of services and to minimise errors.
  As can be seen in Chapters 3, 4 and 5, although complaints procedures are in place within the NHS and each trust is supposed to take steps to learn from past mistakes, there has traditionally been a culture of deference to the medical profession that may have prevented real lessons being learned and disseminated within the organisation. Common law jurisprudence on clinical negligence allowed one doctor to support another in court and effectively remove any examination of that doctor's practice by the court for many years.[7]

- The NHS will support and value its staff.
  Just like any other large organisation, some staff feel very undervalued. Nurses in particular have complained of poor pay and working conditions and junior doctors are notoriously overworked in the early years of their career. Administrative staff also report feeling undervalued. Indeed, the NHS is regularly the subject of employment tribunal claims for unfair dismissal and harassment. In particular, staff who 'whistleblow', that is report poor practice by other staff, have often reported to have been treated very poorly.

---

[7] See, for example, *Bolam v Friern HMC* [1957] and Chapter 3.

- Public funds for healthcare will be devoted solely to NHS patients.
  Over 40% of the NHS budget goes on payment of staff salaries. Many of these staff are in management roles and much of the money is spent on issues that are not always obviously seen to be connected to patient care.

- The NHS will work with other bodies to ensure a seamless service for patients.
  Many legal provisions, especially around confidentiality, prevent this from being possible in many cases. Devastating examples include those of Victoria Climbié and Baby P, in which, despite multiple contacts with various NHS personnel and departments, that information was not shared between departments or with other organisations such as social services and the police.[8]

- The NHS will help to keep people healthy and work to reduce health inequalities.
  The NHS does provide education and information programmes on issues such as nutrition, breastfeeding, smoking cessation etc., although the effectiveness of these programmes is debatable. In 2009 in the Northumberland area, only 8% of mothers were still breastfeeding six weeks after the birth of their child (the recommendation is that breastfeeding should continue for at least six months after a child is born) despite there being dedicated breastfeeding counsellors, classes, support personnel (including a buddy system), information services and support groups in the local area.

- The NHS will respect the confidentiality of individual patients and provide open access to information about services, treatment and performance.
  Generally, the NHS is very aware of its responsibilities regarding confidentiality, but there will be cases in which other concerns override that. For example, where a patient is under 18 and divulges evidence of abuse, that information must be communicated to the relevant bodies. Where a patient poses a danger to the public, the doctor will be able to share that information. (For more details, see Chapter 7.)

As can be seen from this, while the aims of the NHS are very positive, its ability to fulfil them can be questioned, especially as it becomes a larger body providing services to a growing population, under increased economic pressure.

Legal framework

The current legal framework was laid down initially by the NHS Act 1977, but has been substantially amended and was subject to a consolidating Act in 2006 that tried to bring all provisions together. Section 1 states:

---

[8] See the Victoria Climbié Inquiry Report, 2002–2003 HC 570 and 'The Protection of Children in England – A Progress Report', Lord Laming, March 2009 available at http://news.bbc.co.uk/1/shared/bsp/hi/pdfs/12_03_09_children.pdf.

(1) It is the Secretary of State's duty to continue the promotion in England and Wales of a comprehensive health service designed to secure improvement –

    (a) In the physical and mental health of the people of those countries, and

    (b) In the prevention, diagnosis and treatment of illness, and for that purpose provide or secure the effective provision of services in accordance with this Act

Note that he is only under a duty to continue the 'promotion' of such a service, not directly to provide the services themselves. This is significant as it means services can be brought in from private providers or even other countries. Of equal note is the duty to provide 'comprehensive' services, but who decides what constitutes a comprehensive set of services? The Act does go on to provide further details of the sorts of service that should be available, such as accommodation in hospital, medical, dental, nursing and ambulance services, maternity services etc.,[9] but there is a discretion in section 3(1) which states that such services need only be provided 'to such an extent as he (the Secretary of State) considers necessary'. Does this then mean that if the Secretary of State feels that certain services are not 'necessary' he is under no obligation to ensure they are provided? That is certainly the implication from the way the section is drafted.

Who's who in the NHS?

Department of Health

The NHS is not technically a part of the Department of Health (DH) but it is managed by it in that the DH sets targets and monitors performance. The DH has the task of supporting the government in developing and carrying out its health and social care policies through the NHS.

Special health authorities

These were set up by statute[10] and, although independent, can be subject to ministerial direction like the NHS itself. An example is the National Institute for Health and Clinical Excellence (NICE), which sets standards of good practice for trusts on various areas of healthcare and makes decisions about which drugs and treatments should be funded by trusts.[11]

---

[9] Section 3 NHS Act 2006.
[10] See section 28 and Sch. 6 NHS Act 2006.
[11] See http://www.nice.org.uk.

NHS trusts

There are various types of trust within the NHS. A primary care trust (PCT) is a trust providing primary care, such as GP services, dentists etc. An NHS trust is a trust providing secondary care such as hospital treatment – such services may often be commissioned by the PCT.[12]

The NHS Act sets out that the power to create trusts rests with the Secretary of State.[13] Each trust is a body corporate. This means that it has a separate legal personality from the individuals running it. Thus, if you were to bring a claim in negligence it would be the trust itself that would be the defendant, not the individual doctor or chief executive. Trusts are run by a board of directors, which is headed by a chairman appointed by the Secretary of State. Money is not given directly to the trust to spend on providing services. Rather, the trust will negotiate contracts with the commissioning bodies (the PCTs) in order to fund their activities. Thus, if they do not fulfil their contracts and provide the requisite services, they do not get paid.

More recently, some trusts have opted to convert to foundation trust status. This new type of trust has its performance monitored by a new independent regulator, Monitor, rather than the DH. It is a different type of legal entity in that it is owned by its members and its relationship with other trusts and NHS bodies is governed by contracts. In order to operate, a foundation trust must be granted a licence by Monitor. The idea is that this will lead to tighter performance monitoring and higher standards of care. Whether this actually is the result remains to be seen.

NHS v private healthcare

Contract claims

The essential difference between an NHS patient and a private patient surrounds the relationship the patient has with the healthcare provider. The NHS patient is dealing with a body that has a statutory obligation to provide healthcare (but not specific treatments), which means that, if something goes wrong, the patient can only sue using common law rules in negligence. The private patient, however, has a contractual relationship with her healthcare provider. In this case, should something go wrong she can choose to sue in negligence using common law principles, she may sue in contract for breach of a term of the contract or she may sue in both. This, arguably, gives the private patient more options although, in practice, it will become clear that the principles and tests applied in both areas are very similar.

---

[12] Commissioning is set to change following the Health and Social Care Act 2012, which received Royal Assent on 12 March 2012.

[13] Sections 25–27 and Sch. 4 NHS Act 2006.

Clearly, the fact that a particular treatment has not succeeded in fixing the patient's medical problem does not necessarily mean that the private healthcare provider has breached its contract. It will depend what the terms of the contract were and it is unlikely that any organisation or individual doctor would ever contractually guarantee a successful outcome to a patient. For example, in *Thake v Maurice*,[14] a patient's vasectomy spontaneously reversed, as does occasionally happen. There was no indication that the doctor had performed the procedure incorrectly. The couple sued for breach of contract and negligence in relation to the unplanned pregnancy that resulted. The court held that no contract could contain an implied term guaranteeing a successful outcome to a particular treatment and rejected the claimant's evidence that such a guarantee had been made orally in addition to the written contract. Neil LJ stated quite clearly: 'I do not consider that a reasonable person would have expected a responsible medical man to be intending to give a guarantee.' The only term that could be implied was one to act with reasonable care and skill (very similar to the common law test in negligence – see Chapter 3). The operation *had* been carried out with such care and skill. However, the court did find that the failure of the doctor to warn the couple about the possibility of such occasional reversals was negligent and they could recover damages on that basis in tort, just as an NHS patient could have done. This point is explored in more detail in Chapter 3. There are also various statutory provisions governing the contract for medical services that could be viewed as giving a private patient some extra protection over an NHS patient. For example, any medical devices that are supplied to a patient must be of satisfactory quality and fit for purpose[15] and a healthcare provider will be unable to limit their liability in the contract for death or personal injury caused by negligence.[16] Such differences between private and NHS patients have always been controversial, with many arguing that it creates a two-tier system whereby the more affluent in society can afford to buy better healthcare with more legal protection if things go wrong. For example, Lord Donaldson has stated:

> 'I am . . . unable to detect any rational basis for a state of law . . . whereby in identical circumstances, Dr A who treats a patient under the national health service and whose liability falls to be determined in accordance with the law of tort, should be in a different position from Dr B who treats a patient outside the service and whose liability . . . falls to be determined in accordance with the law of contract'.[17]

This argument is further strengthened by the fact that there are different limitation periods for tort and contract claims. An NHS patient who only has the option of a tort claim has just three years from the date of the incident or the date that he or she knows of the incident in which to bring a claim. A private patient has six

---

[14] [1986] 2 WLR 347.
[15] Sections 4 and 9 Supply of Goods and Services Act 1982.
[16] Section 2(1) Unfair Contract Terms Act 1977.
[17] Per Lord Donaldson in *Hotson* v *East Berkshire Area Health Authority* [1987] 1 AC 750 at p. 760.

years to bring a contract claim.[18] It has also been argued that it may be easier to claim damages for loss of a chance in contract.[19] As we will discuss in Chapter 3, claiming such damages in tort for clinical negligence is extremely difficult and leaves many victims of breaches of duty without recompense.

Judicial review

One way in which the playing field is somewhat levelled, at least theoretically, for the NHS patient is the availability of a judicial review claim against an NHS trust. Such a claim is available because the NHS is a public body, carrying out public functions delegated to it by the Secretary of State. Private providers are not subject to judicial review unless the claimant can show that even though the provider in question is a private organisation, it is carrying out public functions.

The important thing to note about a judicial review is that it is not asking the court to make a judgment about the decision that has been made, but about the decision-making process the public body has gone through. The process can be challenged on any of three main grounds, namely that it was illegal, irrational or procedurally incorrect in some way,[20] but not because someone feels it was the 'wrong' decision.

KEY CASE

R v Cambridge District Health Authority ex parte B [1995]

B was a 10-year-old girl suffering from an aggressive form of leukaemia. She had undergone various treatments including rounds of chemotherapy and although she had experienced periods of remission, the disease had always come back. When it returned this time, her father heard about an experimental and very aggressive form of chemotherapy that was being used to treat the disease and wanted the health authority to fund this treatment for his daughter. Medical evidence suggested that she had around a 10% chance of its having any impact on her disease and if it did, then only another 10% chance of its preventing a further relapse. It was an unpleasant treatment to endure with many side-effects that would cause her distress and pain. The cost of one round of the treatment was £76,000. The Health Authority refused to pay for the treatment on the basis that within its limited resources, it was not a good use of the money given the small chance of success and the trauma it would cause to the patient. Her father argued that they were putting a price on his child's life and no patient should be allowed to die because of the cost of treatment. ➡

---

[18] See the Limitation Act 1980 and Chapter 5.
[19] See Jones, M., *Medical Negligence*, 2nd edn, Blackstone Press Ltd 1996, p. 69.
[20] See Lord Diplock in *Minister for the Civil Service* v *CCSU* [1985] AC 374.

Legally, he brought the claim on the grounds that the decision had been irrational. The test for irrationality is that the decision was so unreasonable that no reasonable decision maker could possibly have arrived at the same conclusion.[21] This is a difficult test to satisfy and in this case, the fact was that the Health Authority had gone through the proper procedures, looked at their available budget and all the other demands on it from other patients and departments and determined that there was not sufficient benefit to using the money for this purpose.

Sir Thomas Bingham MR was clear that making decisions about resource allocation was not the role of the court. The court had merely to establish that the decision maker was going through the proper processes and making the decision in the right way. He stated: 'Difficult and agonising judgments have to be made as to how a limited budget is best allocated to the maximum advantage of the maximum number of patients. That is not a judgment which the court can make.' Here, the decision was valid.

The case attracted much academic and other comment. The chief executive of the trust involved later stated that: 'The case took on a symbolic importance, helping people to grasp the reality that expectation and demand had now outstripped their publicly funded systems without regard to the opportunity cost'.[22] In the end, after the family was unsuccessful at court, an anonymous benefactor donated the money to fund the treatment and it was carried out in the United States. Unfortunately, it was ultimately unsuccessful and B died soon after.

ETHICS QUESTIONS

Is the resources argument a valid one when it comes to denying certain treatments to certain people? Is it acceptable for a trust to say that £76,000 is too much money to spend on trying to save a child's life? Does it depend where that money ultimately gets spent? What if that money is instead spent on treating a long-term smoker with lung disease? Who should decide *where* the money is best spent?

Over the years, bringing a claim against a health authority or NHS trust on the basis that a decision regarding the provision of care has been illegal, irrational or procedurally incorrect has been difficult. Case law is littered with failed attempts to set aside decisions not to fund a particular drug or not to provide a certain type of

---

[21] Ibid.
[22] Reflections of a Chief Executive (1997) 314 BMJ 1838.

treatment. For example, in *ex parte Walker*,[23] a non-urgent operation on a premature baby was delayed several times due to a shortage of nurses and his mother sought a judicial review of the decision. However, the court made it very clear that it was not prepared to substitute its view for that of the health authority when it came to allocating inevitably finite resources. Similarly in *ex parte Collier*,[24] where a heart operation on a 4-year-old boy had been repeatedly delayed due to staff shortages and lack of availability of a bed in the acute care unit, the court refused to interfere with the decision. In this case, the court also made the point that if cases were given leave to apply for judicial review over decisions made on allocation of resources, 'We should ourselves be using up the NHS resources by requiring the authority . . . to meet the complaints of their patients'.[25] This view can, to some extent at least, be understood in the sense that tying NHS bodies up in litigation does drain resources that could be better used elsewhere and often, decisions regarding allocation of resources will be better made by those with the requisite medical and local knowledge. However, other decisions have appeared more arbitrary. For example, in *ex parte Harriott*,[26] a woman suffering from fertility problems and who had been refused permission to adopt a child (on the grounds that she had been convicted of a minor prostitution-related offence some 20 years earlier) sought IVF treatment at St Mary's Hospital. The hospital refused to provide the treatment on the same grounds as those behind the unsuccessful adoption application. The court decided that the decision of the hospital had not been irrational.

Recently, the court does seem to have been more willing to subject the decisions to some degree of scrutiny or at least to examine the decision in more depth. This may well be in large part down to the introduction of the Human Rights Act 1998 (which came into force in October 2000). For example, in *Coughlan*,[27] the court held that where the decision maker had induced a 'legitimate expectation' in the claimant and then failed to deliver the expected benefit, this would be likely to constitute irrationality. The decision in this case involved the closure of a unit for elderly and disabled people after they had been assured it would be their 'home for life' when they moved in, only a year earlier. It is clear that the court had in mind the fact that the residents' Article 8 rights were engaged (the guarantee of respect for private life under the European Convention on Human Rights) when they made the decision and previous cases had suggested that where human rights issues were involved, the courts should subject the decision maker to a higher level of scrutiny.[28] Another

---

[23] (1987) 3 BMLR 32.
[24] Unreported, 6 January 1988.
[25] Ibid. per Sir John Donaldson MR.
[26] *R v Ethical Committee of St Mary's Hospital ex parte Harriott* [1988] 1 FLR 512 and discussed further in Chapter 7.
[27] *R v North East and Devon Health Authority ex parte Coughlan* [2001] QB 213.
[28] *Smith v UK* (2000) 29 EHRR 548.

important example of the changing approach of the court came in *ex parte A, D and G*,[29] where several transsexual patients had been turned down for gender reassignment surgery. It turned out that the health authority had a policy that categorised treatments according to priority and need. Although the court accepted the need for such categorisation to take place and that it made sense for gender reassignment surgery to fall below other treatments such as heart surgery, the evidence was that this particular health authority grouped it alongside cosmetic procedures such as breast enhancements. As Auld J stated: 'In establishing priorities comparing the respective needs of patients suffering from different illnesses and determining the respective strengths of their claims to treatment, it is vital for an Authority: (1) to accurately assess the nature and seriousness of each type of illness; (2) to determine the effectiveness of various types of treatment for it; and (3) to give proper effect to that assessment and that determination in the formulation and the individual application of its policy.'[30] Essentially, it was fine to have a policy, but that policy had to be based on a realistic assessment of the condition and the individual patient. In this case, the policy amounted to an outright ban on this particular procedure.

Perhaps the most well-known recent case on the application of a policy regarding provision of treatment is that of Mrs Rogers and her battle to obtain the breast cancer drug Herceptin.

KEY CASE

R (on the application of Rogers) v Swindon[31]

Mrs Rogers was suffering from breast cancer and was one of a small number of patients for whom a new drug called Herceptin was thought to be clinically appropriate. The Department for Health had issued a circular that stated it was down to individual physicians to decide whether a patient was eligible for the drug and that PCTs should not refuse to fund it solely on the basis of cost. However, there was no getting away from the fact that the drug was very expensive and the PCT, while stating that it was complying with the DH circular, had put in place a policy whereby Herceptin would only be provided where the patient could demonstrate 'exceptional personal or clinical circumstances'. Mrs Rogers initially used her own savings to pay for the drug, but when they ran out she went back to the PCT to ask them to fund the rest, at a cost of over £26,000. The PCT refused and she challenged that decision as being irrational. At first instance, Mrs Rogers lost. The court upheld the PCT's decision, primarily because the drug had not at that point been cleared by the European Medicines Agency. Mrs Rogers' argument about the many women who

---

[29] *A, D & G v North West Lancashire Health Authority* [2000] 1 WLR 977.
[30] Ibid. at para. 992.
[31] *R (Rogers) v Swindon Primary Care Trust and Secretary of State for Health* [2006] EWCA Civ 392.

would benefit from the provision of the drug was dismissed by Bean J. He stated that 'rationality in law is not determined by counting heads'. However, she persevered and was successful on appeal. The case turned on the fact that the policy stated that a patient had to show exceptional personal or clinical circumstances but then completely failed to give any guidance on what would constitute 'exceptional circumstances'. It was held that the policy was, in effect, a blanket ban on providing the drug. Sir Anthony Clarke stated: 'In short . . . once the PCT decided it would fund Herceptin for some patients and that the cost was irrelevant, the only reasonable approach was to focus on the patient's clinical needs and fund patients within the eligible group who were properly prescribed Herceptin by their physician. This would not open the floodgates to those suffering from breast cancer because only comparatively few satisfy the criteria so as to qualify for the eligible group.' He also pointed out that within the policy as it was drafted, there was 'no rational basis for preferring one patient over another'.

The *Rogers* case is significant because it subjected the policy of the PCT to real scrutiny and assessed for itself, almost reading between the lines, that it was in real terms a prohibition on funding Herceptin due to its cost. Whereas previously the court had very much shied away from getting involved where the decision was one of resource allocation, here it was prepared to require the PCT to demonstrate that its policy was fair, reasonable and proportionate – again this reflects the fact that it is a post-HRA decision.

It has not been all success for claimants in recent years, despite what one may be led to believe by occasional overhyped press coverage. In *Eisai Ltd* v *NICE*,[32] the manufacturer of a drug used in the treatment of Alzheimer's disease challenged NICE's recommendation that it be used only for those patients with moderate severity of the disease, as determined by their mini-mental state examination (MMSE). The case was hailed as a great success for patient groups when the court ruled the decision procedurally flawed and required NICE to look at it again. However, what was not always clear in the reporting was that the only criticisms the court made of the decision were of the reliance solely on the MMSE to determine severity of disease and the failure to provide the guidance in formats for those with disabilities, such as Braille. The court upheld the right of NICE to determine that some treatments, including this particular drug, were not cost effective for those with early or late stage disease. Thus, many patients hoping the drug would slow down the progression of their recently diagnosed illness or those hoping it would give them a precious few more weeks or months with their loved ones, were still left having to try to fund it themselves.

[32] *R (on the application of Eisai Ltd)* v *National Institute for Health and Clinical Excellence* [2007] EWHC 1941.

Another limitation to be considered when looking at judicial review claims is the lack of effective remedies. Essentially, the decision maker is being asked to go back and retake the decision, correcting whatever errors were made the first time around. This may involve setting aside an original decision or obtaining an injunction to prevent its being acted on until it has been looked at again. Generally, financial remedies are not available and the court will never reverse the decision or step into the decision-maker's shoes and determine what the outcome should be, especially where the issue is one of resource allocation. Therefore, despite rhetoric such as that of Laws J in the *Re B* case at first instance that: 'Where the question is whether the life of a 10-year-old child might be saved by however slim a chance, the authority must do more than toll the bell of tight resources' and despite the more recent cases where courts have scrutinised the decision-maker and hospital policies more stringently, it remains something of a blunt instrument for claimants.

Summary

For all these reasons, it is important to get a clear understanding early in a case about the relationship between the patient and the healthcare provider, as, quite often, private care will be provided in NHS hospitals and the same doctor may have NHS and private patients at the same time. While the complex structure of the NHS and the problem of limited resources mean that patients do not always get the treatment they want as early as they want it, the fact remains that we still have a free healthcare system that is envied by many other countries. How long we manage to maintain that system in its current form remains to be seen. At the time of writing, the government has just announced plans to have £1 billion worth of certain key services provided by private companies.[33] Those who opt for private care may open up other options for themselves in terms of being able to sue in contract for substandard care, but, of course, they may also find that it is more difficult to pinpoint exactly who the defendant should be. There are also ethical questions around whether limited resources should be a reason for denying certain treatments or an excuse when things go wrong.[34]

To end, have a look at the following quote from Lewis, which is typical of a view shared by many academics about the state of the NHS and its future:

[33] http://www.guardian.co.uk/society/2011/jul/19/nhs-services-open-to-competition?CMP=twt_gu.
[34] See Chapter 3 for more on this argument.

The NHS, in the hands of the current government (not to say any other would be better though), undergoes ceaseless change, restless like Homer's ocean. Health bodies are forever merging and separating in a hypnotic eddy of tides, with names and nomenclature forever changing, services reviewed and altered, targets disastrously introduced leading to serious distortion of clinical priorities, meaningless (indeed harmful) comparisons of hospitals and of practitioners created by eager bureaucrats, 10-year plans proudly proclaimed and vote catching initiatives started with flags flying and political tails wagging only to be quietly forgotten in due course. Quangos proliferate, administrators outnumber practitioners and rules and regulations for the governance of society spew forward endlessly from the legislative maw in this as in every other aspect of community life.[35]

He paints a rather bleak picture. Do you agree with him? What is certain is that within the current healthcare system, a whole new and fascinating area of law has developed into its own distinct discipline and the rest of this book attempts to guide the reader through this evocative, fast changing and often controversial subject.

Self-test questions

1 What are the main differences between an NHS trust and a foundation trust?

2 Who is ultimately in charge of the NHS?

3 How is the NHS funded?

4 What are the key legal differences between an NHS patient and a private patient?

5 Give two reasons why a patient bringing a contract claim could have an advantage over one bringing a tort claim.

6 What are the three grounds on which a patient can bring a judicial review?

---

[35] Lewis, *Clinical Negligence* 6th ed, 2006, Tottel Publishing, p. 9.

2 Introduction to medical ethics

Introduction

Every legal provision drafted, every case decided and every piece of guidance issued regarding the legality of a particular act of a medical professional requires the author to grapple with ethical questions that go to the very heart of human existence. As Dr David Jenkins has remarked, put simply, 'ethics is about being human'.[1] Given that medicine is about treating human beings at the most vulnerable and fundamental points in their lives, the simple fact is that medical law and medical ethics are inevitably and inextricably linked. Yet there is no escaping the fact that as disciplines, law and ethics are very different. While the law requires clarity, overall good for the many rather than for every individual and some idea of a common and shared standard from which to work, ethics, by its very nature is a much more complex beast, combining the ideal of individual rights and freedoms with the overall good of society. As will become clear in later chapters, this is why the law and ethics surrounding a particular medical issue often diverge. The ideal scenario is one where intelligent and informed ethical debate informs and shapes the law, but all too often and especially in emotive areas such as abortion, euthanasia and neonaticide, the ethical debate becomes too heated and impassioned to contribute constructively to the law-making process. In some situations, lawmakers can feel restricted in the kind of law they are able to make for fear of political ramifications. Compounding this is the fact that Britain is increasingly a multicultural and multi-faith society, meaning there are no accepted ethical norms on the more controversial practices mentioned earlier.

The subject of medical ethics is a vast one and, in a book such as this, it is only possible to give an introduction to the key issues that impact most often and most meaningfully on medical law. The aims of this chapter are to:

- set out the background and development of medical ethics
- consider the sorts of medical topic most affected by ethical arguments
- examine some of the key ethical schools of thought and how each might apply in a medical context

---

[1] Dr David Jenkins, former Bishop of Durham.

- provide some real-life scenarios for the reader to consider in light of the various ethical theories described.

History and Hippocrates

Ethics is something that has been associated with the practice of medicine since the time of the ancient Greeks. Hippocrates was born around 460 BC and is generally credited as being one of the first recognisable 'physicians'. He chronicled and described many medical conditions for the first time, but is probably most famous for his 'Hippocratic Oath', which serves as a basis for the oaths taken by newly qualified medical practitioners today. For Hippocrates, being a physician was about being a professional and this is evident in the six key duties outlined in the oath.

THE HIPPOCRATIC OATH

Six basic duties

- to do no harm
- not to assist suicide or administer euthanasia
- not to cause abortion
- to refer patients for specialist treatment
- not to abuse professional relationships (particularly for sexual motives)
- to keep the patient's confidences.

It is interesting to look at these principles against the backdrop of our modern society and think about where they came from. They reflect the consensus about right and wrong at the time in which they were written but it is rather strange to reflect on the ones that have fallen by the wayside and the ones that have been maintained. As can be seen in Chapter 7, confidentiality is still considered to be a very important duty for a medical professional and the circumstances in which medical information can be divulged are very limited.[2] Conversely, the prohibitions on causing abortion and administering euthanasia are regularly dismissed as both those practices can now be facilitated without incurring legal liability in certain circumstances.[3] Another point of note is that there is no mention of individual autonomy (that is, the right of each person to determine what should happen with their own body). In our modern, rights-based culture, the oath can appear too paternalistic.

Continuing on from the time of Hippocrates and even up to the eighteenth and nineteenth centuries, medicine was still very much an upper-class preserve practised

[2] See for example *Attorney General* v *Guardian Newspapers* [1990] 1 AC 109 and *R (Stevens)* v *Plymouth City Council* [2002].
[3] See Chapters 10 and 11, respectively.

in a society that viewed lower-class citizens as inferior. Therefore, much of the ethics surrounding it was very paternalistic and closely resembled the model Hippocrates had set out. However, the twentieth century definitely marked a turning point and the emergence of medical ethics as a more rounded discipline with more of a focus on the individual. Two key factors played a fundamental part in this change: the Nuremberg trials and the dramatic changes in technology.

Nuremberg

The Nuremberg trials took place between October 1945 and August 1946 and involved 23 Nazi officers being charged with war crimes for carrying out extensive medical experiments on human subjects. None of these was carried out with the consent of the subject and all ended with either the death of the subject or permanent damage and disfiguration. Judgment was handed down on 19 August 1947 and reiterated the six points for legitimate research on human beings accepted by the Council for War Crimes earlier, along with four other recommendations. These 10 points constitute what we now call the Nuremberg Code. The document is the basis of modern medical ethics.

The 10 points are:

1 The voluntary consent of the human subject is absolutely essential. This means that the person involved should have legal capacity to give consent; should be so situated as to be able to exercise free power of choice, without the intervention of any element of force, fraud, deceit, duress, over-reaching, or other ulterior form of constraint or coercion; and should have sufficient knowledge and comprehension of the elements of the subject matter involved as to enable him/her to make an understanding and enlightened decision. This last element requires that before the acceptance of an affirmative decision by the experimental subject there should be made known to him the nature, duration, and purpose of the experiment; the method and means by which it is to be conducted; all inconveniences and hazards reasonable to be expected; and the effects on his health or person which may possibly come from his participation in the experiment. The duty and responsibility for ascertaining the quality of the consent rests on each individual who initiates, directs or engages in the experiment. It is a personal duty and responsibility and may not be delegated to another with impunity.

2 The experiment should be such as to yield fruitful results for the good of society, unprocurable by other methods or means of study, and not random and unnecessary in nature.

3 The experiment should be so designed and based on the results of animal experimentation and knowledge of the natural history of the disease or other

problem under study that the anticipated results will justify the performance of the experiment.

4 The experiment should be so conducted as to avoid all unnecessary physical and mental suffering and injury.

5 No experiment should be conducted where there is a prior reason to believe that death or disabling injury will occur; except, perhaps, in those experiments where the experimental physicians also serve as subjects.

6 The degree of risk to be taken should never exceed that determined by the humanitarian importance of the problem to be solved by the experiment.

7 Proper preparations should be made and adequate facilities provided to protect the experimental subject against even remote possibilities of injury, disability or death.

8 The experiment should be conducted only by scientifically qualified persons. The highest degree of skill and care should be required through all stages of the experiment of those who conduct or engage in the experiment.

9 During the course of the experiment the human subject should be at liberty to bring the experiment to an end if he has reached the physical or mental state where continuation of the experiment seems to him to be impossible.

10 During the course of the experiment the scientist in charge must be prepared to terminate the experiment at any stage, if he has probable cause to believe, in the exercise of the good faith, superior skill and careful judgment required of him, that a continuation of the experiment is likely to result in injury, disability or death to the experimental subject.

It is clear when reading the Code that the background situation that led to its creation has had a great influence on the wording used and the tone and spirit of the document. Nevertheless, the principles espoused in it have echoed in professional guidance and codes of practice ever since.

Technology

Advances in medical technology have never been as rapid and as spectacular as they were in the last half of the twentieth century. We can create babies in testtubes, replace vital organs, perform a face transplant, identify defects in a child before birth and keep a person alive with machines when their body is incapable of sustaining life by itself. All these advances have brought many advantages and prevented much suffering but they also come with difficult moral and ethical dilemmas that physicians simply did not have to face in the time of Hippocrates or even when the Nuremberg Code was being drafted. Ebert perhaps summarises it best when he states:

Advances in medicine have created ethical dilemmas not previously of concern to moral philosophers. When is a birth control method an abortifacient? When is the foetus viable? What are the ethical issues created by amniocentesis and the resulting ability to diagnose genetic defects in utero? How should society view the possibility that the sex of an unborn child can be chosen in advance of artificial insemination with appropriately selected sperm?[4]

Such advances in technology require new approaches to ethical standards. We are now dealing with issues that would have been unthinkable to those who created the documents that formed the basis of medical ethics and this means that the last couple of decades have largely involved the adapting of old concepts and the creation of new ethical rules in an attempt to keep pace with the scientific developments. The danger with this, however, is that what is considered 'ethical' is changing very quickly and there is a danger that society may be seen to be making up the new ethical rules as it goes along.[5]

Modern practice

What we now need to ask ourselves is how the ethical framework and values apply in modern medicine and how the courts approach the issue at hand. The following quote from Ian Kennedy sums up key concerns about the role of doctors in ethical decision making:

> I submit that the majority of decisions taken by doctors are not technical. They are instead moral and ethical. They are decisions about what ought to be done, in light of certain values . . . But if I am right that it is a fundamental feature of medical practice that doctors are making ethical judgments, it means that ethics, to the extent that they touch on how doctors choose to practise medicine, are something for them and them alone. This is a surprising and even dangerous notion.[6]

Kennedy seems critical of the notion that medical practitioners alone should concern themselves with deciding what is or isn't ethical. Of course, there are technical instances where the medical profession provides the best measure of acceptable behaviour – for example, in negligence cases, the courts will apply the Bolam test which, put simply, says that as long as the doctor has acted in accordance with the accepted practice of other doctors, he has not behaved negligently. But what makes a doctor any more qualified to take moral or ethical decisions than you or I? Five years of medical school do not provide a magical insight into the human condition or the greater universe. Perhaps the answer is simply that the doctors are the

---

[4] Quoted in 'Medical Law and Medical Ethics–Complementary or Corrosive?' Miola J., MLI Sept 2004 vol 6 no. 3 251–274.

[5] See Chapter 13 for discussion of illustrations of this, such as the consultation on egg sharing and the creation of chimera embryos.

[6] Kennedy, I. and Grubb, A., *Principles of Medical Law.*

ones at the coalface, having to make these ethical decisions regularly in the course of their jobs.

There can be serious consequences for doctors who fail to act ethically, but these are usually more professional than legal. The Bolam test allows doctors to escape legal liability in most circumstances as long as they can show that other doctors would also have acted as they did. However, in cases where a doctor has acted unethically they will almost certainly have breached a professional code of conduct, such as that of the General Medical Council (GMC). In its preamble the Code[7] states that 'serious or persistent failures to meet the standards in this booklet may put your registration at risk'. To complicate things further for the medical profession, it is often very difficult to separate what is a legal requirement and what is merely ethical guidance. As the British Medical Association warns its members:

> The reader must constantly bear in mind this necessary and implicit distinction between 'Legal' – which is relatively easily determined by statute, 'Ethical' – which is a more difficult assessment of what is currently accepted as proper to the group of which the reader is a par, and 'Moral' – which requires the reader to view the problem in relation to the authority which the reader accepts personally, even in opposition to other members of the same profession.[8]

It is interesting that, even here, the BMA seems to think that the determination of what is ethical should lie with the medical profession.

Throughout the rest of this book, the ethical issues surrounding legal provisions will be highlighted and discussed, but to give an idea, ethics will be a central discussion in the following topics:

- consent
- children and consent
- confidentiality
- resource allocation
- mentally incapacitated patients
- reproductive medicine
- medical research
- neonaticide
- euthanasia
- surrogacy
- abortion.

[7] 'Good Medical Practice', 2006, available at http://www.gmc-uk.org/guidance/good_medical_practice.asp.
[8] Medical Ethics Today – The BMA Handbook of Ethics and Law 2012, BMJ Books.

Ethical schools of thought

In order to make sense of some of the ethical arguments that will be covered in the book, it is necessary briefly to introduce the reader to some of the key ethical schools of thought and the fundamental differences between their approaches to the determination of what is or is not ethical. Set out in the following are summaries of the main ethical approaches; Table 2.1 provides a quick reference guide.

Table 2.1 Summary of the ethical schools of thought

School	Explanation
Consequentialism	• Looks at the consequences of a person's actions
	• There is no inherent right or wrong act
	• A framework of rules can lead to actions with ethical consequences
Deontological	• We all have certain duties towards one another and society
	• Actions that intend to comply with those duties are inherently ethical actions
Virtue ethics	• Looks at each type of action on a case-by-case basis
	• Assesses the virtue of a particular act by looking at all the surrounding circumstances and deciding if the person acted ethically
	• Who decides what is virtuous?
Vitalism	• Life has intrinsic value and should be preserved at all costs
	• It does not matter what the quality of that life will be
	• Life has a magic 'spark' or 'soul' that cannot be broken down scientifically and must be preserved
Quality of life	• Only life of a certain quality should be preserved
	• Life itself is not the goal – it must have some pleasure or positive factor in order to have value
Sanctity of life	• Generally, human life is sacred and should be preserved because it is not for humans to give or take away
	• There can be exceptions where a person is suffering and ending of life can be justified
Futility	• If treatment is futile, i.e. it is not likely to result in improvement or cure, it should not be provided
	• How is the assessment of futility made?
	• Does treatment that is futile for the patient mean it is futile in general or will other consequences count such as benefits to the family?

Consequentialism

This determines the right thing to do by looking at the consequences of the action. If the consequence is bad, then it is not ethical to proceed. Of course, a key question to ask of this approach is who decides whether a consequence is good or bad. A doctor intervening and saving a very premature infant from death may consider her survival a good outcome and therefore feel he acted ethically. However, the child herself and/or her parents may feel that a life of pain, disability and hospitalisation is a bad outcome and it would have been more ethical to allow her to die.

The term 'consequentialism' was coined by British philosopher G.E.M. Anscombe[9] and covers several different ethical theories that broadly have in common the fact that they define what is ethical or unethical by reference to the consequences of the action. For example, classic utilitarianism, as advocated by writers such as John Stuart Mill and Jeremy Bentham, would hold the view that the happiness of society as a whole, rather than particular individuals, is the ultimate goal and that acts which will have the consequence of increasing overall happiness and pleasure are therefore ethical. Indeed, Mill describes happiness as 'one of the criteria of morality'.[10] Such a purist utilitarian view invites much criticism, however, not least because there may be many various consequences to any particular action, some of which may be good and others not so good. This is especially true in medical law, where a doctor may set in course consequences that are good for some patients and not others, for example, deciding which patient goes to the top of the transplant list. It may be good for society if the younger, more 'useful' members who potentially have many years of valuable life left to contribute to society are prioritised for transplant over those who are older and less able to contribute. Would we consider that to be ethical, however? It is argued that it is difficult to support such pure utilitarian views in post-Human Rights Act Britain today.

Other consequentialist schools of thought try to address the criticisms of Mill and Bentham regarding the arbitrary nature of deciding what are 'good' consequences and what are 'bad' by framing ethics around a series of rules. By following the rules it is hoped that one ensures the consequence is ethical. Rule consequentialism was advocated by writers such as Nozick during the 1970s and more recently Brad Hooker, who has stated:

> The best argument for rule consequentialism is not that it derives from an overarching commitment to maximise the good. The best argument for rule consequentialism is that it does a better job than its rivals of matching and tying together our moral convictions, as well as offering us help with our moral disagreements and uncertainties.[11]

It is suggested that the problem with rule consequentialism is that in order for the actions arising out of that set of rules to be ethical, the rules themselves must be framed in an ethical way. We return to the familiar question of who decides what rules should be deemed ethical. It is not always possible to align ethical rules with legal rules; while many laws may be ethical, certain governments throughout history have put in place laws that we now consider extremely unethical, such as laws in the

---

[9] 'Modern Moral Philosophy', 1958, *Philosophy*, 33(124).
[10] See Bentham, J., *The Principles of Morals and Legislation* (1789) and Mill, J.S. and Bentham, J., *Utilitarianism and Other Essays*, 1987, Penguin, p. 308.
[11] Hooker, B., *Ideal Code: Real World*, 2000, Oxford University Press, p. 101.

United States in the 1950s preventing African American children from attending the same schools as white children. Neither is it possible to determine an ethical framework of rules by reference to a religious approach, as this would only be accepted by those citizens holding that particular religious view. The danger with the rule of consequentialism is that the person or organisation setting the rules would also be dictating what is and what is not ethical.

Deontology

The word 'deontology' derives from the Greek word *deon*, meaning 'duty' or 'obligation'. The theory starts an assessment of ethical behaviour from the point of view of certain duties and argues that some acts are wrong, irrespective of the consequences. Thus, in our earlier scenario about a doctor intervening and saving the life of a very premature infant, a deontological approach would be to say that a doctor has a duty to preserve life if he can and therefore the ethical thing would be to save her, regardless of the consequences or the quality of her life going forward. Of course, this makes the assumption that the duty to save life is always an ethical one.

Many deontologists criticise utilitarianism on the basis that it oversimplifies our relationships with others. For example, Ross argues that:

> Utilitarianism seems to simplify unduly our relations to our fellows. It says in effect that the only morally significant relation in which my neighbours stand to me is that of being possible beneficiaries of my action. They do stand in this relation to me, and this relation is morally significant. But they may also stand to me in the relation of promise to promisor, of creditor to debtor, of wife to husband, of fellow countryman to fellow countryman, and the like, and each of these relations is the foundation of a duty.[12]

The position voiced by Ross is really the foundation of modern deontological theory. One noted deontologist, Immanuel Kant, argued that the only absolute good is what he described as 'good will' so the factor determining whether an action is morally right is the will or intention of the person doing it.[13] This would mean that if a person's intention in doing the particular act was to fulfil their duty to their husband or to their patient, their action would be ethical. However, how do you define the scope of any given duty? A wife may consider it her duty to end the pain and suffering of her terminally ill husband by giving him extra morphine in an attempt to end his life. The intention would be to fulfil what she perceived was her duty as a wife and therefore her act could be viewed as ethical from a deontological perspective. By the same token, another person may argue that a wife has a duty to take care of her sick husband for as long as he is ill and to protect him when he is vulnerable. Thus, the ethical status of the act depends on how you define the duty.

---

[12] Ross, W.D., *The Right and The Good*, 1930, Clarendon Press, p. 19.
[13] See Kant, I., *Groundwork of the Metaphysic of Morals*, 1964, Harper & Row.

Virtue ethics

Virtue ethics has a central code of virtuous behaviour that dictates ethics. It is similar to the deontological school in the sense that it focuses on the individual person carrying out the act, rather than the recipient or the consequences, and requires the person to act in a virtuous way. As with consequentialism, however, the question must be asked about who decides what is virtuous. Should you adopt, for example, a religious view of virtue? If so, which religion provides the night set of virtues?

The key difference between virtue ethics and the two approaches described already lies in its case-by-case approach to acts that may or may not be ethical. Rather than classifying a certain act, such as ending the life of a terminally ill patient, as either *always* ethical or *always* unethical, virtue ethics will look at the individual doctor and all the surrounding circumstances. Did he stand to benefit from the person's death? Was the person in such a large amount of pain that mercy dictated action being taken? Did he act purely in the interests of the patient? Did he consider the views of the family? Depending on the answers to these and other questions, a view would be formed about whether the act in question in that particular instance was virtuous or not.

The idea of virtue is a very old one and philosophers such as Plato laid down the basis for a theory based on an intrinsic set of moral values that determine the ethics of an individual's behaviour. It can be argued that virtue ethics has been sidelined somewhat over the last 20 or 30 years, with much of the core writing on it ending before the 1980s.[14] This may well have been partly due to the difficulty in establishing a core or inherent set of moral values in an increasingly pluralistic and permissive society. However, some writers are coming back to the idea that a core instinct for 'virtue' may well influence behaviour.[15]

The problem faced by advocates of virtue ethics is similar to that faced by proponents of other theories, in that someone has to define the framework (in this case, what is virtuous and what is not) in order for the theory to work and increasingly, virtue is becoming something of a subjective concept.

Vitalism

In medical ethics, vitalism requires that patients' lives should be preserved at all costs. For example, a vitalist would require a premature baby to be saved, even where there were no hope of her ever breathing unaided, where her organs were not developed and where she would be in constant pain. Life prevails over all other arguments.

---

[14] See for example Foot, P., *Virtues and Vices and Other Essays in Moral Philosophy*, 1978, Oxford University Press.
[15] See Hursthouse, R., *On Virtue Ethics*, 1999, Oxford University Press.

The true origin of the concept of vitalism is that life cannot purely be reduced to processes of science but that there is some vital element that renders life to some extent self-determining. Many equate this concept with that of having a 'soul' or 'spirit' and the theory thus often finds supporters among members of various religions across the world. In previous centuries, when religion played a much more central role in society and science was not at the stage where life processes could be explained or recreated, vitalism was a significant ethical force and one that was not able to be scientifically disproved. However, as a concept it has faced challenges in recent times. Francis Crick, one of the scientists who discovered the structure of DNA, stated in the 1960s: 'And so to those of you who may be vitalists I would make this prophesy: what everyone believed yesterday and you believe today, only cranks will believe tomorrow.'[16] Indeed, many elements of life that vitalists have traditionally attributed to this vital and undefinable 'spark' or 'soul' have indeed been scientifically recreated. For example, sperm and eggs can now be harvested from the body, made to combine and be reintroduced to a woman's body, resulting in a normal pregnancy and a live baby. The advent of human rights legislation has also impacted on the vitalist theory, with Article 3 protecting citizens against 'inhuman and degrading treatment' and placing an obligation on states to ensure people are not subjected to such treatment.[17] The preservation of life at all costs, regardless of the amount of pain or suffering experienced by the patient, is becoming an increasingly difficult position to maintain.

So is the position of vitalists now untenable? Not necessarily. Science has by no means unravelled the mysteries of life. If the creation of a baby really has been reduced to a simple scientific process in a testtube, why do 70% of properly carried out IVF cycles result in no pregnancy? Commentators have argued over the years that vitalism is nothing more than a holding position, until science develops to a point at which all of these things can be logically explained. However, if and until such a time comes, vitalism remains an important school of thought in medical ethics.

Quality of life

This requires a value judgment to be made about the quality of a patient's life in order to determine whether or not it should be saved. In the case of the premature infant, people taking this ethical standpoint would look at how much pain she would be in, the chances of improvement or recovery, the level of disability likely etc. and decide whether her life was worth living or not. The difficulty with such an assessment is that it is inherently subjective. A life that is not worth living

---

[16] Discussed in Hein, H., 'Molecular Biology v Organicism: The Enduring Dispute Between Mechanism and Vitalism', *Humanities, Social Sciences and the Law*, 20(2), 238–253.
[17] See HRA 1998 section 6 and Article 3 European Convention on Human Rights.

to one person may be acceptable to another and takes us back to the question we have asked many times before – who should decide?

The term 'quality of life' in relation to healthcare was first coined by American President Lyndon B. Johnson in the 1960s – it is a rather modern idea compared to some of the other schools of thought that have been discussed in this chapter. It is arguable that post-World War II, as society has developed beyond a situation where people struggled to meet their essential 'needs', we began to have greater freedom and ability to pursue our 'wants' and that this has led away from a view that maintaining life is the ultimate goal towards a position that life is only worth saving if it is pain free or useful or enjoyable. Such a development can be seen as a positive or a negative depending on your perspective. Either it represents a success that we are now able to go beyond just mere survival to determine the quality of the life we live or, conversely, we have lost touch with the basic premise that life itself is the ultimate aim.

The Vatican, not surprisingly, supports the latter view very strongly. It has stated:

> After satisfying their needs, people affirmed the urge to satisfy their desires; however, these have no predetermined limit . . . the message converged with the utilitarian philosophy widespread in English speaking societies . . . to become an ideal: ethical good must produce pleasure and eliminate pain. The political programme based on the quality of life concept thus becomes an ethical obligation.[18]

However, despite such objections, the quality of life argument is a popular one and has indeed been legitimised in England and Wales by being the basis on which the National Institute for Clinical Excellence (NICE) decides whether to fund new treatments for individual patients. Using a complex formula involving analysis of number of years the treatment may give the patient with the perceived quality of the life that patient will have (known as QUALYs), a score is reached that determines whether the treatment is worth the money or not.[19] It seems that the quality of life school of ethics is now embedded in legislation and administration of healthcare. However, the fundamental question remains about who should decide what amounts to a 'quality life'.

Sanctity of life

Often confused in everyday language with vitalism, this approach does not advocate preserving life at all costs. It does, however, work on the assumption that human life has an intrinsic value and should generally be preserved if possible. The key

---

[18] Mons Elio Sgreccia, H.E., 'Examining Quality of Life Ethics of Health', 2005, available at http://www.vatican.va/roman_curia/pontifical_academies/acdlife/documents/rc_pont-acd_life_doc_20050223_report-health_en.html.

[19] A full explanation of how QUALYs are calculated can be accessed on the NICE website at www.nice.org.uk/newsroom/features/measuringeffectivenessthequaly.jsp.

distinction between this and vitalism is that the sanctity of life approach allows for certain circumstances in which there might be justification for allowing life to end. In our example regarding the very premature baby, where a vitalist approach would require everything possible to be done to save the baby's life, a sanctity of life approach would be to say that all steps should be taken to save her life unless she would be in so much pain and would suffer to such an extent that an exception can be justified.

Although part of the sanctity of life argument involves a belief that life is sacred because it comes from God, there are other elements to it. It also incorporates the idea that human life is a good in itself, rather than a means to an end good and also the premise that all human life is equally valuable, regardless of age, sex, social status, disability or other factor.

At its basic level, the principle says that all human life should be treated as sacred and is one that this author leans strongly towards. However, valid criticisms of this approach mean it is by no means a straightforward issue. Consider the following situations:

- Someone is in great agony and no longer wants to live.
- Someone has a severe disability, both physical and mental.
- An embryo is at its earliest stages, devoid of personality, the ability to reason etc.
- Vital research that would improve the quality of life for millions requires experimentation on embryos.
- A person has tortured and killed other people.

Many would argue that in these situations outlined, life should not be treated as sacred because of the perceived 'good' that might be achieved in ending their life, be that relief of suffering, benefits to others or a notion of 'justice'. Such a view accords more with a consequentialist ethical position and is virtually irreconcilable with a sanctity of life position.

Futility

This looks at a proposed treatment and where that treatment has no possibility of achieving its aim, i.e. it is considered futile, then it should not be given. So with the premature infant, if resuscitation and intubation are not going to save her life, they should not be attempted. But how is futility to be assessed? We have mentioned the great advances in medical technology and science in the last half century, but it is by no means a precise science and the media regularly report on stories of patients defying the odds and surprising their doctors. Can anyone really be certain enough of an assessment of futility to withhold lifesaving treatment? The concept of futility in medical ethics was debated in recent years in the light of the case of Stephanie

Keene, a baby born in the United States in 2002 with a condition called anencephaly. This basically means that a large part of her brain was missing – it had failed to develop in the womb – and thus only the brainstem was present. This controls motor functions such as respiration and circulation but it meant that Stephanie had no higher brain function. The condition was diagnosed prenatally and her mother was advised to have a termination but refused due to her firm Christian beliefs. After birth, several court battles ensued as the hospital tried to enforce 'do not resuscitate' orders and sought permission of the court to refuse to intervene if respiratory difficulties developed. However, the court refused to be drawn on the ethical dilemma presented by the baby and simply interpreted legislation and guidance in place in the USA at the time to mean the hospital had to continue to treat her while it searched for a more suitable long-term facility that would be willing to take her. The hospital had argued that it was not a good use of taxpayers' money to use technology, drugs and staff time on Stephanie when there was absolutely no hope of any improvement in her condition and when she would die within a short space of time whatever they did. The overwhelming opinion among ethical commentators seems to be that the court made a bad decision and that it prevented the doctors from making sound judgments about what was in the best interests of their patient.[20] However, from the perspective of Stephanie's parents, they were able to spend two and a half years with their precious daughter. They cared for her and she became a part of their family and a part of their lives. After she died, they had memories of holding her, dressing her and caring for her that sustained them in their grief. In other words, her being kept alive allowed them to be parents, albeit for a relatively short time. Therefore, can it really be said that her life had no value? Does the value have to be experienced by the patient themselves in order for the life to have value? Does the fact that she was never going to be cured of her condition equate with the concept of futility? Surely, futility requires that *nothing* can be achieved, whereas here, a great deal was achieved for Stephanie's family. Indeed, there may well have been some value in her life for Stephanie herself, although impossible to determine due to her inability to communicate.

Futility is one of the more difficult concepts in medical ethics because it requires doctors to make hard and fast predictions about things that are inherently uncertain. If Stephanie can't communicate, we do not know whether she experienced positive things during her life, negative things or nothing at all. If it were the last, then the question of what was in her best interests is profoundly difficult because she was not experiencing any pain or suffering, neither was she experiencing pleasure. However, it may well have been in her parents' best interests that she was kept alive. Is that a valid basis on which doctors should proceed?

---

[20] See for example Flannery, Ellen J., 'One Advocate's Viewpoint: Conflict and Tensions in the Baby K Case', *Journal of Law, Medicine & Ethics* (American Society of Law, Medicine & Ethics) 23(1), 7–12.

These are the main schools of thought in medical ethics, but there are other sources we can look to for guidance on what is ethical and that appear throughout the rest of the book.

Religion and theology clearly have a huge role to play. Although religion appears to be in decline in modern society, a recent poll suggested that nine out of 10 Americans believe in God,[21] so it is clear that it is still an important factor in ethical discourse for many people. In *Re A*,[22] an incredibly difficult case in which the court had to decide whether to authorise the separation of conjoined twins where the operation would inevitably lead to the death of the weaker twin, the court allowed the Roman Catholic Archbishop of Westminster to make a submission to the court.[23] However, Britain is made up of people with a broad range of different religious beliefs and some who have none at all. In a case in which a blood transfusion was required, could the court legitimately take a Catholic view into account (which would advocate saving the life of the patient because life is precious and is for God to give and take, not humans) as opposed to a Jehovah's Witness view (which may prohibit transfusions even where the patient will die). If you let religion guide the formation of ethics, which religion would you use in a multicultural society?

There is also the idea of patient autonomy. In recent years and especially since the advent of the Human Rights Act 1998, the focus in medical ethics has very much been on the rights of the individual to determine what should happen with their body. The idea of autonomy has been taken to some rather troubling extremes, such as allowing a schizophrenic who believed he was a world-renowned surgeon to refuse surgery to cure a gangrene infection, ultimately leading to his death, because he had a right to decide not to undergo the operation.[24]

However, after many years of justifiable concern over the degree of paternalism exhibited by the medical profession,[25] the idea of allowing patients autonomy to make what may appear to be unwise decisions has gained much support and is undeniably a central tenet of modern medical ethics. That is not to say it is without criticism, however. The lawyer and academic writer Charles Foster is scathing in his assessment of society's blind adherence to the concept of autonomy and argues that it has hijacked ethical discourse in this area.[26]

In light of the sheer complexity of the issues involved in medical ethics, it should be clear that medical professionals have a very difficult task in navigating the law

---

[21] Gallup poll published 3 June 2011.
[22] [2001] Fam 147.
[23] The case is discussed fully in Chapter 7.
[24] Re C [1994] 1 WLR 290.
[25] See cases such as Sidaway, discussed fully in Chapter 3.
[26] Foster, C., *Choosing Life, Choosing Death: The Tyranny of Autonomy in Medical Ethics and Law*, 2009, Hart.

and guidance they are supposed to be following, as well as giving due consideration to their own ethical instincts and the oath that they all take to act in the best interests of the patient. The Nuffield Council on Bioethics advises that:

> There is no set method for addressing an ethical issue. However, there are some generally accepted guidelines which can be applied to an issue. As a starting point for any discussion it is essential that information is accurate and from an objective and reliable source. It is important to be able to distinguish between facts and opinions. Clarity of terms and expression is crucial.[27]

Real-life application

Many of the ethical arguments and schools of thought discussed earlier are difficult fully to understand and explore until a working knowledge of their operation in practice is acquired. In order to stimulate thought and discussion around these issues, the rest of this section sets out some questions about situations that may be faced in everyday life.

When does life begin?

This is one of the most fundamental ethical questions that must be addressed in medical law, but is also one that is least likely to ever achieve a workable consensus. There are numerous options available for a person to choose when they feel 'life' begins. Is it at conception? Is it when the fertilised egg implants at around day 10? Is it when the primitive streak appears at day 14? Is it at viability at 24 weeks? Is it at birth? Think about the ethical theories in Table 2.1. Assume that a vitalist holds the view that life begins at conception. Such a person would argue that the life deserves protection from this point onwards. However, a consequentialist argument may be that the ultimate harm of a woman having to carry a child she does not want or that is the result of rape permits the destruction of the foetus any time before birth.

Using a similar approach, think about the questions that follow.

---

[27] Critical Care Decisions in Fetal and Neonatal Medicine – Ethical Issues. Nuffield Council on Bioethics, Nov 2006, p. 24.

- Research conducted on a human embryo will 'kill' it – is such research ethically acceptable?

- Y and Z are husband and wife and have two embryos created in-vitro. The two embryos are twins. One is implanted and nine months later the couple have a baby boy. Three years later the other embryo is implanted and the second child is born. The twins are born three years apart. Is this procedure ethically justifiable?

- Was it ethical when the court sanctioned the operation on the conjoined twins (*Re A* earlier) or would it have been better had they respected the wishes of the parents and let nature take its course?

- Is it ethical to allow abortion on demand?

- Is it ethical to refuse a foetus legal rights?

- A grandmother aged 75 is suffering from a terminal illness. She is incontinent and in terrible pain. Her health carers give her 12–18 months before she dies. She wants to go now and asks them to give her a lethal injection – is it ethical for them to comply with her request?

- The research team at a hospital is convinced that if it acquires sufficient organs from dead babies, it could learn enough to ultimately cure severe illnesses in young children so, unknown to the parents, the research team has been removing the hearts of dead babies. They argue that the ends justify the means. Is their behaviour ethical?

- If you were infertile would you believe it was ethically acceptable to use a surrogate?

- Is it ethically acceptable to be a surrogate?

Summary

There are certainly no easy answers to these questions. There are, arguably, no 'right' answers to these questions. The best that can be hoped for is an open and intelligent discourse on the various ethical arguments that apply in a given situation so that those arguments can inform and, it is to be hoped, improve the law that results. In such a context, medical ethics is one of the most fascinating and challenging disciplines that can be studied. On a medical law and ethics course, students often make the mistake of thinking that the law is the most important bit and the ethics are just arguments tagged onto the end of an essay. In fact, the ethical arguments are just as important, if not more so, and without due consideration of them, the law would be ineffective and inapplicable.

Self-test questions

1 What is the difference between vitalism and sanctity of life?

2 What are the key elements of a consequentialist approach to ethics?

3 What is autonomy?

4 How relevant is the Hippocratic Oath today?

Practice essay question

'Medical ethics has often focussed on the tension between rights based and duty based reasoning' (Pattinson, S.D., *Medical Law and Ethics*, 2011, 3rd edn, Sweet and Maxwell, p. 13).

Critically assess the extent to which medical law achieves a balance between these two ethical positions.

3 Clinical negligence I: duty and breach

In this chapter, we will cover:

- the circumstances in which the duty of care arises
- who can owe a duty and to whom the duty may be owed
- the scope of the duty
- the standard of care required and the test for breach of duty
- the issue of causation
- human rights implications and issues arising out of the duty.

Introduction

Students who have studied tort law, and, in particular, the law of negligence at an earlier stage of their degree course, often make the mistake of thinking that clinical negligence is merely the tort of negligence applied in the medical setting. While this may well have been the prevailing view of practitioners and academics alike at one time, in the last 20 years or so, clinical negligence has developed separately from the law of tort and rightly gained recognition as a distinct discipline in its own right. Although clearly based around traditional tort principles, the application of those principles has developed through complex case law and against a backdrop of professional guidance and ethics to form a specialised and involved area of law that aims to balance the rights of the often ill and vulnerable patient against the professional and practical requirements of the job being undertaken by the doctor. As we will see, that balance is difficult, if not impossible, to achieve and judges often struggle just as much as medical professionals with the application of legal rules in often sensitive and ethically complex situations.

There are several main reasons why the law of clinical negligence differs so substantially from negligence in general tort law. First, the identity of the defendant plays a crucial role. In most circumstances, the claim will be brought against the NHS trust and this has certain unavoidably difficult consequences. As we saw in Chapter 1, resources in the NHS are finite and extremely difficult decisions regularly have to be made by those responsible for the budget about how those resources can best be used to benefit the maximum number of patients. We saw in the *Cambridge* case[1] that the trust could not justify spending £75,000 on a 10-year-old girl who had less than a 10% chance of survival because that would mean that they would not have funds available to provide lifesaving treatment to other patients with a better chance of recovery. Even before the recent economic downturn, trusts were struggling to prioritise inadequate funds and the courts were initially very reluctant to encourage patients to bring claims.[2] There is at the very least an ethical question to be asked about the merits of large amounts of those very limited budgets going towards legal fees and compensation payouts and it is almost inevitable that some patient care must be compromised as a result. There is also a more intangible but nevertheless compelling ethical question about the nature of the doctor–patient relationship and the effects of large numbers of claims and a high level of awards of damages on public trust in the medical profession.

Another reason for the differences between general and clinical negligence is the nature of medicine itself. In a general tort claim, where one party has behaved negligently and caused harm to another, perhaps by leaving a tripping hazard or not maintaining equipment correctly, the situation is largely within the understanding and general experience of the public and of the judge hearing the case. This makes the assessment of whether a person or organisation has fallen below the standard of care required and breached its duty of care relatively straightforward to establish. However, medicine is a complex and extremely specialised art, full of uncertainties and contradictory opinions and positions. Fundamental disagreements can exist between eminent professionals in any one field and judges are often no more able to unravel such differences than the average layperson would be. Legal tests that would be simple in another area of law may not be appropriate in the context of such a mismatch between the knowledge of the defendant and the knowledge of the claimant and/or the court. This leads to a much heavier reliance on expert witnesses, something that has resulted in no shortage of controversy over the years[3] and makes authoritative judgments much harder to deliver. Supplementing this is the additional problem that any harm caused to the patient must be viewed in the light of an underlying illness or injury that may also have caused or contributed to the damage that results, and, as we will discuss further in Chapter 5, discovering with absolute certainty the extent to which any negligence caused or contributed to any harm suffered by the patient is, generally, extremely difficult.

Before going on to look in detail at the individual components of a clinical negligence claim, we need to cover the basic structure and content. In terms of potential defendants, where the person who has allegedly been negligent is an employee of the NHS trust, under the principles of vicarious liability the NHS trust will assume liability and will be the defendant in the case. However, there are some special situations that merit mention:

---

[1] *R v Cambridge District Health Authority ex parte B* [1995] 2 All ER 129 CA and see p. 9 for a full discussion of the case.

[2] *R v Central Birmingham Health Authority ex parte Walker* [1987].

[3] See for example the case of Professor Roy Meadows, who was struck off the medical register by a Fitness to Practise Panel at the GMC in 2005 for giving evidence in the trial of a mother accused of murdering her two infant sons that the GMC described as 'misleading' – he later challenged and overturned that decision: http://www.timesonline.co.uk/tol/news/uk/article731947.ece.

- *The general practitioner (GP)* – GP surgeries tend to be arranged as a partnership, so will either sue the individual GP or, more usually, the partnership as a whole. The trust is not technically his employer so the rules on vicarious liability will not apply.

- *The locum doctor* – locums are temporary doctors brought in to cover when someone is off sick or on holiday. They will often be from another area or even another country and are generally classed in law as independent contractors rather than employees. It is therefore usual to sue the locum doctor individually as opposed to the trust.

- *The private hospital* – where the patient is receiving private rather than NHS treatment, the situation is different because, unlike an NHS patient, the private patient has a contractual relationship with the health professional and/or the clinic at which the treatment is provided and therefore the defendant will be whomever the contract names as the party providing the treatment. The private patient therefore has the option of whether to sue in tort, by way of a clinical negligence claim, or to sue for breach of contract (see Chapter 2 for further discussion of contract claims).

- *The Department of Health* – it is theoretically possible for the Department to owe a direct duty of care to the patient. In *Re HIV Haemophiliac Litigation*,[4] 962 claimants argued that the Department was in breach of its statutory duty under the NHS Act and also negligent in importing blood products from the United States and not providing for those products to be tested for HIV contamination. The court decided it was at least arguable that a direct duty of care was owed and the case should proceed. However, the government settled the claim before any further hearings could take place, leaving the theoretical possibility not fully explored.

Once a claimant has established who the defendant is going to be, the starting point is that they must establish the basic elements of a negligence claim. They are:

- that a duty of care existed
- that the defendant breached its duty of care by falling below the standard required by law
- that the claimant suffered actionable damage and that damage was caused by the defendant's breach of duty

Duty of care

In looking at the duty of care owed by a medical professional to a patient, three key questions need to be addressed:

- What is the nature of the duty?
- When does the duty begin and end?
- Who owes the duty and to whom?

[4] [1996] PIQR P220.

The nature of the duty

Does the health professional owe a duty to provide a specific treatment or produce a particular result or is the duty merely a more general requirement to act in the best interests of the patient and provide the best treatment they can reasonably provide in the circumstances? This fundamental question has been addressed in several cases and will largely depend on whether the patient is receiving private or NHS treatment – in other words whether or not there is a contractual duty in existence to provide a certain treatment or result.

In an NHS setting, the answer is fairly straightforward. The provider of care will only be liable for falling below a general standard of care required by law (see p. 47). A private patient could theoretically establish that the provider had guaranteed a particular outcome or type of treatment but so far the courts have been reluctant to find this. In *Eyre v Meadsay*,[5] a patient who had undergone a failed sterilisation operation in a private clinic was unsuccessful in her attempt to argue that the doctor had guaranteed permanent sterility. It would be a foolhardy doctor who made such a promise and unless it was expressly recorded in a written contract it is unlikely that a court is going to find that such a guarantee has been given. In its absence, the duty under a contract for private care is largely the same as that owed in the NHS – it is a duty to take reasonable care.[6]

One of the main debates when it comes to the nature of the duty of care centres around whether there is one duty that applies to all forms of treatment and care received by a patient or whether the duty differs depending on the situation. For example, does a doctor owe the same duty when he is conducting open heart surgery as he does when he is discussing the risks of a particular treatment with a patient? The official answer to this question is that there is only one, indivisible duty that applies to all aspects of patient care. However, when it comes to disclosure of information about risks of treatment options to a patient, case law seems to disclose a rather different approach to how the duty operates. The leading example of this is *Sidaway*.[7]

KEY CASE

Sidaway v Board of Governors of Bethlem Royal Hospital

This case concerned an operation carried out in 1974 to try to relieve the claimant's persistent back pain. The operation carried an inherent risk of damage to the spinal cord of between 1 and 2%, even where the procedure was carried out with appropriate care and skill. The claimant alleged that she had not been informed by the surgeon of this inherent risk and if she had been so informed, she would not have ➡

---

[5] [1986] 1 All ER 488.
[6] See also *Thake v Maurice* [1986] 1 All ER 497, CA.
[7] *Sidaway v Board of Governors of Bethlem Royal Hospital* [1985] AC 871.

consented to the procedure. In fact, the operation was carried out competently but the risk materialised and left her with disabilities. On the facts, the court held that the surgeon was only under a duty to disclose the risks that a reasonably competent surgeon would disclose to a patient and in accordance with that test (discussed in more detail later), there was no breach of duty.

However, the court also indicated that there could be a situation where the nature of the risk meant that regardless of whether there was a responsible body of medical opinion that would testify to the contrary, liability would attach for failure to disclose that risk to the patient. That situation was described by Lord Scarman as 'where the risk is such that in the court's view, a prudent person in the patient's situation would have regarded it as significant'.[8] In other words, the court could foresee a situation where the risk could be so important that the duty imposed on a doctor in relation to disclosure may be higher than the duty imposed in other contexts.

It should be noted that this prediction by Lord Scarman has been confirmed by the more recent case of *Chester* v *Afshar*,[9] where, on similar facts, there was found to have been a breach of duty. The case will be discussed at great length in Chapter 4, but for now, the words of Lord Steyn in *Chester* sum up the change in approach to duty of care in risk disclosure situations. He stated: 'In modern law, medical paternalism no longer rules and a patient has a prima facie right to be informed by a surgeon of a small but well established risk of serious injury.'[10]

This duty to inform a patient of risks involved in treatment extends to a duty to inform of the comparative risks of an alternative treatment option. So, for example, in *Birch UCL*,[11] the patient was advised of the risks associated with the catheter angiography that was carried out, ultimately resulting in a stroke, but was not informed of the much lower risks involved with the alternative treatment option using MRI. Thus, there was a breach of duty even though the actual clinical decision not to use MRI was not negligent.

The beginning and ending of the duty

The duty of care will begin when treatment begins. This is considered to be when the medical professional takes responsibility for the patient and will apply to each individual professional who takes responsibility for or begins treating the patient. In *Wyatt* v *Curtis*,[12] a woman contracted chicken pox when she was 14 weeks' pregnant but her GP breached his duty of care by failing to advise her of the risks of damage to the foetus. Four weeks later, when she saw an obstetrician as a normal

[8] See n. 7 above at 889.
[9] *Chester* v *Afshar* [2004] UKHL 41, [2004] 3 WLR 927.
[10] See n. 8 above at 933.
[11] *Birch* v *University College London Hospital NHS Foundation Trust* [2008] EWHC 460.
[12] *Wyatt* v *Curtis* [2003] EWCA Civ 1779.

part of her antenatal care, that obstetrician was held also to be under a duty to inform her of the possibility of damage and to make sure she understood the risks. The case raises some interesting issues that we will return to when we deal with standard of care, as, on the facts, it was decided that the first doctor was negligent because if she had been informed at 14 weeks she would have had a termination, but the second doctor was not because, at 18 weeks, even had she been informed of the risk of damage, she would not have had a termination. Does this effectively mean that past a certain point in pregnancy, there can never be a breach of duty for failure to warn or inform the woman of possible damage to the foetus?

The leading case on when the duty of care begins is *Barnett*.

KEY CASE

Barnett v Chelsea and Kensington HMC[13]

Three nightwatchmen were feeling very ill after their shift and went to the accident and emergency department of the defendant's hospital. The house officer on call did not attend the men but relied on information relayed to him over the telephone by the nurse. He diagnosed food poisoning and told them to go to their GP when the surgery opened later in the morning. One of the men later died from what turned out to be arsenic poisoning and his wife brought a claim against the hospital. The defendant argued that as the doctor had not actually seen the patient and admitted him, no duty of care existed, but this argument was rejected by the court. As soon as the men arrived at the unit and were examined and discussed by the nurse and the doctor over the phone, the duty of care existed and had therefore been breached.

(The case later failed on the issue of causation which we discuss in Chapter 4.)

Who owes the duty?

In most straightforward situations regarding inadequate care in a hospital environment, establishing who owes the duty of care will be fairly simple (it will be the medical professional caring for the patient and their employer will be vicariously liable for their actions), but set out in the following are some examples where the duty has been a little more difficult to allocate appropriately.

Inexperienced staff

In principle, all those involved with the care of the patient will owe the same duty regardless of their level of experience or their seniority. For example, in *Wilsher*,[14] a

---

[13] *Barnett v Chelsea and Kensington Hospital Management Committee* [1968].
[14] *Wilsher v Essex Area Health Authority* [1986].

junior house officer who had only been working on the ward in question for a couple of days inserted a catheter into the vein of a premature baby. The catheter was supposed to be inserted into an artery and the result was that too much oxygen was administered to the baby. The doctor did ask a senior colleague to check his efforts and the colleague failed to spot the mistake. The court held that the duty owed to the patient is a duty to adhere to the standard reasonably expected of a doctor working in that post and was the same regardless of the experience of the individual concerned. (See Chapter 3 for further discussion of this case.)

Direct liability of the trust

We have talked up until now about the duty being owed by the individuals providing the care to the patient and the trust being liable for their actions vicariously as an employer, but in some circumstances, the trust itself may owe a duty directly to the patient. In *Bull v Devon*,[15] the court found that the trust owed individual patients a duty to operate an effective system at their two hospital sites. Mrs Bull had been in labour with twins and was being cared for by midwives at a hospital run by the defendant health authority when complications arose. A registrar was bleeped but he was attending to another patient at the other site which was over a mile away. Because of resourcing issues, the authority did not provide for registrar cover overnight at both sites and when the delay in his arrival was shown to have caused the subsequent damage to one of the twins, Mrs Bull was successful in her claim against the authority for what the court called a 'system error'. In other words, the damage was caused by the inadequate system that the authority had implemented, not by the individual actions of the medical staff involved. However, the court made clear that it was not saying that someone should have been able to attend to Mrs Bull immediately and it appreciated the resourcing challenges facing the authority. Had there been a 10- or 15-minute delay in the registrar arriving because he was busy with another patient, that would not have been sufficient to show a systematic failure on the part of the trust, but the hour-long delay was indicative of such a failure. The unanswered question in this case is, of course, where exactly that line is to be drawn . . . what would the outcome have been if there had been a 25-minute delay? Does it depend on the reason?

Alternative facilities

This direct duty of care can also extend to a duty to provide alternative facilities where a trust cannot afford to operate its own facilities to full capacity and a direct duty on the provider of that alternative. For example, in *Hardaker*,[16] a diver was suffering from decompression illness and needed to be treated in a decompression

---

[15] *Bull v Devon Area Health Authority* [1993] 4 Med LR 117.
[16] *Hardaker v Newcastle Health Authority & Chief Constable of Northumbria Police* [2001].

chamber, but the chamber at the defendant's hospital was closed overnight due to staff shortages. Arrangements had been made between the trust and the police so that the chamber at the police diving school could be used in such situations and the diver was taken there instead, but they had not had advance warning of his arrival and the chamber was not ready, which caused further delay in his treatment. The court found that both the trust and the police owed the patient a direct duty of care. It found that the trust had not breached that duty because it had put appropriate arrangements in place for a suitable facility to be available and that the police had not breached their duty because they were not a medical service and therefore the duty was lower than it would be for the trust – they did not have the information they needed in advance and could not therefore have readied the chamber any more quickly than they did.

Independent laboratories

When tests are carried out on patients and samples taken for analysis, those samples are often analysed, not in the hospital where they are taken, but increasingly by independent laboratories that have contracts with the trust. This had led to disputes over who owes the duty to the patient when mistakes are made or samples analysed incorrectly. In *Farraj* v *Kings*,[17] a couple were both carriers of a gene for a blood disorder and were concerned about the condition being passed to their unborn child. A test called chorionic villus sampling (CVS) was carried out where a sample of fluid is taken and analysed to assess the genetic profile of the baby to see if it has the disease. The defendant trust had a contract with a reputable, independent cytogenetics laboratory to carry out the testing of such samples. Mr and Mrs Farraj were assured that the sample had been negative and the baby was healthy but when it was born, it did, in fact, have the inherited blood disorder. The court held that the duty owed by the trust in such circumstances is a delegable duty, meaning that it can effectively pass that duty over to someone else provided that it reasonably believes that other person will discharge it properly, so here it was the laboratory that was liable to the couple. However, the court was keen to distinguish the duty in relation to testing of samples and to stress that the duty in relation to actual patient care is non-delegable. Is this yet another chink in the armour of the argument still officially adhered to by the courts that there is but one duty of care that applies equally in all medical cases?

Healthcare funded by insurance companies

West Bromwich Albion Football Club had medical insurance to cover medical treatment that might be needed by any of its players. One player was badly injured on

---

[17] *Farraj* v *Kings Healthcare NHS Trust and anor* [2009] EWCA 1203 CA.

the field and was treated by a doctor who was paid for by the insurance company. The doctor negligently misdiagnosed the problem, which led to a significant delay in appropriate treatment, ultimately resulting in the player having to retire from professional football and abandon what had been a very promising and lucrative career for both him and the club. The club sued the doctor, seeking compensation for the financial loss they had been caused. The question for the court was whether the doctor owed a duty of care to the club. It was held that he did not – his fees were paid by the insurance company and he was not engaged to provide advice or treatment to the club but to the individual player, to whom he did owe a duty. This ruling seems a little harsh, even if it is based on sound legal reasoning. The player may have arguably lost future earnings, but the club also lost any future money it would have made from the player (for example, in transfer fees), as well as the money it had already paid to sign and train him. Its loss is greater and more easily quantifiable but it has no cause of action against the person whose negligence has caused that loss. In practice, of course, there may well be contractual duties in place between a club and an insurance company whereby the company will agree to indemnify the club for such losses. In this author's opinion, the contractual freedom of a party to protect its position by other means does not necessarily mean that the law of negligence should be allowed to choose not to offer them protection.

Prison doctors

Are prison doctors under a duty to individual prisoner patients and does the prison itself owe a duty to a prisoner? The answer to both questions is yes. So, for example, in *St George* v *Home Office*,[18] a prisoner who was going through drug withdrawal was left alone in a cell unrestrained, and during a fit caused by the withdrawal, fell from the top bunk and injured himself. It was held that the prison owed him a duty of care which it had breached by not providing an appropriate standard of care during his withdrawal. Similarly, in *Ministry of Justice* v *Carter*,[19] a female prisoner had been to three separate prison doctors on three separate occasions complaining that she could feel a lump in her breast. None of them could feel anything unusual and she was not referred for further investigation. On release it was discovered that she did, indeed, have breast cancer. At first instance it was held that the initial and second doctors owed a duty but had not breached it because there were no outward signs to alert them to her cancer. However, the third doctor should have referred on the basis that she had complained twice before and he should have realised it warranted further investigation. This was overturned on appeal, on the basis that each of the prison doctors owed the same duty – it was not appropriate to impose

---

[18] *St George* v *Home Office* [2008] EWCA Civ 1068.
[19] [2010] EWCA Civ 694.

a higher duty on the third doctor when the lump was still not palpable and he was looking at the same clinical presentation as the other two.

Pharmacists

Where a doctor has given a patient a prescription, that doctor clearly owes a duty to prescribe the appropriate medication in the appropriate dose. But is there also a duty on the pharmacist who dispenses the medication to check that it is suitable? Yes, according to the case of *Horton v Evans*, where a patient who had been to the same pharmacist on seven previous occasions for medication to control a long-term condition presented that pharmacist with a prescription for the same medicine but at a much larger dose. The court confirmed that the pharmacist had a duty to check with the patient and with the doctor if necessary whether a mistake had been made.[20]

Who is owed the duty?

Again, in most cases, this will be straightforward because the person suing will be the patient who has received the faulty treatment (or their representative if the patient is dead or unable to bring the claim himself). However, there are certain patient groups that warrant further discussion.

Third parties

The question here is whether a health carer can, in law, owe a duty to someone injured by his patient. The general tortious principle that such a duty to third parties can only be imposed where the damage they have suffered is foreseeable applies equally in medical law.[21] However, as medical staff are often privy to more intimate and detailed information about a patient due to the nature of the relationship, the question of exactly how foreseeable the damage has to be becomes a complex one to answer. In *Palmer v Tees*,[22] the defendant trust had released a patient who had been receiving psychiatric treatment on the advice of the doctor who was treating him that he did not pose a threat to society. Just a few days after his release, the former patient abducted, sexually assaulted and killed a 4-year-old girl, Rosie Palmer, in Sunderland. Rosie's mother sued the trust for the distress caused to her by its decision to release this patient. The question the court had to answer was not whether his ultimate violence was generally foreseeable but whether it was foreseeable that if he was released, he was likely to cause such damage to Rosie and/or Mrs Palmer – in other words, the foreseeable risk had to attach to a particular

---

[20] *Horton v Evans; Lloyds Pharmacy Ltd* [2006] EWHC 2808.
[21] See, for example, *Smith v Littlewood Organisation* [1987] and *Home Office v Dorset Yacht Co Ltd* [1970].
[22] *Palmer v Tees & Hartlepool & East Durham NHS Trust* [1999] Lloyds Rep Med 151.

identifiable person and in this case, there was nothing in the patient's behaviour for the trust to identify the Palmers as being at risk, so no duty was owed to them on the basis that a duty cannot be owed to the world at large. This can be contrasted with American cases such as *Tarasoff*,[23] in which the student patient told the university psychiatrist that he was going to kill his ex-girlfriend, a threat he then proceeded to carry out. Although he did not name the girl in the consultation, it would have been quite easy for the doctor to establish her identity on the information he had and the court therefore held that he had owed her a duty of care and his failure to warn her was a breach of that duty. Whether such an approach would be taken in the UK, or whether the potential victim actually needs to be named or otherwise specifically identified is debatable. The key problem with our approach to third-party duties at the moment was summed up nicely by a student who asked: 'Does that not mean that they could just let all the psychiatric patients out as long as they had not named a victim and they wouldn't be liable if they killed someone because they don't owe a duty?'

The embryo/foetus

As we will see in later chapters, an embryo or a foetus is not classed as a legal personality and, as such, attracts very limited legal protection. As such, the issue of whether a duty of care can be owed in respect of harm done to a pregnant woman that causes damage to the foetus or harm done directly to the foetus before birth is a difficult one. The general approach is that such a duty can exist, but only if the child is subsequently born alive. In *Burton v Islington*,[24] a baby had been born with severe disabilities due to the alleged negligent treatment of its mother during the labour and delivery. As a preliminary issue, the court had to consider whether the health authority owed a duty to the foetus at the time of the labour and delivery. Balcome LJ stated that:

> Although not a person in the eyes of the law when the injury took place, an unborn child is deemed to be born whenever its interests require and is therefore clothed with all the rights of action when born that it would have had if in existence at the date of the accident to its mother.[25]

The events in this case pre-dated the implementation of the Congenital Disabilities Act 1976 (which we will look at in more detail in Chapter 5) but the Act confirmed the court's reasoning and placed the duty in such circumstances on a statutory footing.

There is, however, a rather large caveat to this duty owed to a child in respect of damage sustained before birth, which is best illustrated by the case of *McKay*.

---

[23] *Tarasoff* v *Regents of the University of California* 551 P 2d 334 (Cal, 1976).
[24] *Burton* v *Islington Health Authority* [1993] QB 204.
[25] n. 24 above at 232.

KEY CASE

McKay v Essex Area Health Authority **[1982]**[26]

Mrs McKay became aware that she had been in contact with the rubella virus during the first trimester of her pregnancy and went to see a doctor, who took a blood sample. This sample was lost and another had to be taken some time later. The trust subsequently informed Mrs McKay that neither she nor the baby had contracted the virus. In actual fact, they had and the baby, a girl named Katherine, was born with significant disabilities. Various claims were brought by the family, including one by the mother for wrongful birth, alleging that she had been deprived of information necessary to allow her to choose whether or not to terminate the pregnancy and for the distress caused by having a child with disabilities and also a claim by Katherine for wrongful life. Essentially Katherine was seeking damages for the negligence that allowed her to be born into a life of pain and suffering and it was here that the court drew the line in terms of the extent of the duty that can be owed to the foetus. Here, the doctor had not caused the damage to the child, it was the rubella infection that had been causative, so effectively Katherine was arguing that he had been under a duty to enable an abortion. The court's concern with this was summed up by Stephenson LJ:

> An obligation to abort would mean regarding the life of a handicapped child as not only less valuable than the life of a normal child, but so much less valuable that it was not worth preserving . . . these are the consequences of the . . . assumption that a child has the right to be born whole or not at all, not to be born unless it can be born perfect or 'normal', whatever that may mean.[27]

On a more practical note, the court also stressed the difficulties in assessing damages. The usual approach is to compare the situation of the claimant before the negligence with the situation after and try to provide compensation for the difference, but how do you assess and quantify the difference between existence and non-existence, between life and death? While difficulty in assessing damages is not of itself prohibitive of a duty of care arising, in this case it was useful added weight to the already firm line taken by the court that such a duty could not be imposed on a health carer. This did not impact on the duty owed to Mrs McKay however and she was able to succeed in her claim for damages.

It should be noted that if the damage to Katherine had been caused by negligence rather than rubella, she could have claimed against the health authority for the pain and distress and financial impact of her disabilities, because their breach of duty caused the harm that she suffered. The reason her claim failed was that the breach she was alleging was not causing the harm but causing her to be born instead of being aborted.

---

[26] *McKay v Essex Area Health Authority* [1982] QB 1166, [1982] 2 All ER 777.
[27] n. 26 above at 781.

The ambulance service

As members of the public, are we owed a duty of care by the ambulance service to attend promptly when called or can such a duty not be imposed because, as discussed earlier, a duty cannot be owed to the public at large? This was the question facing the court in *Kent v Griffiths*.[28] A pregnant woman, who was severely asthmatic, had a bad attack and an ambulance was called at 4.27 p.m. The ambulance took 38 minutes to arrive by which time the patient was in full respiratory arrest. The delay in treatment led to her suffering a miscarriage and lasting after-effects such as personality change and memory impairment. The ambulance service argued that it had not had any contact directly with her and therefore no duty of care arose until it arrived at the scene. As Lord Woolf stated: 'The issue on this appeal is whether an ambulance service can owe any duty of care to a member of the public on whose behalf a 999 telephone call is made if, due to carelessness, it fails to arrive within a reasonable time.'[29] The court acknowledged the general rule that a duty is not owed to the wider public where no individual subject of the duty is identified, but distinguished circumstances where an emergency call has been made and personal details of the patient have been accepted by the ambulance service. At that point, the patient is identifiable and the service has taken responsibility for their care and they have a duty to respond in a reasonable time.

◼ Summary – duty of care

As we have seen, it is often fairly easy to establish the existence of a duty of care in medical settings (with some notable exceptions discussed earlier) but defining the scope and limits of that duty can be extremely difficult. There is also a tension between the strict legal position and policy considerations that tend to influence judicial reasoning. Such policy considerations can be seen clearly in judgments such as *Chester v Afshar* (patient rights to information) and *McKay* (sanctity of life) and more recently in relation to child protection in cases such as *JD v East Berkshire*[30] and *RK and AK v United Kingdom*[31] where it was held that where a doctor owes a duty to a child patient and there is a suspicion of child abuse by the parents, even if the parents are also his patients, he will not owe a duty to those parents because the duty to protect the child outweighs any duty he may have had to the parents. It is impossible to grapple with such life- (and death-) defining issues without policy considerations creeping in, but the problem with this is that policy is changeable

---

[28] [2001] QB 36.
[29] n. 28 above at 41.
[30] *JD (FC) v East Berkshire Community Health NHS Trust and others* [2005] 2 AC 373.
[31] [2008] ECHR 38000/05.

and dependent on societal views on a particular issue at a particular time and indeed on the individual views of judges in particular cases. In other areas, the law cuts through all this by being very clear and dispassionate, but even the law cannot be dispassionate over the issues thrown up by the cases we are looking at in this chapter, making hard and fast answers to these difficult legal questions increasingly elusive.

Standard of care

Now that we have looked at the circumstances in which a duty of care arises, we need to think about how we decide when and whether that duty has been breached. This involves an analysis of the standard that medical professionals should adhere to and how it should be established whether they have fallen below that accepted standard. Should we look to NICE clinical guidelines for the required standard,[32] or allow judges to set the standard, or perhaps allow the medical profession them-selves to tell us what is and is not good and acceptable practice? Given the inherent mismatch in knowledge between a medical practitioner and the general public (including judges), this is one of the most difficult questions to answer in medical law. In this section, we will look at:

- how the standard of care is defined in law
- how that test has been applied in cases over the years
- the role of other influences such as clinical guidelines and increased patient knowledge
- human rights implications on the standard.

What is the standard of care?

The standard expected of medical practitioners cannot be assessed in the normal tortious way, by looking at the theoretical 'man on top of the Clapham omnibus'[33] because quite obviously, medicine is a skilled art and an ordinary man would gener-ally perform open heart surgery to a rather poor standard. So if we cannot use that test, what test should we use? The answer came in what must have appeared at the time a rather lowly and straightforward medical negligence case in the 1950s but which has come to be one of the defining legal cases of all time – the *Bolam* case.

---

[32] For discussion of these, see Chapter 1.
[33] Term coined by Sir Richard Henn Collins MR in *McQuire* v *Western Morning News* [1903] 2 KB 100 at 109.

KEY CASE

Bolam v Friern Hospital Management Committee[34]

Mr Bolam had been a psychiatric patient at the defendant's hospital and had been subject to the controversial treatment of electro-convulsant therapy (ECT). During this treatment, he was not given a muscle relaxant, neither was he restrained in any way, and this led to his suffering a hip injury while undergoing the treatment. He brought a claim for damages for the pain and suffering caused and the court had to decide whether the failure to administer a relaxant or to restrain him constituted treatment that fell below the accepted standard of care.

At the time, medical evidence was that opinion was divided within the profession. The claimant had several doctors who claimed that they would have taken such precautions but the defence had equally well-respected doctors who claimed they would not have considered it necessary. McNair J set out what has become the defining test in clinical negligence cases:

> The test is the standard of the ordinary skilled man exercising and professing to have that special skill. A man need not possess the highest expert skill; it is well established law that it is sufficient if he exercises the ordinary skill of an ordinary man exercising that particular art.[35]

In other words, the standard to be expected of a doctor is the standard of an ordinary competent doctor. How do we know what that standard is? By asking doctors. McNair J acknowledged this as he went on:

> A doctor is not guilty of negligence if he has acted in accordance with a practice accepted as proper by a responsible body of medical men skilled in that particular art . . . Putting it the other way around, a doctor is not negligent if he acted in accordance with such a practice, merely because there is a body of opinion that takes a contrary view.[36]

As the defendant had medical experts that testified that he had acted in accordance with a practice that they themselves would have adhered to, there was held to have been no breach of duty.

Note that McNair J does include the word 'responsible' when talking about the body of medical men to be used as a comparator, indicating at least some sort of objective analysis should be carried out by the court. We will come back to this point later in the chapter.

⬤ Case law since *Bolam*

The dangers inherent in this test are clear to see. The risk is that you establish a system of 'trial by expert', where as long as a doctor has a colleague who will testify that

---

[34] [1957] 2 All ER 118.
[35] n. 34 above at 119.
[36] n. 34 above at 122.

they would have acted in the same way, a doctor is never going to be liable in negligence, and indeed case law after *Bolam*, at least initially, seemed to confirm this concern. The idea of the *Bolam* test is for like to be compared with like and ensuring that there is an evenness to the approach. As we examined earlier in this chapter, no distinction is made for a junior doctor; the standard is that of a reasonably competent doctor.[37] This will also apply irrespective of the identity of the patient group, so prisoners can expect the same standard of care as a patient on any hospital ward.[38] However, problems with the test soon began to emerge.

The numbers game

Crucially, the number of doctors who supported the defendant's position was irrelevant, so in *De Freitas* v *O'Brian*,[39] it was held that a body of medical men did not have to be 'substantial' to be 'responsible' and that here, where there were only two spinal surgeons in the country who could be found who would have carried out the operation the way the defendant had carried it out, that was sufficient to constitute a responsible body of medical men.

Defining accepted practice

There is also case law establishing that the accepted medical practice must be current. In *Roe* v *Ministry of Health*,[40] checking glass ampoules containing spinal anaesthetic by sight was the accepted practice at the time of the damage caused to the patient by a contaminated product. A such, it was appropriate to judge the behaviour of medical staff against accepted practice at the time of the incident, not at the time of the trial when knowledge had advanced to the point where that would no longer be considered responsible practice. This does not mean, however, that a doctor must keep up to date with every new development in the field, so in *Crawford* v *Charing Cross*,[41] a blood transfusion was given with the patient's arm held at 80° from his body which caused a brachial palsy in that arm. This was general practice but an article had appeared in the *Lancet* six months prior to his treatment indicating that such a palsy was a danger if transfusions were carried out in this way and recommending an alternative. The court held that a doctor could not be expected to have read every article in his chosen field and there was no breach of duty.

On the issue of whether departure from an accepted practice will automatically mean a breach of duty, we have the case of *Clark* v *MacLennan*.[42] A woman was suffering from stress incontinence after the birth of her first child and just one

---

[37] *Wilsher* v *Essex Area Health Authority* [1988] AC 1074.
[38] See *Brooks* v *Home Office* [1999] 2 FLR 33.
[39] (1995) 25 BMLR 51.
[40] *Roe* v *Ministry of Health* [1954] 2 QB 66.
[41] Unreported, April 22 1953.
[42] [1983] 1 All ER 416.

month after the delivery, the defendant performed an operation called an anterior colporrhaphy. Generally accepted practice was to wait at least three months post-delivery to carry out such a procedure due to the risk of haemorrhage, a risk that did, in fact, materialise in this instance. The woman was left with a permanent disability and the court was required to determine whether the defendant was liable and had fallen below an acceptable standard because he had not complied with normal practice. Of course, the danger in such an assertion is that medicine would never advance at all if doctors were confined to doing things as had always been accepted practice, and in certain fields, doing things in a new way can lead to new treatments and better outcomes for patients. In this case, the court held that where there is a general duty of care and a defendant fails to act in accordance with an accepted practice, the burden of proof shifts from the claimant to the defendant to prove that he was not negligent. The doctor in this case was negligent because he failed to justify his departure from the normal practice and that departure was shown to be causative of the damage.

Bolitho – a revolution?

After a series of cases post-*Bolam* such as *De Freitas* and others,[43] it began to appear that it was virtually impossible to find a doctor who could not produce a colleague willing to provide him with his body of responsible men who would support his practice. As such, allegations that the *Bolam* test was virtually meaningless were rife.[44] Subsequently, the *Bolitho* case was heard, which has been heralded by some as a revolution in clinical negligence law and by others as nothing more than a restatement of the *Bolam* test within its original parameters.

KEY CASE

Bolitho v City & Hackney Health Authority[45]

Two-year-old Patrick Bolitho was admitted to the defendant's hospital with breathing problems. After several episodes of deterioration and improvement, his condition took a turn for the worse and nursing staff bleeped the oncall registrar, Dr Horn, but she failed to attend. Patrick's condition continued to deteriorate and he subsequently died. Dr Horn admitted breach of duty by not attending, but alleged that the only thing that would have saved Patrick's life would have been intubation and even had she attended, she would not have intubated such a young child who had previously improved without it. She duly called upon her medical experts who confirmed that they too would have refrained from intubating him (although the

---

[43] See particularly *Whitehouse* v *Jordan*.
[44] For detailed discussion see Brazier/Miola: *Medical Law Review*. Spring 2000, pp. 85–114.
[45] [1998] AC 232, [1997] 4 All ER 771.

claimant also had an equal number of expert witnesses expressing the contrary view). The question therefore became whether Dr Horn should have intubated had she attended Patrick. Given the case law that came to light between *Bolam* and *Bolitho* along with the credibility of Dr Horn's experts, liability looked very unlikely. However, Lord Browne-Wilkinson revisited the *Bolam* test and focused particularly on the need for the accepted practice to be responsible. He interpreted this to mean that the practice had to have some logical basis and stated that a judge, before accepting that a practice was proper, should look at whether the experts have addressed their minds to the comparative risks and benefits and have reached a 'defensible conclusion on the matter'.[46] This was potentially a robust move away from the deferential approach the courts had previously adopted; however, two things should be noted. First, the important caveat added by Lord Browne-Wilkinson:

> In the vast majority of cases the fact that distinguished experts in their field are of a particular opinion will demonstrate the reasonableness of that opinion . . . But if, in a rare case, it can be demonstrated that the professional opinion is not capable of withstanding logical analysis, the judge is entitled to hold that the body of opinion is not reasonable or responsible . . . I emphasise that, in my view, it will very seldom be right for a judge to reach the conclusion that views genuinely held by a competent medical expert are unreasonable.[47]

This essentially gives with one hand and takes away with the other – it reminds us that the body McNair J was talking about must be responsible and the court must assess that, but it also reminds us of the very deferential treatment of the medical profession in the courts and defends that position very strongly. Second, the actual outcome in the case rather undermined the rhetoric as Mrs Bolitho failed to secure any damages for the breach of duty by Dr Horn on the basis that, regardless of what she *should* have done, had she attended she would not have intubated, therefore her breach of duty did not cause the damage. No doubt Mrs Bolitho was baffled by the subsequent hailing of her case as a revolutionary step forward for claimants in clinical negligence cases.

Post-*Bolitho* case law

The best way to assess the effect of *Bolitho* on this area of law is to look at a selection of cases, but as we will see, the response has been mixed to say the least. Whilst there are numerous cases that support the view held by academics such as Brazier[48] that *Bolitho* has heralded a new dawn and revolutionised the way judges approach medical standards of care, it is just as possible to find cases where the old attitudes

---

[46] n. 45 above at 778.
[47] n. 45 above at 779.
[48] See n. 44 above.

appear to cling on and the claimant is still struggling to overcome the apparent power imbalance facing them in court.

One of the more interesting post-*Bolitho* cases is *Penney* v *East Kent*.[49] Here, cervical cancer screening tests had been carried out on women (in accordance with national policy) but some slides had been misinterpreted by the screeners as negative when, in fact, several women went on to be diagnosed with cancer of the cervix. It was argued for the defendant health authority that the screeners had followed accepted practice and had interpreted the slides as other competent screeners could have done. However, the court was dismissive of this argument, stating that it was less about accepted practice and more about what was actually on the slide and whether or not it was indicative of cancer. The court made a factual finding that there had been evidence of cancer on the slides and the screeners had therefore fallen below the required standard of care by failing to identify that evidence. Whilst it will be rare for such clear-cut factual evidence to be available to the court in a clinical negligence case, it does show a new willingness by the court to actively question and probe the actions of the medical staff and subject those actions to analysis.

Other post-*Bolitho* cases such as *Kingsberry*[50] and *Purver*[51] indicate an increasing willingness by the court to investigate the detailed medical information that was available to the doctors and to subject their actions to close scrutiny. Both cases were to do with labours that failed to progress and the use of forceps to deliver the baby. In each case, the court made up its own mind about the number of minutes the baby had been deprived of oxygen and whether it was acceptable for the doctor to have allowed such a time delay before proceeding to caesarean section. In addition, in *Kingsberry* the court criticised the doctor for carrying out the trial of forceps on the ward instead of in the theatre prepared for a caesarean and in *Purver*, criticised the doctor for being unaware of the '10-minute rule' – a guideline which, perhaps unsurprisingly, dictates that a baby could probably survive without lasting damage if deprived of oxygen for anything up to 10 minutes prior to birth, but if the oxygen deprivation went on any longer than that, damage was likely to result. The court decided the doctor should have proceeded to deliver the baby as soon as that 10-minute window was coming to an end, despite the fact that the defendant produced witnesses who testified that they were also unaware of the 10-minute rule.

Before we decide that the courts have completely turned around and become entirely claimant friendly, we need to look at other cases, such as *Pearce*,[52] which concerned risk disclosure.

---

[49] *Penney v East Kent Health Authority* [2000] Lloyds Rep Med 41.
[50] *Kingsberry v Greater Manchester Health Authority* [2005] EWHC 2253 (QB).
[51] *Purver v Winchester & Eastleigh Healthcare NHS Trust* [2007] EWHC 34 (QB).
[52] *Pearce v United Bristol Healthcare NHS Trust* (1999) 48 BMLR 118.

KEY CASE

Pearce v United Bristol Healthcare NHS Trust

Mrs Pearce was pregnant with her fifth child and had gone past her due date by 14 days. She begged the consultant at the defendant's hospital for either an induction of labour or a caesarean but was told that it would be much better to allow nature to take its course and for labour to begin naturally. The baby died in the womb soon after this and was delivered by an induced labour three days later.

The risk of stillbirth where a pregnancy progresses more than two weeks past the due date is in the region of 0.02%. The issue for the court was whether the claimant should have been informed of this small risk and, in failing to do so, whether the doctor had breached his duty of care. While the court paid lip service to the idea that where there is a significant risk the patient has a right to be informed of that risk, it defined a significant risk as in the region of 10% or more. In this case, given the small risk and the claimant's distressed state during the consultation, there was no breach of duty in the failure to disclose the information.

The crucial point about this case is that, again, where risk disclosure is concerned the paternalistic attitude of doctors seems to be supported by the courts, reinforcing the notion that the decision of whether or not to inform a patient of a particular risk should be left to the clinical judgement of the doctor. That practice was not subjected to any real, detailed analysis in the way that the practices in *Kingsberry* and *Purver* were in a case where, potentially, the claimant had been deprived of information necessary to make a decision that ultimately determined whether her child lived or died.

Summary

It is clear that establishing a duty of care in medical cases can often be straightforward, although the scope and nature of the duty can be tricky to pin down. However, the real difficulties lie in trying to determine whether or not the duty has been breached. The challenge for a layperson, such as a judge, is to determine what a doctor should have done in the specific situation that he was faced with. In the absence of detailed medical knowledge, this is not an easy assessment for the court to make. Over-reliance on medical evidence and expert witnesses leads to accusations of the medical profession setting its own standards and policing itself, but overly critical judges are accused of encouraging nervous doctors to practise defensive medicine. The *Bolam* test, while certainly open to a defendant-friendly interpretation, has probably been reined in to a certain extent by a combination of the judgment in *Bolitho* and the increasing availability and accessibility of medical information which has led to more knowledgeable and demanding patients (and courts). At the same time, the rise of clinical guidelines such as those issued by NICE appear to set ideal standards that medical practitioners should be adhering to. As Teff[53] points out, there is a possibility that as these standards become more accepted and influential they could overshadow or completely replace the *Bolam* test, requiring a doctor to show why it was not negligent to deviate from the prescribed practice. As ever, the standard the law expects of a doctor is continuing to change.

Self-test questions

1 What are the essential ingredients of the *Bolam* test?
2 What is the major criticism levelled at the *Bolam* decision?
3 What is the significance of the *Bolitho* decision?
4 Is risk disclosure treated differently and, if so, in what way?
5 What is the impact of NICE guidelines?

Practice essay question

Although there is said to be one standard of care in clinical negligence to cover all types of treatment, when it comes to sharing information with patients the courts have interpreted the standard very differently.

To what extent do you agree with this statement? Use cases to support your answer.

Practice problem question

In August 2010 Ann, a healthy 35-year-old woman, fell over a rock while out walking on some open moorland in Northumberland with her husband, Brian, and severely lacerated her lower left leg.

She was immediately driven by Brian to the accident and emergency (A&E) unit of West Northumberland NHS Trust Hospital where the casualty doctor on duty, Dr Lee, inserted three stabilising sutures and gave her an injection of tetanus toxoid. Ann was sent home with clear instructions to return in seven days.

Within 48 hours Ann's left leg had become increasingly painful and swollen and she was unable to put any pressure on the leg. Brian went back to the A&E unit to enquire about a wheelchair or crutches for Ann but the casualty doctor on duty, Dr Norman,

[53] Teff, H., 'The Standard of Care in Clinical Negligence: Moving on from *Bolam*', *OJLS*, 18(3), 473–484 (1998).

having heard what treatment Ann had received, refused saying that from Brian's description of events his wife did not seem to be in need of any walking aids. No further arrangements or alternatives were discussed between Brian and Dr Norman.

Ann's condition continued to get worse. She became febrile and confused. Brian tried to telephone Ann's general practitioner, Dr Richards, but was told by the practice's receptionist, Caroline, that Dr Richards was away on an American lecture tour but that a locum, Dr Peters, was looking after Dr Richards' patients. Brian was then put through to Dr Peters and he described Ann's condition to him and in due course (some 10 hours after the call was made) a nurse from the practice, Kelly, visited Ann. The nurse was so alarmed by the state of Ann's leg that she immediately arranged for an ambulance to take Ann to the Mount Wansbeck NHS Trust Hospital.

At the hospital, Ann was seen immediately by a senior house officer (SHO) in general surgery and a senior house officer (SHO) in orthopaedic surgery. Both noticed a discolouration of her left foot, blistering, swelling, an absence of sensation and a foul-smelling discharge from the wound. Ann was immediately admitted to a general surgery ward. No treatment was given overnight, although her blood pressure was 100/60, she had a tachycardia of 140 and pyrexia of 38.7 °C.

Ten hours after her admission Ann was seen by a consultant, Mr Miller. Assessing her to be in immediate need of surgery, Ann was within a short time taken to the operating theatre where an emergency guillotine above-the-knee amputation was performed. Ann subsequently went into acute renal failure and was dialysed.

In October 2010 Ann consults you about the possibility of a claim in clinical negligence.

4 Clinical negligence II: causation

In this chapter, we will cover:

- the concept of causation and the purpose of it as a criterion of clinical negligence
- the basic tests for causation and how they are applied
- the difficulties with particular issues, such as loss of a chance of recovery and failure to warn a patient of the risks of a procedure
- the idea of hypothetical causation
- remoteness of damage and intervening acts.

Introduction

In Chapter 3, we established that in order for a healthcare professional to be liable for damage caused to a patient, it is necessary to demonstrate, first, that they owed a duty of care to that patient and, second, that they breached that duty of care by falling below the standard that could reasonably be expected of a competent medical professional in such circumstances.[1] However, there is one final and extremely complex hurdle still to overcome and that is the need to show that the breach of duty actually caused the damage that the patient ultimately suffered. In other words, liability is not attributed to every breach of duty that occurs but only to those breaches that can legally be shown to have caused damage. The rationale behind this approach is clear: medical professionals should only be held accountable in law for harm that they cause, not for every mistake or every instance where their standard of care falls below the expected norm – doctors are only human, the argument goes. However, this also means that potentially culpable behaviour on the part of those professionals often goes unchecked because of a failure to overcome the hurdle of causation. Does this mean that negligent care and poor standards per se are tolerated to a certain extent within our healthcare system?

---

[1] See Chapter 3.

The key problem with causation in clinical negligence cases is that inherent in the nature of the case is the fact that there was a medical problem with the patient to begin with, i.e. another potential cause of the damage will normally have been present before any breach of duty occurred. This makes proving that the breach, rather then the underlying illness or condition, caused the damage inevitably problematic.

In this section, we will look at the various legal tests that have developed for establishing whether a breach of duty has caused the damage to the patient. We will then go on to consider some more specific problem areas, such as claimants who allege not actual, physical damage but loss of a chance of recovery and the somewhat esoteric notion of hypothetical causation.

General themes

As the specific details of the rules on causation are examined, it will become apparent that there are some key underlying themes that pervade this entire area of law. These themes should be borne in mind when analysing the case law in particular and threads of these arguments can be seen running through most of the key judgments we will examine.

Policy decisions (conservatism v equity) – the courts visibly wrestle with the opposing ideas of, on the one hand, rigid application of the legal tests for causation, resulting in certainty and coherence, and, on the other, the principle of an equitable outcome for the patient. This tension can most obviously be seen in cases such as *Fairchild* (discussed at p. 62) and *Chester* v *Afshar* (discussed at p. 65).

Corrective justice v distributive justice – should liability be imposed for the breach of duty itself, in order to attempt to correct the inappropriate behaviour, or should liability be apportioned in society only to those whose breach of duty can be shown to have caused a particular negative outcome?

Labelling a case – the way a case is framed before the court may have a big impact on the way the law is interpreted and the tests applied. For example, in *Gregg* v *Scott*, the case was framed as a loss of a chance of recovery, but might have been decided very differently if the claimant had instead argued failure to provide him with sufficient information about his condition.[2]

Information available to the court – as always in medical cases, the court is required to rely on scientific medical evidence to decide whether a breach of duty has caused the damage to the patient. Can such evidence always be relied on? For example, if a claimant is arguing that his chances of being alive five years after diagnosis have been reduced by, say, 20% as a result of the doctor's negligence, how meaningful are such statistics and should the court be basing decisions of liability on them?

---

[2] See Green, S., 'Coherence of Medical Negligence Cases', *MLR* 2006, 14 (1).

Tests for causation

Traditionally, there have been three basic legal tests applied by the courts to establish causation. These are:

1 the 'but for' test
2 the material contribution test
3 materially increasing the risk of harm.

The 'but for' test

This test simply requires the claimant to establish that the damage they suffered would not have occurred but for the defendant's breach of duty.

Barnett v *Chelsea and Kensington Hospital Management Committee*[3]

We looked at this case when we examined the rules on duty of care. Three night-watchmen had been poisoned with arsenic and attended the defendant's hospital but were sent home with instructions to see their general practitioner in the morning. The men subsequently died and a claim was brought in clinical negligence. It was established, as we saw at page 39, that the duty of care arose and it was further established that the duty had been breached. The signs of such severe poisoning should have been spotted and the men should have been admitted to hospital immediately. However, the medical evidence suggested that even if they had been hospitalised and treatment begun immediately, it would still have been too late to prevent their deaths. In other words, it could not be said that but for the defendant's negligence, the men would not have died, therefore it was the arsenic that was the operative cause of their deaths, not the negligence. The claim failed.

Robinson v *Post Office*[4]

A doctor administered a dose of anti-tetanus serum but failed to give a test dose first to check for any potential allergic reaction. Although it was established that the failure to administer a test dose was a breach of the doctor's duty of care, the medical evidence before the court was that even if he had given a test dose, it was highly unlikely that the type of allergic reaction the patient experienced would have revealed itself in time to prevent him administering the full dose. As in *Barnett*, it was not possible to say, on the balance of probabilities, that the breach of duty caused the damage – the operative cause was the allergic reaction which would have happened either way.

---

[3] [1969] 1 QB 428; [1968] 2 WLR 422; [1968] 1 All ER 1068.
[4] [1974] 1 WLR 1176.

One of the main criticisms of the 'but for' test was that it would only ever really work where there was only one potential cause of the damage, because whenever there was another possible cause or contributing factor, it would be extremely difficult to show that, but for the negligence, the damage would not have resulted. As we have already noted, it is rare for there to be only one potential cause in clinical negligence and this led to the development of other, more appropriate tests to be applied in such cases.

The material contribution test

This test acknowledges that there may be more than one potential cause of the harm to the patient. In order to establish liability, the claimant need only prove that the defendant's breach of duty materially contributed to the damage he has suffered, even if other causes also contributed.

Bonnington Castings Ltd v *Wardlaw*[5]

The claimant in this case had worked at the defendant's foundry for eight years and while working there, had inhaled silica particles that were released into the air when large machines called swing grinders were being used to grind metal. It was agreed by both parties that the inhalation of the silica dust caused the claimant to develop pneumoconiosis (a fatal lung disease). However, although there would have been some silica in the air regardless of the conduct of the defendant, there had been a breach of duty in that the extraction equipment that would have taken a large amount of the dust out of the air was not kept free of obstruction and was frequently blocked and ineffective. This meant that there had been in effect both 'innocent' dust and 'guilty' dust in the air at any one time and there was no way of establishing which had caused the claimant's condition – it would certainly not have been possible to argue that but for the defendant's negligence the damage would not have occurred. The court therefore decided the issue of causation on the basis that the silica particles in the air as a result of the defendant's negligence had made a material contribution to the damage ultimately caused to the claimant and that was sufficient to establish liability.

Brown v *Lewisham and North Southwark Health Authority*[6]

The claimant underwent heart bypass surgery at the defendant's hospital and was treated afterwards with heparin (a drug which thins the blood and prevents clotting). He was then discharged eight days after his surgery and left alone to travel by train and taxi to the trust's facility in Blackpool to continue his treatment and recovery. He developed a deep vein thrombosis and heparin was restarted at Blackpool but

[5] [1956] AC 613.
[6] [1999] Lloyds Rep Med 110; [1999] 48 BMLR 96.

caused an adverse reaction which ultimately led to the loss of the leg. The claimant argued either that, but for his undergoing the journey, the damage would not have occurred or that making him undergo the journey had materially contributed to him losing the leg. However, the Court of Appeal held that the journey was not a materially contributing factor because there was no evidence of symptoms being aggravated afterwards and the Blackpool hospital would have given him heparin anyway.

Materially increasing the risk

In the case of *McGhee v National Coal Board*,[7] the claimant had contracted dermatitis after working in hot, dusty conditions. The defendant failed to provide washing facilities so the claimant regularly cycled home from work covered in sweat and grime. Because of the nature of the condition, he may well have developed it even if showers had been provided, so it could not be said that the failure definitely caused the condition. However, the evidence was that their absence materially increased the risk of him developing the ailment. Was this enough to establish liability or did the claimant need to show that the failure had actually materially contributed to the harm? The House of Lords decided that causing the disease and increasing the risk of contracting it by more than a negligible degree through breach of duty had equivalent legal results:

> I can see no substantial difference between saying that what the defender did materially increased the risk of injury to the pursuer and saying that what the defender did made a material contribution to his injury.[8]

In other words, the court was equating materially contributing to the damage and materially increasing the risk of the damage occurring and making no distinction between the two in law. An illustration of the problem with that approach is provided by the case of *Wilsher v Essex Area Health Authority*.[9] Martin Wilsher was born extremely prematurely and was being cared for in the defendant's special care baby unit. He required oxygen but a junior doctor inserted the catheter into an artery instead of a vein. Realising the mistake, he consulted his superior, who repositioned the catheter but again, it was mistakenly inserted into an artery and this time, the mistake was not noticed. When the oxygen was administered through the catheter, the baby received too much, too quickly and the defendant admitted breach of duty in this regard. The baby developed a condition called retrolental fibroplasias which led to near complete blindness. The medical evidence showed that there are several potential causes of this condition in a premature infant, of which administration of excess oxygen was one. However, there were four other possible causes and it was

[7] [1973] 1 WLR 1.
[8] Per Lord Reid at 5.
[9] [1988] AC 1074.

Table 4.1 Summary of the causation tests

Causation test	Advantages	Disadvantages
'But for' test	• Simple • Relatively easy to apply • Ensures that liability is only attributed where the causal link is very clearly established	• Only really works where there is only one possible cause of the damage
Material contribution	• Covers situations in which there is more than one potential cause of harm • Allows culpable defendants to be liable even where an underlying condition may also have contributed to the damage	• Difficult to apply if there is more than one defendant, especially where the damage is not caused by an accumulation but by one isolated event
Materially increasing the risk	• Useful where there are multiple causes and it is impossible to prove which one caused the damage • Helpful where there are multiple defendants	• Extent of test is uncertain and it is often used interchangeably with material contribution test • Potentially attributes liability to a defendant that did not actually cause the damage suffered by the claimant

not possible to establish which of these had, in fact, led to Martin developing this condition. Making clear that the onus is on the claimant to show that the negligence caused or materially contributed to the damage, the court pointed out that just because negligence is one of the potential causes does not automatically mean it is the most likely cause and therefore liability was not established.

One interesting point to consider is that the claimant failed because it could not be shown that the negligence materially contributed to the damage, i.e. it could have been any one of the possible causes that actually led to Martin's blindness. However, consider the concept of materially increasing the risk: if there were four risk factors present for his developing retrolental fibroplasia and the defendant negligently adds a fifth, could that not be said to have materially increased the risk of the condition resulting? In other words, the outcome could be different depending on which test you use, yet *McGhee* says there is no difference between the two tests. It is submitted that there is actually a very significant difference between the concepts of materially contributing to the damage and materially increasing the risk of the damage resulting and that using the latter test would have resulted in a different outcome for the Wilsher family.

Interpretation of the tests – some policy issues

The material contribution test is fairly straightforward when you are dealing with more than one potential cause of the damage but only one potential defendant. However, complications arise where there are several possible defendants who may have materially contributed to the damage. How do you apportion the contribution and therefore the liability?

> ## KEY CASE
>
> ### *Fairchild* v *Glenhaven*[10]
>
> The claimants in this case had all developed the fatal lung disease mesothelioma. The condition was caused by inhalation of asbestos fibres and each claimant could prove that they had been negligently exposed to such fibres in the course of their employment. However, they had all worked for several employers over the years, all of whom had negligently exposed them to this material and it was not possible to establish which defendant had been responsible for the single fibre that entered the lungs and caused the disease in each of them. The House of Lords held that it could not be argued that each employer materially contributed to the damage because only one fibre could have caused the condition, but said that each employer had materially increased the risk of the claimants developing the disease and therefore it would hold the defendant liable.

Controversially, the claimant was able to recover his entire damages from the defendant despite the fact that several other defendants had also materially increased the risk and, it could be argued, the causal link was not established, as in *Wilsher*. Just because this particular defendant had been negligent did not necessarily mean that his negligent exposure was the precise exposure that led to the crucial fibre being inhaled. The Lords acknowledged that they were basing their decision in *Fairchild* largely on policy grounds, in that it was felt that claimants in this position should have some redress for a situation they found themselves in through no fault of their own:

> The men did nothing wrong, whereas all the defendants wrongly exposed them to the risk of developing a fatal cancer, a risk that has eventuated in these cases. At best it was only good luck if any particular defendant's negligence did not trigger mesothelioma.[11]

While this reasoning has some merit, it is difficult to understand why the same reasoning was not applied in *Wilsher* where, at best, it was only good luck on the defendant's part if their breach of duty did not actually cause the baby's blindness. As Lord Hoffman stated in *Fairchild*: 'When a decision departs from principles normally applied, the basis for doing so must be logical and justifiable if the decision is to avoid the reproach that hard cases make bad law.'[12]

It is submitted that the reasoning behind the approach of the Lords in the *Fairchild* case is not entirely logical and justifiable and reflects more the keenness of the courts to provide a remedy to those people affected by negligent exposure to asbestos, which occurred on such a massive scale in the UK for many years. Also

[10] [2002] UKHL 22.
[11] ibid above at 116.
[12] n. 10 above at 70.

relevant is the identity of the defendant. Lord Hoffman specifically distinguished *Wilsher* from *Fairchild* and *McGhee* by stating that: 'The political and economic arguments involved in the massive increase in the liability of the National Health Service . . . are far more complicated that the reasons given by Lord Wilburforce [in *McGhee*] for imposing liability upon an employer who has failed to take simple precautions.'[13]

Not only were they willing to impose that liability in *Fairchild*, they were not prepared to limit the extent of the defendant's liability to reflect his relative contribution to the risk. It has since been argued that this is unfair:

> The defendant was a wrongdoer, it is true, and should not be allowed to escape liability altogether, but he should not be liable for more than the damage he caused and, since this is a case in which science can deal only in probabilities, the law should accept that position and attribute liability according to probabilities.[14]

Some problematic issues with causation

In order to illustrate some crucial problems with the application of the causation tests in clinical negligence, consider the following two cases and, applying your knowledge of the tests, decide whether liability is established in each case.

Case study 1

The claimant visited his GP complaining of a lump under his arm. The GP misdiagnosed the lump as benign and a further year went by before the claimant went to another GP who referred him to hospital for investigation. In fact, he was suffering from cancer of the lymph gland which had by now spread to his chest. He argued that if the first GP had not misdiagnosed him (which it was admitted by the defence was a breach of duty) and he had begun treatment after that first visit, his chance of surviving for 10 years from diagnosis would have been 42%. After the year-long delay, his chance was now 25%.

Case study 2

The claimant suffered from repeated bouts of lower back pain and was referred to a surgeon who specialised in lumbar disc surgery. The surgery was explained to her in some detail, but she was not informed of a small risk (around 1 to 2%) that she would develop a complication called cauda equine syndrome as a result of the surgery. She agreed to the surgery, the complication did, in fact, occur and she was left with significant nerve damage and partial paralysis. She argued not that the surgeon

---

[13] n. 10 above at 68.
[14] *Barker* v *Corus Plc and Ors* [2006] UKHL 20 – this approach has been overruled in relation to mesothelioma cases by section 3 of the Compensation Act 2006. For earlier cases in favour of apportionment of damages between all potential defendants, see *Thompson* v *Smiths Shiprepairers (North Shields) Ltd* [1984] QB 405 and *Holtby* v *Brigham and Cowan (Hull) Ltd* [2000] 3 All ER 421.

had carried out the operation negligently, but that his failure to fully warn her of the risks was negligent and that if the risks had been properly explained to her, she would not have had the operation on that particular day, she would have waited, considered other options and perhaps sought a second opinion.

Case study 1 – loss of a chance

In the first case,[15] the House of Lords, by a 3:2 majority, confirmed the Court of Appeal decision that the claimant could not recover damages because causation was not established. It is established law in England and Wales that where a claimant is alleging that the defendant's negligence resulted in a loss of a chance of recovery, the claimant must be able to show, on the balance of probabilities, that he would have recovered if not for that negligence. For example, in *Hotson v East Berkshire Health Authority*,[16] a 13-year-old boy fell from a tree, injuring his leg. He was taken to hospital and x-rayed, but they found nothing wrong and sent him home. It was only after five days of increasing pain that he was taken back to hospital and a hip injury was discovered and promptly treated. The child went on to develop a condition called avascular necrosis, where blood supply to the area is restricted, leading to joint pain, disability and the development of osteoarthritis in later life. He alleged that there was a 25% chance that if he had received the correct treatment immediately, the avascular necrosis could have been avoided. At first instance, he was awarded full compensation but this decision was quashed by the House of Lords, because he needed to show that it was likely that he would have had a problem-free recovery but for the negligence of the defendant. In this case, there was a 75% chance that he would have developed the avascular necrosis anyway so it was not shown, on the balance of probabilities, that the negligence caused the damage. The effect of this was that in order to recover for loss of a chance, a claimant had to prove that he had a 50% or better chance of recovery to begin with. Lord Donaldson dissented in *Hotson* and expressed the view that such a rule led to an inequitable outcome and should be approached in a similar way to contract claims, where all the claimant needs to show is that he had a *significant* chance in the first place that was then reduced by the actions of the defendant:[17]

> What is the damage that the claimant has suffered? Is it the onset of the avascular necrosis or is it the loss of a chance of avoiding that condition? In my judgment it is the latter . . . I can see no reason why the loss of a chance which is capable of being valued should not be capable of being damage in a tort case just as much as in a contract case . . . it was amply proved in the present case that the choice which the claimant on the judge's finding had was lost by the admitted negligence of the doctor.[18]

[15] *Gregg v Scott* [2005] UKHL 2 [2005] 2A. C176.
[16] [1987] 2 All ER 909.
[17] See, for example, *Allied Maples Group Ltd v Simmons & Simmons* [1995] and *Stovold v Barlows* [1996].
[18] Per Lord Donaldson at 760.

The arguments put forward in *Gregg* supported the view that it comes down to burden of proof and that where the claimant has a fairly low chance of recovery, it is not possible to establish the causal link between the breach of duty and the damage – it is more likely that the underlying condition caused the damage. As Lord Hoffman has observed, we cannot know the exact cause and that lack of knowledge is dealt with by having the burden of proof.[19] However, there is an inescapable effect of such an approach, which is that the law then provides 'a blanket release from liability for doctors and hospitals any time there was a less than fifty per cent chance of survival, regardless of how flagrant the negligence'.[20] In effect, as far as the law is concerned, the patient's chances of recovery simply do not exist unless they are greater than 50%. Any lower than this and the claimant has not shown recoverable loss.

One question raised by this decision is the importance of the way a case is framed. For example, if instead of alleging a loss of 17% of his chance of recovery, Mr Gregg had alleged that the doctor had negligently failed to give him all the necessary information about his condition that he needed, would the case have been decided differently?

Case study 2 – *Chester v Afshar*

Here, by a 3:2 majority, the House of Lords found in the claimant's favour, despite the fact that she was not arguing that if she had received a full and complete warning of the risks of the surgery she would not have gone ahead. If that had been her argument, then she might have succeeded on the basis of the 'but for' test. However, she was alleging that if the defendant had not breached his duty, she would possibly still have had the surgery but would have had it on a different day. She succeeded in her claim on the basis that the injury she suffered was the product of the very risk of which she should have been warned and it could therefore be regarded as having been caused by that failure to warn. This is an extremely tenuous argument and possibly a distorted application of the causation tests. The Lords acknowledged that, on a strict application, her claim would fail and that policy played a strong role in their ultimate decision. As Lord Hope stated: 'To leave the patient . . . without a remedy . . . would render the duty useless in cases where it is needed most . . . I would hold that justice requires Miss Chester to be afforded the remedy that she seeks.'[21] Lord Steyn agreed, saying 'This result is in accord with one of the basic aspirations of the law, namely to right wrongs.'[22]

---

[19] Per Lord Hoffman at 196.

[20] Per Dore J, *Herskovitis v Group Health Cooperative of Puget Sound* (1983) 664 P2d 474, 477 quoted by Lord Nicholls in Gregg at 190.

[21] Per Lord Hope at 162.

[22] Per Lord Steyn at 146.

Not surprisingly, the case has come in for a lot of criticism, particularly in the light of the seemingly inequitable outcome in the *Gregg* case. Sarah Green argues that the law of negligence simply cannot accommodate both decisions and that in order to retain some coherence in the law, you either have to take the strict interpretation approach favoured in *Gregg* or you have to look at each case on a broad, equitable basis as demonstrated in *Chester*, but the courts cannot simply choose one of these approaches each time depending on the scenario presented to them.[23] Lord Hoffman observed in *Gregg* that: 'a wholesale adoption of possible rather than probable causation as the criterion of liability would be so radical a change in our law as to amount to a legislative act'[24] but arguably, that is exactly what the Lords did in *Chester*.

Chester is a difficult case to reconcile with the rules we associate with causation and in subsequent cases the courts have been cautious about attaching too much weight to it as a precedent, instead equating it with *Fairchild* as an example of rare cases in which the rules can be modified on policy grounds.[25] Even so, it presents the student of clinical negligence law and the lawyer advising clients in such litigation with a challenge in trying to predict just how a court will deal with the issue of causation in a situation where the long-established tests cannot easily be satisfied. It also brings us back to the question of how you frame a case. If Miss Chester had argued that the surgeon's negligence had resulted in the loss of a chance of pursuing a different treatment or an operation at a different time, would the outcome have been different? Perhaps an even better approach from a legal certainty perspective would have been to argue that the operation itself was carried out negligently because it was done without full and valid, informed consent (for a detailed discussion of the rules on consent, see Chapter 6).

Hypothetical causation

So far, we have been talking about a situation in which there has been some negligent act on the part of the defendant that is, if not the only cause, then a possible, partial or contributory cause of the damage suffered by the claimant. How then will the law deal with a situation where the negligent act is failure to attend? The actual failure to turn up may not be an operative cause, but can failure to administer the treatment that the doctor would or should have given if they had attended be an operative cause of damage in law?

---

[23] See n. 2 above.
[24] Per Lord Hoffman at 198.
[25] See *White v Paul Davidson & Taylor* [2005] PNLR 15.

Bolitho v City & Hackney Health Authority[26]

We analysed the *Bolitho* decision in some depth when we considered the *Bolam* test in relation to assessing the appropriate standard of care to be required of healthcare professionals (for a detailed discussion of the facts, see p. 50). Here the admitted breach of duty on the part of Dr Horn was her failure to answer her bleep and attend the child to assess his condition. Clearly the *Bolam* test as modified by Lord Browne-Wilkinson in this judgment is relevant to the assessment of whether failure to answer the call and attend the child was negligent, but should that test play any part in the assessment of whether that failure caused the child's death?

In effect, the defence was arguing that even had Dr Horn not been negligent and had in fact attended Patrick when she was bleeped, the only thing that would have prevented his ultimate respiratory arrest was intubation and she alleged that she would not have intubated him at that stage – in other words, the negligence did not cause the damage because even if she had attended, the outcome would have been the same. Given this argument, the court in *Bolitho* decided that it needed to consider both the factual question of whether Dr Horn would have intubated had she attended Patrick and the hypothetical question of whether it would have been a breach of duty not to intubate. How did the court make that assessment? Well, it made it quite clear that the *Bolam* test has no application to the factual assessment of whether or not she would have carried out the procedure, but it could only resolve the second question by asking what a reasonable, competent doctor would have done in those circumstances.[27] As it turned out, medical opinion was divided, with experts for the claimant advising the court that failure to intubate Patrick at that time given the symptoms he was presenting with would have been a breach of duty and one very eminent medical expert for the defence stating that in that situation, he would not have opted for the invasive, uncomfortable and risky option of intubating such a young child. The House of Lords ultimately decided that a reasonable doctor may not have intubated and therefore, they could take Dr Horn at her word and if indeed she would not have performed the procedure, her breach of duty in not attending had not caused Patrick's death.

The *Bolitho* case raises some interesting questions about how the courts should approach the issue of causation when the defendant doctor's breach is a failure to attend, because realistically, although it may be possible using the *Bolam* test to hypothesise about what they *should* have done if they had been present, it is impossible to say with any certainty what they *would* have done had they not breached their duty and come to the patient's bedside. Should they take the view of Lord Hoffman in *Gregg* v *Scott* that where knowledge is lacking the court must employ

---

[26] [1998] AC 232.
[27] [1998] AC 232 at 240.

the notion of probability[28] and decide the issue of causation based on the fact that a reasonable doctor would have acted in a certain way, therefore it can be assumed that the defendant would have acted in that way, or should they accept that because they cannot know what would have unfolded, causation cannot be established in such cases? It is submitted that neither approach guarantees an equitable outcome. Perhaps a better argument in *Bolitho* would have been that Dr Horn's failure to attend materially increased the risk of the damage that resulted because she was not physically present and able to assess his condition as she should have been. This once again illustrates the different outcomes that can be reached depending on which particular test is employed.

Remoteness of damage

The normal tort rules on remoteness of damage will apply in clinical negligence claims, so the harm caused must generally be foreseeable, but the egg shell skull rule will apply. This states essentially that you take your victim as you find them, so if as a result of the defendant's breach of duty the claimant suffers more damage than somebody else would have, perhaps due to an underlying condition or predisposition, this will make no difference to the liability of the defendant.[29]

Similarly, intervening acts may break the chain of causation and take over from the defendant's breach of duty as the operative cause of the damage. Such acts are often referred to as a 'novus actus interveniens'. However, these will be limited to unforeseeable interventions. For example, in *Emeh* v *Kensington Area Health Authority*,[30] the Court of Appeal held that where a sterilisation operation had been carried out negligently and the patient was claiming for the damage of an unwanted pregnancy and birth, the defendant could not argue that the claimant's failure to have an abortion was an intervening act that broke the chain of causation. This was partly because it was not unforeseeable that once she was pregnant she might feel unable to terminate that pregnancy, but also for policy reasons in that the court would never be seen to be forcing or encouraging a woman to have an abortion.[31]

The concept of contributory negligence will also apply and is discussed more fully in relation to its impact on the remedy of damages in Chapter 5. This principle states that where the claimant has contributed to the extent of the damage by his own negligent act, although the defendant who has breached his duty will still be liable, the amount of damages available to the claimant will be reduced. For example, in *Crossman* v *Stewart*,[32] the damages paid to the victim of a road traffic accident

---

[28] See Lord Hoffman at 196.
[29] See *Smith* v *Leech Brain* [1962] 2 QB 405 and *Page* v *Smith* [1996] AC 195.
[30] [1985] QB 1012.
[31] Also on intervening acts, see *Corr* v *IBC* [2008] 1 AC 884.
[32] [1977] 5 CCLT 45 (BC SC).

were reduced by 25% to reflect the fact that she was not wearing a seatbelt. Clearly this raises extremely complex questions in the context of medical law, such as whether a claimant suffering from lung disease should have damages reduced because he smoked all his life, especially if the smoking continued after medical advice to stop.[33]

Summary

As noted in the introduction, causation is probably the most difficult hurdle that a claimant in a clinical negligence claim has to overcome and many factors can influence the extent to which the breach can be linked to the damage. Although general tests have been established over the years, they are merely the starting point for anyone studying this area of law, and the case law discussed in this chapter makes it very clear that decisions are often very fact specific and heavily influenced by policy. The concept of having a requirement to show damage in tort claims, in order to avoid punishing defendants indiscriminately for every drop in standards is a legitimate one, but in medical cases in particular, it begs the question: where there is fault, should there be liability?

Self-test questions

1 Explain the material contribution test.
2 Can a claimant bring a claim in clinical negligence for loss of a chance of recovery?
3 Explain the concept of materially increasing the risk of harm.
4 What is the significance of the *Fairchild* case?
5 What is meant by the term 'hypothetical causation'?

Practice essay question

'While the principles of causation may ordinarily be relatively straightforward, it is fair to say that causation in the context of medical law is fraught with difficulty.'

By looking at decisions such as *Chester v Afshar* [2004] UKHL 41, comment on whether you regard this statement as true of causation in clinical negligence.

---

[33] See *Badger v Ministry of Defence* [2005] EWHC 2941 QB.

Practice problem question

Graeme, aged 25, is a professional cricketer and has just been called up to the national team. During the course of one match, Graeme was batting when the bowler bowled a very fast ball at a bad angle and Graeme fell badly on his knee as he tried to manoeuvre out of the way. He continued with the game but after the match, as a precautionary measure, he attended the accident and emergency department of Northcastle District Hospital. Sarah, a junior doctor, who had been on duty for the past 18 hours, began to examine Graeme but was called away to an emergency. As she left, she called to the nurse, 'X-ray department.' The nurse thought that she was saying that Graeme had just come back from the X-ray department and therefore simply bandaged his knee and sent Graeme home with the instruction that he must rest.

Despite this instruction Graeme played in the following mid-week practice match as he did not want to be dropped from the team. After the game he was again in pain and the next day visited his GP, who simply prescribed rest. One week later he again visited his GP with the same complaint and was once more told to rest. Eventually, three weeks later, Graeme collapsed in severe pain and underwent emergency surgery. As he was recovering from the anaesthetic he thought he heard a doctor say: 'It has gone reasonably well considering it should have been done very much earlier.'

Over the next few months Graeme repeatedly visited his GP, complaining of tenderness and pain in his knee. During this period Graeme was dropped from the team and he has never regained his place. The pain in his knee has continued to date.

It is now March of the following year and Graeme is playing for a local cricket club and the chance of a promising international career seems remote. He has been informed that he will continue to suffer pain in his knee and that he now has a degenerative condition that will eventually stop him playing altogether in about five years' time. Graeme believes that the degenerative condition may have been caused by poor medical care and wants to know if he can bring a claim against the hospital and/or his GP.

Advise Graeme whether he can bring a claim in clinical negligence against any of the parties concerned.

5 Clinical negligence III: procedure and damages

Introduction

As well as the fundamental legal principles that were discussed in detail in Chapter 3, there are multiple complex procedural hurdles that must be overcome if a claimant is to bring a clinical negligence claim. In this chapter, we will focus on the following three key areas:

- the NHS complaints procedure
- the procedure for bringing a clinical negligence claim
- assessing damages.

As the chapter progresses it will become clear the extent to which financial considerations have become fundamental to issues around clinical negligence. This is not just in terms of the level of damages that may be awarded, but also the way in which the claim is brought and, indeed, whether it is brought at all. Public funding for such claims is very limited and conditional fee arrangements (discussed later) are perceived as risky and complicated by the public. High costs can eat into any award of damages, leaving the value of bringing the claim at all open to debate and behind this, the long-running criticisms of the time-consuming and complex system as a whole continue to be valid, despite repeated attempts at reform.

The complaints procedure

Background

While the NHS as a whole has seen its fair share of reform and upheaval over the years, the complaints process has been by far the most reformed area. In the space of 13 years, between 1996 and 2009, the complaints process in the NHS was completely overhauled not once but twice. The main impetus for change came from continued criticism of the process from complainants who had been through the system and found it incomprehensible, intimidating, inefficient and ultimately ineffective. The key problems identified with the system in a 1994 report[1] included:

- not knowing to whom to complain
- not knowing how to complain
- language barriers caused by professionals using medical jargon
- lack of understanding of clinical procedures
- difficulty expressing concerns clearly
- confusing and complex procedures
- impersonal and unhelpful process
- lengthy, time-consuming system
- fear of impact on ongoing care
- ultimately not worth it as little was achieved.

As a result, the system was changed in 1996 to comprise a two-stage process: local resolution (where the complainant dealt directly with the NHS body) and independent review (carried out by a convener). However, the old criticisms detailed here still applied to this system, especially in light of the fact that the convener was often a non-executive director of the trust. After various reviews and reports,[2] the system was overhauled again in 2004. This new system consolidated the local resolution stage and established the (now obsolete) Healthcare Commission to deal with the independent review stage. However, many of the reforms were phased in as the government was waiting for the fifth Shipman Report, looking at complaints to see if further changes were going to be necessary.[3] Indeed, when that report was published in 2007,[4] it made various recommendations and another consultation process began. The current process is now outlined, but the reader should bear in mind the criticisms made about previous systems when assessing whether the current one is satisfactory.

The new process

The system is now governed by the Local Authority Social Services and National Health Service Complaints (England) Regulations 2009[5] and the Amendment Regulations 2009.[6] The new complaints procedure applies to all complaints brought

---

[1] 'Being Heard: Review of NHS Complaints Procedure', 1994.
[2] Including 'NHS Complaints Reform – Making Things Right', April 2003 and draft Regulations published for consultation in December 2003.
[3] See Chapter 11 for further discussion of the Shipman reports.
[4] Safeguarding Patients: Lessons from the Past – Proposals for the Future, 9 Dec 2004, cm6394.
[5] 2009/309.
[6] Local Authority Social Services and National Health Service Complaints (England) (Amendment) Regulations 2009/1768.

after April 2009. The idea behind these latest reforms is that a single complaints system should encompass all social care, NHS care and primary care (including GPs and NHS foundation trusts), thus addressing the problem highlighted by the Shipman Report, in which complaints had been made by various people to various bodies but that information had never been collated. The aim is to have a more personal approach so that communication between the complainant and the organisation is better and to encourage organisations to learn from complaints to improve the services they offer.

GUIDING PRINCIPLES OF THE NEW SYSTEM

The new system is governed by the following six key principles:

- Getting it right.
- Being customer focused.
- Being open and accountable.
- Acting fairly and proportionately.
- Putting things right.
- Seeking continuous development.

Organisations are also encouraged to follow some basic good practice guidelines to improve the relationship with the complainant. These include:

- Publicising the complaints process.
- Acknowledging the complaint and offering to discuss it.
- Dealing with the complaint efficiently and investigating it properly and appropriately.
- Writing to the complainant after the complaints has been investigated to explain how it has been resolved and what they can do if they are not happy.
- Having a senior officer responsible for the complaints process and ensuring lessons are learned from it.
- Helping the complainant to understand the process.
- Producing an annual report.

All trusts must have a system in place to deal with complaints in accordance with these principles.[7] The chief executive officer of the trust is the 'person responsible' under the regulations, though they can delegate certain of the functions to others and they must appoint a complaints manager.[8]

[7] Reg. 3.
[8] Reg. 4.

Who can complain?

This is governed by Regulation 5 of the 2009 Regulations. Essentially, any person can complain who:

1 is receiving or has received services

2 is affected, or is likely to be affected, by the act/decision/omission of the trust.

The first category is fairly self-explanatory. Anyone that has received treatment that they are not happy with may make a complaint about it. The second category would include, for example, those people who have been refused certain treatments or drugs because of cost concerns or due to staff or bed shortages.

There is also provision made for a representative of the patient to bring a complaint on their behalf, where the patient is unable to do so. This would apply where the patient is a child or an adult lacking mental capacity, or where the patient has requested a representative to bring the complaint on their behalf. As we will see in Chapter 6, some children have mental capacity to consent to treatment and to handle some of their own affairs, even when they are below 16 years of age. Therefore, the Regulations state that where a representative is bringing a complaint on behalf of a child, the trust needs to be satisfied that there are reasonable grounds for the representative acting, rather than the child. Presumably, this would be satisfied where the child was extremely young and not able to understand the process, or where they were too ill to bring the claim themselves. In addition, where a representative is bringing a claim on behalf of a child or an adult lacking mental capacity,[9] the trust is not required to consider the complaint if it is satisfied that the representative is not conducting the complaint in that child or adult's best interests. There is no further guidance given in the Regulations about determining 'best interests'. The Mental Capacity Act gives some guidance on assessing this[10] and there is a body of case law on assessing best interests of children in relation to consenting to or refusing medical treatment, but nothing specifically on how a complaint would be conducted in someone's best interests. Presumably, the Regulations are referring to vexatious or unsubstantiated complaints brought by a relative or representative with a particular axe to grind. However, such vague provisions that could potentially be seen to advantage a trust that seeks to avoid dealing with a particular issue are not helpful and not really in keeping with the spirit of the new system.

In terms of whom the complaint is made to, for the first time, the Regulations give the complainant some choice.[11] They can complain directly to the trust as the provider of the services, but they can also choose to complain to the primary care trust (PCT) as the commissioner of the services.[12] A patient may feel uncomfortable

---

[9] Assessed by means of the test set out in the Mental Capacity Act 2005, which is discussed in full in Chapter 6.
[10] See section 4 MCA 205.
[11] Reg. 7.
[12] See Chapter 1 for an explanation of the relationship between trusts and PCTs.

complaining directly to the trust, especially if the relationship has completely broken down. They may also feel that complaining to the PCT will prevent such services being provided in the same way in other hospitals and settings as opposed to just the hospital or place where they received their treatment. In any event, Regulation 9 requires that the different bodies cooperate in relation to the complaints process and share information and lessons learned where appropriate.

Practical considerations

The complaint must be brought within 12 months, either from the date of the incident or from the date at which the patient had knowledge of the incident. Complaints brought outside that time limit may sometimes be considered, but only if the trust is satisfied that the complainant had a good reason for not bringing the claim within the time limit and it is still possible to investigate the matter effectively and fairly.[13]

In terms of methods of lodging a complaint, there are three ways in which it can be done:[14]

1 orally – however, where this is done, the trust needs to make a written record of the complaint and send a copy of that to the complainant

2 electronically

3 in writing.

However the complaint is lodged, the trust must acknowledge receipt of the complaint within three working days and must offer to discuss with the complainant how the complaint will be handled and what the timescales will be. If the complainant does not take up the offer of such a discussion, then the trust sets the timescale and informs the complainant.

Regulation 14 then sets out the general obligations on the part of the trust when conducting the investigation.

GENERAL OBLIGATIONS ON THE TRUST

● To investigate and deal with the complaint in an appropriate manner to resolve it speedily and efficiently and so far as is reasonably practicable to keep the complainant informed of progress.

● To send a written response as soon as reasonably practicable after the conclusion of the investigation, setting out conclusions reached, remedial action taken and whether there are any further actions still to happen.

---

[13] Reg. 12.
[14] Reg. 13.

> - To inform the complainant of his or her right to take the matter to the ombuds-man (see later).
> - To provide all this information in the form of a report within six months of the complaint (unless a different timescale has been agreed between the parties) and, if this cannot be done, to write to the complainant explaining why there is a delay and when the report can be expected.

It is hoped that these new Regulations will do away with some of the dissatisfaction with the complaints process in the past and will make trusts and other organisations more accountable to patients and the public. However, it is important to remember that not all types of complaint will be dealt with by these Regulations. Complaints excluded from this system include:

- those about treatment or services made by other trusts or responsible bodies
- those made by employees
- an oral complaint resolved by the next working day
- a complaint already investigated under this procedure
- a complaint already being investigated or having been investigated by the ombudsman
- those about freedom of information (FOI) issues.

Thus, some vital and valid complaints will not have the benefit of this more streamlined system and the tight timescales imposed and may be dealt with under several different systems. Freedom of information complaints systems tend to be well administered and fairly efficient as the Act required such systems to be set up and organisations were fairly well prepared for them. In contrast, complaints by staff are notoriously badly dealt with and difficult to make, for various practical and political reasons.[15] Therefore, despite the positive reforms that these new Regulations have put in place, it may still be that a person's experience of the complaints process will vary depending on the nature of their complaint.

The final stage

The post of ombudsman (also known as the health service commissioner) was created by the Health Service Commissioner's Act 1993 and is a last resort for complainants who feel that their grievance has not been properly dealt with by the trust.

---

[15] For some examples, see the comments on the Nursing Times website regarding tightening up of whistleblowing policy – real NHS workers anonymously relating tales of failed attempts to raise concerns – http://www.nursingtimes.net/whats-new-in-nursing/news-topics/whistleblowing/greater-protection-for-nhs-whistleblowers-outlined/5020423.article.

At the outset it should be noted that the availability of a complaint to the ombuds-man is limited. Complainants must be able to show that they have suffered some injustice or hardship and that they have exhausted all NHS procedures (i.e. they must have already gone through the procedure as detailed). However, the most important limitation is that there must not be a remedy available in court or, if there is, there must be a good reason for not taking legal action. This is potentially very limiting as often, where services have been provided to an inadequate standard, an action will lie in negligence. However, as we will see later in this chapter, claims are time consuming, expensive and extremely stressful and damages are often very small. With this in mind, many claimants would rather complain to the ombudsman after an unsuccessful complaint though the NHS process but will not be able to unless there are overwhelming reasons why they are not bringing a legal claim. In a time when the idea is supposed to be to bring claim numbers down, it seems strange to have a final leg of the complaints system that almost appears to encourage litigation.

If a claim is brought to the ombudsman, there are extensive powers set out in the 1993 Act to compel staff to testify and to demand documents and records. This means that the matter is usually investigated more fully and staff are often more forthcom-ing than when they are simply interviewed by their boss. However, the ombudsman has no powers to award compensation or damages of any kind. In some circum-stances, out-of-pocket expenses may be awarded but these will be small amounts.

The ombudsman system is more transparent than the NHS system. A report of the investigation is sent to the complainant and to the NHS body involved, but it also goes to the Secretary of State for Health and if the ombudsman feels the report raises important issues, a special report can be written on it and laid before both houses of parliament.

In light of this discussion, the ombudsman complaints system is really for situa-tions where the complainant feels there is some systemic failure on the part of the NHS body or where there is a higher principle at stake, rather than where they want a specific remedy for themselves.

Summary – the complaints procedure

Overall, the complaints process is greatly improved by the 2009 Regulations, in that NHS bodies are more accountable and held to tighter timescales and principles of good practice in dealing with complaints. There may also be an advantage to patients considering litigation in going through the complaints process first, as explanations and evidence may come to light that either precludes a legal claim or saves time and money during later litigation. There is evidence that patients are more aware of the availability of the system and more willing to use it since the latest reforms came in, with complaints against hospitals increasing by 13.4% in the first years after the Regulations came into force and claims against GPs increasing by

4.4%.[16] Overall, between April 2009 and March 2010 there were over 150,000 complaints about NHS treatment services.[17] It is crucial that these complaints are taken seriously and lessons learned to improve patient care going forward. This is the only way to reduce the huge cost and other detriments associated with the large numbers of clinical negligence claims currently being brought.

Bringing a clinical negligence claim

In order to bring a clinical negligence claim, there are various procedural steps and practical issues that need to be addressed, as well as the complex legal issues examined in Chapter 3. Lord Woolf's reforms that came into effect in 1999 attempted to address the earlier criticisms of the civil litigation system as a whole and clinical negligence claims in particular.[18] He introduced a pre-action protocol, more openness and tighter timescales to ensure efficiency and also piloted controversial practices such as the use of a joint medical expert. We will see as the chapter unfolds whether those reforms and others made since have produced a coherent and effective means of legal redress for those in receipt of poor quality medical care.

The aims of this section are to explain and evaluate:

- how claims are funded
- issues of limitation
- the pre-action protocol
- reliance on expert evidence
- possibilities for future reform.

Funding

It is an unavoidable fact that bringing a clinical negligence claim is expensive. No matter who ends up footing the bill, the costs of solicitors' fees, possible barrister fees if it goes to trial, commissioning of expert reports, court fees and the like put the full cost of a claim way beyond the means of most average members of the public. In November 2010 the Medical Defence Union, which insures members of the medical profession against negligence claims, stated that the average amount of claimant's costs it now pays out is around £44,500, as compared with £1300 in 1981.[19] In order to improve access to legal redress, various alternative methods of

---

[16] See 'Data on Written Complaints in the NHS 2009–2010', available at http://www.ic.nhs.uk/webfiles/ publications/002_Audits/nhscomplaints0910/Written_complaints_NHS_%202009-10_Report.pdf.

[17] See n. 11 above.

[18] See the Right Honourable Lord Woolf, Master of the Rolls, 'Access to Justice Final Report' 1996, which ultimately resulted in the amended Civil Procedure Rules 1999.

[19] MDU quoted in BMJ Careers at http://careers.bmj.com/careers/advice/view-article.html?id=20001606.

funding claims have developed in recent years, as legal firms began to recognise the untapped market in legal accident claims.

One method is to try to attract funding for the claim from the community legal service (CLS) – what used to be called 'legal aid'. However, this has traditionally been difficult to get for clinical negligence claims. It used to be that policy reasons lay behind the reluctance to fund such claims – why encourage people to sue an already overstretched NHS? More recently, it has simply been a lack of availability of public funds that has resulted in tight means and merits testing for assistance. Specific guidance is contained in section 9 of the Funding Code.[20] In particular, it should be noted that funding will not be available where the case is one that is suitable for a conditional fee arrangement (more detail on these later). What this means is that, to qualify for CLS assistance, the claimant must have an income below the threshold in place at the time (this will usually be restricted to those on benefits as it will be at or below the minimum wage) and must be able to show that they have a reasonable chance of success if the case gets to court. However, such cases will usually also be suitable for a conditional fee agreement, which bars them from eligibility for CLS funding.[21] The result of this is that it can be very difficult to obtain CLS funding and while worth exploring with a client, it will not often prove successful.

Another potential and much more widely available method of funding a claim is what is known as a conditional fee agreement (CFA). In this type of arrangement, a firm of solicitors will agree to take the case and will not require any fees to be paid upfront. If the case is won, the firm will obtain its costs from the defendant at an enhanced rate – in other words, it will claim its usual costs and disbursements plus a success fee that has been negotiated with the claimant. Of course, in some cases where the case is won, the court does not award costs against the defendant and in such situations, the fees and the success fee will both come out of the damages awarded to the claimant. In the event that the case is lost, some firms agree that they will not take a fee (so called 'no win, no fee' arrangements) but most will require their basic costs to be paid by the claimant. In order to address this, the claimant is often advised at the outset of a CFA to pay an additional, relatively small premium for 'after the event' (ATE) insurance, which will cover the solicitor's costs in the event that the case is unsuccessful. Both arrangements have their drawbacks. In a 'no win, no fee' arrangement, the firm looks very hard at the available evidence and the strength of the case and only takes cases it feels it has a good chance of winning, meaning worthy but more risky claims are left without representation. They are also likely to have a higher success fee to cover themselves for the few cases that they do lose and for which they receive no fees. With an ATE insurance

---

[20] See http://www.legalservices.gov.uk/civil/guidance/funding_code.asp.
[21] See section 9.2.1 Funding Code.

arrangement, it was for some time unclear as to whether the claimant could recover the premium as part of the costs from the defendant. However, this was settled in the case of *Callery* v *Gray*.[22] Here the claimant entered into a CFA and took out ATE insurance before the defendant responded to the claim. In actual fact, the defendant admitted liability and the case settled very quickly. The issue for the court was whether the ATE premium could be recovered or whether the claimant should have awaited the defendant's response before taking out the insurance. The court made it clear that the claimant had not been premature as it was important to protect himself from the very outset as costs could mount quickly. The cost of the premium could be recovered from the defendant. The court also took the opportunity to discuss CFA cases and to state that in its view, the solicitor's success fee should be no more than a 20% uplift on their normal fees unless there were exceptional circumstances.[23] The following year, in *Halloran* v *Delaney*,[24] the court made it clear that in simple claims settled without the need for court proceedings, the success fee should be no more than a 5% uplift. This went some way to addressing previously mounting concerns regarding unscrupulous firms of solicitors and other volume claims businesses that were charging inflated success fees and taking huge chunks out of the damages won by the claimant. However, there are still those who feel these types of arrangement are risky and can leave claimants with a smaller amount of damage than they may be legitimately entitled to.

One other issue that may impact on the funding situation is the use of alternative dispute resolution (ADR). This involves the parties looking at alternative ways of resolving their dispute other than a legal claim, for example by engaging in mediation or the NHS complaints procedure. The potential impact on funding is highlighted by this extract from paragraph 4.7 of the practice direction on pre-action protocols (which will be discussed further later):

> The parties should consider whether some form of ADR procedure would be more suitable than litigation, and if so, endeavour to agree which form to adopt. Both the claimant and defendant may be required by the court to provide evidence that alternative means of resolving their dispute were considered. The courts take the view that litigation should be a last resort, and that claims should not be issued prematurely when a settlement is still actively being explored. Parties are warned that if the proposal is not followed (including this paragraph) then the court must have regard to such conduct when determining costs.

In other words, parties may be penalised on costs for not having visibly considered and/or attempted forms of ADR. Case law suggests that in order to be penalised on costs, it must be shown that the other party acted unreasonably in refusing ADR.[25]

---

[22] [2001] EWCA Civ 117.
[23] This was affirmed in the case of dental negligence in *Bensusan* v *Freedman* [2001] All ER 212.
[24] [2002] EWCA Civ 1258.
[25] For example, see *Halsey* v *Milton Keynes General NHS Trust* [2004] EWCA Civ 576.

Limitation

Time limits for bringing claims are governed by the Limitation Act 1980. Generally, this states that while the time limit for most civil claims is six years, for personal injury claims it is three years, either from the date that the incident actually happened or from the date when the claimant has knowledge of it.[26]

Defining when the claimant has knowledge is a difficult exercise. Section 14(1) defines actual knowledge as 'a broad knowledge that something has gone wrong'. For example, in *Nash* v *Eli Lilly*,[27] the defendants had been left with various side-effects after taking an anti-arthritic drug manufactured by the defendant. The drug was withdrawn from the market in 1982 and most of claimants issued writs in 1987 and 1988 (clearly outside the 3-year time limit). The court stated that the claimants had knowledge when they 'had, or could reasonably be expected to acquire, knowledge that a possible cause of their photosensitivity was exposure to an unsafe drug'. In all but two of the cases, it was held that they were statute barred by being out of time.

In another example, *Rowbottom* v *Royal Masonic Hospital*,[28] the claimant had originally issued proceedings but at the time of his receiving his first medical expert report, it was stated to be 'uncertain' as to whether or not he had been given antibiotics after his hip replacement. As a result, his solicitor advised that it was not clear he had a cause of action. It was only on receipt of a second report several months later that it became clear he had not been given antibiotics. Therefore, the date of actual knowledge was found to be the date on which he received the second report.

The court also acknowledges the concept of constructive knowledge, i.e. knowledge the claimant might reasonably be expected to acquire. The court pointed out in *Nash* v *Eli Lilly* that the claimants had constructive knowledge from the date their GP became aware of the withdrawal of the drug and the possible side-effects it had caused, as from that point, they could reasonably be expected to find out that information from their GP. In *Haward* v *Fawcetts*,[29] a negligence case against a firm of accountants, the court stated that the relevant date for limitation purposes was not when the claimant first knew he might have a claim for damages, but the earlier date when he first knew enough to set about investigating the possibility that the defendant's advice was defective. Thus, the rules are very onerous on claimants and require them to be proactive in seeking information regarding their treatment and the likelihood that they can bring a claim. Once again, looking at the Woolf reforms, this was not supposed to be the culture that was to be encouraged.

There are some exceptions to these fairly tight rules on limitation. For example, the limitation period will not start where the patient is a minor until he or she

---

[26] See sections 11, 14(1) and 14(2) Limitation Act 1980.
[27] [1993] 1 WLR 782.
[28] [2002] EWCA Civ 87.
[29] [2006] UKHL 9.

attains the age of 18 years.[30] The court also has discretion under section 33 to allow claims that are outside the time limit in certain circumstances. The court will look at various factors when deciding whether to allow a claim that is out of time, such as:

- the length of delay and the reasons for it
- the cogency of the evidence
- the response of the defendant
- whether the claimant was under a disability that prevented them bringing the claim earlier
- whether the claimant had taken steps to progress the claim.

Essentially, the court is looking at whether it would be just and equitable to allow the claim outside the time limit, to both the claimant and the defendant. It is not ideal to have hospital staff working under the shadow of threatened litigation indefinitely and it can be difficult to get good-quality evidence as more time passes between the incident and the claim.

A recent and controversial example of this divided opinion on whether the courts should be able to allow such claims and, if so, how far out of time they should be allowed to go, is described below.

KEY CASE

A v Hoare[31]

The claimant had been seriously sexually assaulted by the defendant 16 years earlier and he had been serving a life sentence in prison with no income. It was therefore not feasible for her to bring a civil claim against him at the time. However, on one of his day releases on licence from prison he bought a lottery ticket and won £7 million. The claimant argued that she should now be able to bring her civil claim and asked the court to exercise its discretion under section 33. She issued her claim 13 years and 10 months after the expiry of the initial three-year limitation period, but the court allowed her claim to proceed. Coulson J stated that although allowing the claim did prejudice the defendant, such prejudice 'was not substantial'. It was felt that the case contained such unusual circumstance that there was no risk of opening the floodgates to other claims and it was noted that the claimant had acted 'promptly' on discovery of the defendant's lottery win!

---

[30] See sections 28 and 38.
[31] [2008] EWHC 1573.

The *Hoare* case clearly shows that the court effectively weighs up the fairness to both parties and, in this case, the fact that the defendant had been convicted of a very violent sexual assault against the claimant meant the scale tipped firmly in her favour. However, it is arguable whether such flexible rules are justified, given the potentially significant consequences of bringing a claim so far out of time. As *Hoare* is a trespass claim in which there was criminal liability attached to the defendant, it may well be that the judge was correct in his assertion that it would not open the floodgates, especially in the realm of clinical negligence. It is still a rather more flexible approach to section 33 than has previously been demonstrated and means that the court is effectively making value judgments about which claims should be allowed and which should not. Is this within their remit?

The pre-action protocol

The pre-action protocol was brought in as part of the Woolf reforms in order to speed up the clinical negligence process and improve transparency and cooperation between the parties. It was also hoped that it would lead to reductions in costs, although as we saw in earlier, this has not proved to be the case. The general aims of the protocol are:

- to maintain or restore the patient/health carer relationship
- to resolve as many disputes as possible without recourse to litigation
- to inform the defendant early of the claim
- to improve systems of incident reporting within the healthcare organisation
- to encourage early disclosure of medical records
- to conduct litigation on a reasonable timescale
- to discourage the pursuit of unmeritorious claims
- to place increased emphasis on ADR.

One of the key protocol steps requires that medical records be obtained early in order to establish the merits of the claim and chances of success.[32] The healthcare organisation must provide these within 40 days of the request and can charge no more than £50 to cover the costs. In practice, these can be extremely useful in revealing the strength or weakness of the claim. Traditionally, there were problems with poor quality of photocopying and atrocious GP handwriting that rendered some pages illegible but with the advent of computerised records, such problems are less prevalent.

CPR 31 also requires disclosure of other records. For example, in the case of *Waugh* v *British Railways Board*,[33] where the plaintiff had died as a result of an

[32] See CPR 31.16 and 31.17.
[33] [1980] AC 521.

accident on the railway line, an investigative report had been commissioned by the BRB to look into the causes of the accident. The report was to be sent to its legal advisors on completion. Because of this, when the court ordered disclosure, the BRB refused, stating that the report was prepared for its legal advisors and as such, was the subject of legal professional privilege. However, the court rejected this argument on appeal, stating that such documents would only be privileged if the dominant purpose was submission for legal advice. In this case, ensuring safety on the railway was at least as important a purpose and therefore, the report had to be disclosed. This principle was extended to reports prepared by a trust or health authority in the case of *Lask* v *Gloucester Health Authority*[34] where it was held that reports produced by the hospital after an incident served two purposes. One was to establish whether or not there was liability in any future claims and the other was to look at ways of preventing further such incidents from occurring. The legal purpose was not the dominant of the two and therefore the document was not privileged.

The protocol also requires that a letter of claim is sent to the defendant. The letter should:

- describe the injuries and prognosis
- indicate the heads of damage
- provide a chronology of events if the case is complex.

The protocol indicates that proceedings should not normally be brought within three months of the letter of claim, unless there is some pressing reason, such as a limitation issue. The defendant is required to provide an initial response within 14 days and a more detailed and reasoned answer within three months.

Expert evidence

CPR 35 governs the issue of using expert evidence and it is an area fraught with difficulty. In the past, cases became battles of the experts, with eminent physicians on either side arguing over very technical medical information and a judge effectively choosing which side's expert he preferred.[35] There were also problems for each side in choosing how many experts to have and from what specialities. Experts can come from various sources. Often, they will be experts whom lawyers have seen in other cases and who are good at giving evidence and explaining complex medical issues to the court. The Law Society keeps a directory of expert witnesses, as do groups such as Action for Victims of Medical Accidents (AVMA) and the Association of Personal Injury Lawyers (APIL).

---

[34] [1991] 1 Med L R 379.
[35] For a stark example of this, see comments in *Bolitho* v *City & Hackney Health Authority* and *Whitehouse* v *Jordan* [1981].

The new rules try to prevent battles of the experts by actively restricting the amount of expert evidence in the case.[36] No expert evidence can be called and no evidence used in the case without the prior permission of the court[37] and permission will only be granted if its use is proportionate in terms of time and costs. However, unlike in other types of case, the court cannot demand that a single joint expert be used in clinical negligence cases.[38] This is in recognition of the fact that medicine is an inexact science and there are often genuine and complex disagreements between professionals that need to be aired in the court.

The main point that the CPR tries to make is that regardless of whether the claimant or the defendant commissions the expert report, that expert owes a duty to the court, not to the party on whose behalf he gives evidence.[39] All instructions provided to the expert by whatever party instructed him must be disclosed to the court.[40] Cases such as *Lucas* v *Barking*[41] make it clear that this includes documents such as other expert reports and background information provided to the expert.

CPR 35.6 allows any party to submit written questions to an expert, whether the expert has been instructed by one party or as a single joint expert. The questions must be answered provided that:

● They have been asked within 28 days of service of the expert report.

● They are proportionate.

● They are solely for the purpose of clarifying some element of the report.

Any answers given are then considered part of the original report.

There are other ways in which the rules try to streamline the process. For example, if there is more than one expert and there are key differences of opinion between them on an important issue, the court may direct that they have discussions to try to reach an agreed position on that point.[42] Ultimately, this is done in an attempt to minimise both the amount of time spent arguing in court and the costs for all concerned. However, it should be noted that any agreement reached between experts at one of these meetings is not binding on the parties unless they agree to it being binding.[43]

---

[36] CPR 35.3.
[37] CPR 35.4.
[38] See *Oxley* v *Penwarden* [2000] 7 Lloyds Rep Med 347.
[39] CPR 35.3.
[40] CPR 35.10(3).
[41] *Lucas* v *Barking, Havering and Redbridge Hospitals NHS Trust* [2004] 1 WLR 220.
[42] CPR 35.12.
[43] *Hubbard & Others* v *Lambeth Southwark and Lewisham Health Authority* [2002] PIQR P14.

ETHICS QUESTION

There is no doubt that the pre-action protocol and the civil procedure rules post-Woolf have sped up the clinical negligence process and have streamlined the system, with time and cost benefits to all concerned. However, forcing parties to agree on medical evidence, factual details and other elements of the case may not be the best way of achieving justice. For example, in *Hubbard* (referred to earlier), the claimant was concerned that because he did not have legal representation (which, of course, he is not required to have), his medical expert would feel intimidated when meeting with the defendant's medical expert and their legal team and would end up agreeing with them on issues rather than standing her ground. Is widening access by making the system cheaper and quicker so important that it justifies the fact that the court does not get to analyse each case in as much detail? Is poorer justice for many better than superior justice for a few?

Regulation in the future

The Kennedy Report[44] stated that:

> Clinical negligence litigation should be abolished and replaced by systems for identifying and analysing errors and learning from them. Expert groups should be appointed to consider alternatives to litigation for clinical negligence litigation and to make proposals for a possible administrative system to compensate those who suffered as a result of substandard care.

Essentially, Kennedy was recommending that a system similar to the no-fault compensation schemes in other countries such as Australia should be implemented. Such schemes set out a statutory framework of awards that can be paid without going through the lengthy and costly process of litigation, on the basis that the defendant does not admit liability but accepts the need to compensate the victim. The advantage of such schemes is that the costs and pressures associated with adversarial litigation are removed and the claimant is guaranteed a (usually smaller) sum of damages. However, it is not clear whether such schemes actually save money in the long run; the number of claimants is likely to increase dramatically despite the fact that payouts are smaller.

In 2006, the National Health Service Litigation Authority (NHSLA) ran a pilot scheme called Resolve. This aimed to deal with claims valued at under £15,000 under a fixed-fee system where the case would be settled within six months. The scheme was organised and run by a company, Resolve Services Ltd, and 20 specialist firms across the country took part in the pilot. Indications were that claimants found the service positive, even where their claims were unsuccessful, but the scheme has not been rolled out.

[44] The final report of the inquiry into Bristol Royal Infirmary 2001, available at http://www.bristol-inquiry.org.uk/final_report/index.htm.

In the same year, the NHS Redress Act was passed. This provides for a scheme to be set up for claims valued at under £20,000, offering an alternative to litigation. If a claimant accepts an offer made under the scheme, they cannot then bring a clinical negligence claim. Initially, the government acknowledges that costs may rise due to more claimants coming forward, but long term, it believes there will be cost savings to the NHS resulting from less litigation. Brazier has argued that the scheme may not be seen as impartial because it will be run by the NHSLA[45] and there are also concerns that only those who cannot afford to bring a negligence claim will use the scheme, which Herring argues will actually lead to a cost increase.[46] In any event, the government made clear at the outset that the scheme would not be introduced until 2010 at the earliest and, at the time of writing, it is still not up and running. In the author's opinion, it will have a profound effect on the clinical negligence litigation landscape, but possibly not in the way the government had intended. Given current economic concerns, further delays in implementation of the scheme seem likely.

Damages

With any clinical negligence claim, although there may well be an element of satisfaction from a finding of liability and a sense of closure achieved by having the defendant admit wrongdoing, the ultimate aim for the claimant is usually to obtain an award of damages. However, it is important for claimants to realise that a finding of liability by no means guarantees a large payout. Despite various sensational newspaper headlines, most claimants will receive a relatively modest amount in respect of their pain and suffering (known as *general damages*). Claimants may also be entitled to certain additional awards for quantifiable losses or required expenditure, such as loss of earnings or future care costs (known as *special damages*). However, there are rules about what types of damages can be claimed in each case. In this section, we will look specifically at:

- general damages
- special damages
- claims for wrongful life, birth or conception
- claims for nervous shock.

General damages

As stated earlier, this is the award the court makes in relation to the pain and suffering caused to the claimant by the substandard care provided by the defendant. For

---

[45] Brazier, M. and Cave, E., *Medicine, Patients and the Law*, 4th edn, 2009, Penguin at p. 236.
[46] Herring, J., *Medical Law and Ethics*, 3rd edn, 2010, Oxford at p. 136.

example, in *Ackers* v *Wigan*,[47] the claimant had the dreadful experience of being incompletely anaesthetised during the caesarean delivery of her first child. She was totally paralysed, but could feel every sensation and experienced intense pain with no way to communicate with the medical team. The court was not merely looking at compensation for the negligence of the anaesthetist and other staff in the performance of the actual operation and the pain experienced in theatre, but was also required to provide a remedy for the associated pain and suffering. She experienced severe postnatal depression for three months after the birth of her child and therefore missed out on the joys of early motherhood. She delayed having a second child. When she faced another caesarean she suffered weeks of extreme fear and anxiety. She refused operations to alleviate other medical conditions due to a fear of surgery. It had a detrimental effect on her sex life because she had a deep-rooted fear of getting pregnant again. In order to treat her, she was going to have to endure therapy sessions requiring her to relive the experience, which would be extremely distressing. Somehow, the court has to make a value judgment about the kind of suffering that has taken place and put a financial 'price tag' on it.

In terms of assessing general damages for the actual medical problems endured by the claimant, there are some useful sources of guidance for the court, including the Judicial Studies Board Guidelines, Butterworth's Personal Injury Service, and Kemp and Kemp, and these allow the court to search a database of similar cases where patients have suffered similar injuries, thus giving an approximate starting point for the assessment of awards.

One of the key areas of general damages that often needs to be calculated, especially in the more serious cases where a claimant has been left with a permanent disability, is loss of future earnings. This is where the court compensates the claimant by looking at what they would have earned had they not been injured by the defendant and tries to put them in the position they would have been in without the negligence. This is assessed by looking at the earning prospects of the claimant at the date of the trial. So for example, in *Collett*,[48] a young footballer in the Manchester United youth academy was permanently disabled by an illegal tackle. Given his ability and the career progression of his peers with equal or less ability, it was envisaged that, barring the incident in question, he would have gone on to play at championship and premiership level. In light of this, his award for future loss of earnings was just under £4 million. However, the court held that it was too speculative to say that he would have later made a career in management and coaching and therefore no award would be made to reflect loss of earnings in that capacity.

Where a larger award is made, such as that in *Collett*, there are additional issues to be considered by the court. It is not simply a matter of taking the average yearly earnings and multiplying that by the number of years of professional life remaining, because:

[47] [1991] 2 Med LR 232.
[48] *Collett* v *Smith* [2008] EWHC 1962 QB.

- A one-off lump sum can be invested – the return on such an investment could mean that the claimant ends up overcompensated.
- The claimant may have died at an earlier date due to some other event.
- The claimant might have become ill or been injured in any event.
- The claimant might have lost his job for another reason.

To reflect such uncertainties, the Damages Act 1996 allows the Lord Chancellor to set a discount rate by which large awards of damages for loss of future earnings will be reduced. It is currently set at 2.5%.[49] Thus, whatever the headline award, if damages are paid in a lump sum, 2.5% will be deducted before the money is paid to the claimant. The court can apply a different rate, but only if there are exceptional circumstances that would justify doing so.[50] In *Warren v Northern General*[51] the claimant (a child injured by medical negligence) tried to argue that a fall in the gross return on index-linked government securities was just such an exceptional circumstance envisaged in the Damages Act and in subsequent case law[52] and should warrant a reduction in the discount rate. The court rejected this, stating that, first, the Court of Protection that was holding the award of damages was a prudent investor and would manage the investment to avoid any adverse impact on the return by a fall in government securities and, second, even if it was not so prudently managed, a 0.5% drop was not significant enough to be an exceptional circumstance.

Special damages

Special damages are quantifiable damages that can be specifically identified and calculated. As such, assessing the value of the award should be a rather easier task than calculating general damages. They relate to things such as accommodation costs, nursing care and medical expenses. However, the calculations are not as straightforward as they may first appear. For example, in *Roberts v Johnstone*,[53] a child was left with catastrophic injuries as a result of the defendant's negligence. The parents had to give up work to provide round-the-clock care and a bungalow had to be purchased and renovated to be suitable for accommodating a person with such severe disabilities. In calculating special damages, the court took into account the fact that compensating the total cost of the property would mean that when the value increased over time, there would be extra value in the claimant's estate and also the fact that the renovations and improvements that had been made had increased the value of the property. Therefore, the claimants were entitled to:

---

[49] See www.lcd.gov.uk/civil/discount.htm.
[50] Section 1(2) Damages Act 1996.
[51] [2000] 1 WLR 1404.
[52] See *Wells v Wells* [1999].
[53] [1988] 3 WLR 1247.

- the value of the income that would have been generated by the money spent on the house if it had been invested – this was calculated at 2% per year over the claimant's estimated life remaining
- the cost of the renovations, less the £10,000 increase in value of the property
- and an award reflecting the cost of one full-time carer (the mother) and 25% of one carer for the father as he had reduced his hours of work to help support his wife but was not providing the same level of care.

It is clear from this that the court is very careful not to overcompensate the claimant.

REFLECT QUESTION

Is this caution about overcompensating the claimant linked to the identity of the defendant (the NHS)? Would the court be so cautious if the defendant were a large private corporation?

In relation to care costs, one issue the court has had to consider concerns whether a claimant who is entitled to local authority or 'state' care is entitled to claim damages for privately funded care instead. In *Peters v East Midlands SHA*,[54] the claimant was a 20-year-old left with profound disabilities due to the negligence of the defendant. She had been awarded around £4 million in damages and the majority of that award was made up of past and future care costs. The defendant appealed on the basis that she would be entitled by statute to care provided and funded by the local authority and therefore it was not reasonable to expect the defendant to pay the full cost of self-funding care. However, the court rejected the defendant's argument and held that the claimant had the right to choose self-funded care if she wished. The court also made the point that in such cases, it is more appropriate for the actual tortfeasor, rather than the local authority, to bear the costs.

One specific point should be made on the issue of special damages. Where the negligence has caused the death of the claimant, damages have been placed on a statutory footing, first by the Law Reform (Miscellaneous Provisions) Act 1934 and later by the Fatal Accidents Act 1976. This former piece of legislation provides for a statutory bereavement award which can be paid to:

- the husband or wife of the deceased
- both parents of the deceased if the deceased were legitimate, unmarried and under 18
- the mother of the deceased if the deceased were illegitimate, unmarried and under 18.

The bereavement award is currently set at £11,800.

[54] [2010] QB 48.

> ## REFLECT QUESTION
>
> Given the awards that are commonplace for other clinical negligence claims, is £11,800 a fair sum to reflect what pain and suffering has been caused by the death of the patient? Given that, in such a situation, the loss to the claimant is not mobility, independence or ability to work but their whole life, should the liability to the estate of the defendant not be a great deal higher? Are there policy issues at play here, again relating to the identity of the defendant and the fact that all the damages are actually coming out of the public purse?

The 1976 Act has extended the scope of compensation available so that further awards can be paid to anyone who is classed as a dependant of the deceased. Under this Act, dependants are defined as:

- the spouse of the deceased (this will now include civil partners)
- a partner who lived with the deceased as man and wife
- parents, grandparents or great grandparents of the deceased
- anyone treated by the deceased as a parent
- children and grandchildren
- anyone who is treated as a child of the family at the time of the death
- brothers, sisters, uncles or aunts of the deceased, or their children.

Section 3 of the Act states that the award shall be calculated to reflect the damage done to the dependants by the loss of the deceased and that an award can be divided between various dependants in such proportions as is deemed appropriate.

One final point to note is that where the claimant is claiming that the defendant's negligence caused them a loss of a chance of recovery that they would otherwise have had, the case of *Gregg* v *Scott* confirmed the longstanding position that the court will require them to show that they had a greater than 50% chance of recovery in the first place.[55] If not, the court will not recognise the lost chance as a head of damage that is recoverable. In other words, a less than 50% chance that has been lost is not classified as a compensatable loss. (For a full discussion of this case and its implications, see Chapter 5.)

Wrongful life, birth or conception

The claim of a child or their parents that negligence on the part of a healthcare professional has led either to the birth of a child that was not planned or to the birth of a disabled child, presents unique legal challenges. In order to try to strike

---

[55] [2005] UKHL 2.

a balance between fairness, equity and the background policy of respecting the sanctity of life, the courts make distinctions between claims for wrongful life and wrongful birth and conception.

Wrongful life

This type of claim involves the child who has been born alleging that it would have been better if she had never been born and that the disabilities caused by the negligence of the defendant before she was born have led to her having a life that is unbearable. The classic case illustrating this type of claim is *McKay*.

KEY CASE

McKay v Essex Area Health Authority[56]

Mrs McKay became pregnant naturally and the early stages were uneventful. Then, several weeks into the pregnancy, she became aware that she had been in contact with rubella and approached her GP with concerns about the possible effect on the foetus. Blood tests were carried out, but as a result of negligence either by the GP or by the laboratory in which the tests were carried out, she was wrongly informed that she had not been infected and that there was no damage to the foetus. When the baby was born, she suffered from severe disabilities. Claims were brought against the health authority by both the child and her mother. The basis of the child's claim was that the negligent failure to identify the exposure to rubella had caused her to be born and to have to live with these dreadful disabilities. She argued (and it was conceded by the defendant) that if the correct information had been given to Mrs McKay, she would have chosen to abort.

In a judgment couched heavily in terms of policy and morals, rather than hard law, the court made it clear that it would not sanction an action by a child along the lines of wrongful life.

The legal rationale for this was stated to be the impossibility of assessing damages. Essentially, what the claimant was asking the court to evaluate would have been the difference between existence and non-existence, between life and death. The court maintained that this was not something that could ever be quantified.

The mother's claim, however, did partially succeed as the essence of that claim was that but for the negligence of the defendant, she would not have experienced the pain and trauma of the birth and the discovery that the child was disabled. General damages are available in such a situation (as we will discuss further later).

McKay is a rather old case but is still of great relevance, partly because the principle that it laid down regarding claims for wrongful life has been maintained to this day by the courts and partly because of what the court had to say in the case about

[56] [1982] QB 1166.

an act of parliament that did not apply to the child in *McKay* because she had been born in 1975, before the Act came into force – the Congenital Disabilities (Civil Liability) Act 1976. Under that Act, if the defendant causes an 'occurrence' prior to the birth that results in the child being born with disabilities, the child may be entitled to compensation.[57] However, the court in *McKay* made it clear that in order to succeed in a claim under the Act, it must be shown that the negligent treatment of the mother during her pregnancy actually caused the disabilities in the child and in this case, clearly it was the exposure to rubella that caused the disabilities. Thus, the *McKay* case would not have fallen within the scope of section 1(2) and would have failed. Any other decision would have meant that in order to escape liability, it would have been necessary for the mother to abort and the court was adamant that such a course of action should never be encouraged or, indeed, mandated. So, the threefold justification for the decision in *McKay* was:

- It was not possible to quantify damages for the difference between existence and non-existence.
- The law should never impose an obligation on doctors to terminate a pregnancy.
- The law should never be seen to devalue disabled persons or imply that it is better not to be born at all than to be born with disabilities.

Wrongful birth and conception

A crucial distinction is therefore made between a claim by the child that they should never have been born and a claim by the mother that she should not have had the trauma of giving birth, either i) at all in the case of failed sterilisation operations, or ii) to a disabled child where the negligence lies in failure to diagnose prenatally. However, the courts have been stringent about restricting such claims to damages for the birth itself and the distress caused at the time.

KEY CASE

McFarlane v Tayside Health Board[58]

Mr and Mrs McFarlane had four children and decided that their family was complete, so Mr McFarlane underwent a vasectomy operation to render him sterile. However, the advice given to the couple after the surgery was deemed to be negligent in that they were not warned of the small chance of the operation naturally reversing itself. This indeed happened and resulted in an unplanned pregnancy. Their fifth child, a girl named Katherine, was born perfectly healthy and became a loved and valued member of the family. However, Mrs McFarlane sued the health board, claiming ➡

---

[57] Section 1(2)(b).
[58] [1999] 4 All ER 961.

damages for the pain and loss of earnings associated with the pregnancy and birth and also the costs of raising Katherine until she attained 18 years of age. She argued that these costs were incurred through no fault of her own as a direct result of the defendant's negligence.

The court ruled that while she could claim for the pain and distress of the pregnancy and birth and for limited associated expenses such as maternity clothes and loss of earnings for the time she had been forced to take off work, she could not recover the costs of raising a healthy child. Running through the judgment is a general reluctance to treat the birth of a child as a damage for which compensation should be payable. Lord Millett stated: 'The law must take the birth of a healthy child to be a blessing, not a detriment.' From a legal perspective, Lord Slynn attempted to clarify the reasoning by explaining that: 'A doctor's duty was only to avoid a pregnancy and that did not extend to the costs of bringing up a child who was born and accepted into the family.'

Several issues must be dealt with in relation to the *McFarlane* judgment. The first is that Lord Slynn's comments leave open the possibility that in a case in which a child who was born was not accepted into the family and had to be taken care of by the local authority or foster parents, the costs of raising him or her may be recoverable. Clearly, this would be difficult to reconcile and would penalise parents who behaved responsibly towards their unexpected addition. Second, while he is correct that the duty was to prevent pregnancy, given the court's view on enforcing or requiring terminations, once that pregnancy has occurred, the costs of raising the child are an unavoidable and arguably directly related expense flowing from the negligence. As Lord Cullen had stated at Court of Appeal level: 'In the result . . . the benefits of the child do not provide an answer to the claim for the costs of her upbringing. Respect for human life should not be allowed to obscure the fact that couples who have decided that they cannot afford to raise another child have been left to find a way to do so'.[59] Another interesting perspective on the court's reasoning is provided by Kirby J in the Australian High Court case of *Cattanch v Melchior*.[60] Kirby stated that 'The coal miner, forced to retire because of injury, does not get less damages for loss of earning capacity because he is now free to sit in the sun each day reading his favourite newspaper. Likewise, the award of damages to the parents for their future financial expenditure is not be reduced by the enjoyment that they will or may obtain from the birth of the child.'[61]

Where the child is born disabled as a result of negligence, the situation is slightly different. For example, in *Parkinson v St James*,[62] the court held that while the general

---

[59] [1998] SLT 307 at 396.
[60] [2003] HCA 38.
[61] Ibid. per Kirby J at 91.
[62] *Parkinson v St James Seacroft University Hospital NHS Trust* [2001] 6 Lloyds Rep Med 306.

costs of raising the child were not recoverable under the *McFarlane* principle, the mother could recover the additional costs of raising a disabled child, such as the cost of specialist equipment. This was a controversial decision. Hale LJ justified it by saying 'This analysis treats a disabled child as having exactly the same worth as a non disabled child. It affords him the same dignity and status. It simply acknowledges that he costs more.'[63] Similarly, in the case of *Rees v Darlington*,[64] in which a child was born healthy as a result of negligently carried out sterilisation, but to a mother who was disabled, the general principle was adhered to that compensation for the upkeep of a healthy child was not available. However, an award of general damages of £15,000 was made to reflect the distress and difficulties experienced by the mother in trying to take care of her child given the disabilities from which she was suffering.

What all this shows is that the courts are treating the birth of a disabled child or the birth of a healthy child to disabled parents differently from the birth of a healthy infant to healthy parents.

ETHICS QUESTION

Is this different treatment by the court justified? Perhaps the costs of raising a disabled child are greater than those of raising a non-disabled child owing to the equipment and resources needed to make her life easier. However, you could argue that the costs of raising a gifted child in music or sport will be more owing to the lessons, equipment, travel, etc. which make her life 'easier'. Should *these* extra costs not be recoverable?

Nervous shock

Where a claimant has suffered emotional distress and pain, this will usually be adequately compensated by an award for general damages, but it is more problematic when a secondary victim wishes to make a claim for such trauma, for example, where a relative has seen the person they love in huge amounts of pain or has witnessed traumatic events and then suffers posttraumatic stress or depression. In general, tort claims for damages for pure psychiatric injury have been difficult and it has always been necessary to prove a genuine psychiatric illness in order to recover damages. Issues about how to compensate distress, anxiety or emotional trauma in secondary victims have taxed the courts for many years. The basic principles were laid down in the *Alcock* case.[65] This requires that the secondary victim has the necessary proximity in time and space to the events and that they prove a recognised psychiatric illness over and above the foreseeable distress caused by injury to their

---

[63] Ibid. per Hale LJ at 325.
[64] *Rees v Darlington Memorial Hospital NHS Trust* [2003] UKHL 52.
[65] *Alcock v Chief Constable of South Yorkshire* [1991] 4 All ER 907.

relative. This is really an assessment that must be made on a case-by-case basis, but the sorts of situations that have given rise to successful claims include a scenario in which a father was shown into a waiting room and told his child had been stillborn, even being given the body of the child to cuddle, until staff realised they had the wrong father and his child was alive.[66] Perhaps the most extreme example of a very lenient interpretation of the rules was a case in which a husband and son of the patient were allowed to recover damages for the trauma of her having an unnecessary mastectomy after a negligent misdiagnosis of breast cancer. The husband said he was traumatised by seeing her naked after the operation and the son by overhearing a telephone conversation in which she discussed her diagnosis of cancer.[67]

Summary

The clinical negligence system, including the complaints process and the availability of damages, has come in for much criticism over the years and numerous attempts at reform have led to confusion and discussion but very little improvement. No-fault schemes are a popular choice in other jurisdictions but may offer little in terms of cost savings and will therefore not prove attractive to the current government. It seems likely that the litigation system will remain unchanged for the foreseeable future. Given all the practical obstacles that the system creates for claimants in addition to the complex legal issues they have to face in establishing a breach of duty, proving causation and assessing damages, it really cannot be said that justice is done or indeed seen to be done in the realm of clinical negligence litigation.

Self-test questions

1 Outline the process for bringing a complaint against a hospital.
2 What is the role of the ombudsman?
3 What are the key stages of the clinical negligence pre-action protocol?
4 What is the difference between general and special damages?
5 Explain the difference between a claim for wrongful life and a claim for wrongful birth.
6 Can a relative bring a claim for psychiatric harm resulting from the negligent treatment of the claimant?

---

[66] *Farrell v Avon Health Authority* [2000] 2 LGLR 69.
[67] *Froggatt v Chesterfield & North Derbyshire Royal Hospital NHS Trust* [2002] All ER 218.

Practice essay question

Harris argues that where a child has a life that is worth living, the child has made a net benefit whereas a child whose life is truly not worth living should be compensated as of right (quoted in Pattinson, *Medical Law and Ethics*, 3rd edn, Sweet & Maxwell, 2011 at p. 338).

Discuss the extent to which Harris' approach would be possible under English law.

6 Consent

Introduction

It is a well-known and generally accepted rule of medical law that in order for a medical professional to carry out any treatment on a patient, that patient must first have given consent to such treatment. This rule makes perfect sense in a post-Human Rights Act society that, as discussed in Chapter 1, no longer holds the medical profession in the high esteem it once did and approaches medical care with an increasingly consumerist focus. The thought of a doctor or nurse performing a medical procedure on a person without his consent, simply because that doctor or nurse believes it is in the patient's best interests, offends modern society's deeply held belief that we all have a right to determine what happens to our own bodies.[1] It also plays to our fears in light of recent high-profile scandals involving medical practitioners abusing their power over us.[2] Having said this, the recognition of the importance of consent to medical treatment is by no means a modern phenomenon. As far back as 1914, Cardozo J stated in the important US case of *Schloendorff* v *Society of New York Hospital* that: 'Every person being of adult years and sound mind has a right to determine what shall be done with his own body and a surgeon who performs an operation without his patient's consent commits an assault.'[3]

However, this simple-sounding rule actually presents the most challenging legal and ethical dilemmas to the medical lawyer once it has to be applied in practice. While the generally accepted ethical stance that patient autonomy should always be the guiding principle is applied almost as a matter of course now in the UK, it is by no means the only ethical issue that arises. How do you ensure that a person is not being coerced by family members into consenting to or refusing a particular treatment? How do you deal with consent issues where the patient is mentally incapacitated or is under 18? What about patients taking treatment decisions based on deeply held religious views – is such consent or refusal valid? How do you define 'valid' or 'informed' consent?

---

[1] For a fascinating, if controversial discussion of this issue, see Foster, C., *Choosing Life, Choosing Death*, 2009, Hart.

[2] Cases such as Harold Shipman and the Bristol and Alder Hey scandals drastically undermined public confidence in the medical profession – see Chapter 1 for full discussion.

[3] (1914) 211 NY 125.

Given the complex nature of this area of law, the aims of this chapter are to:

- evaluate and explain the various ethical arguments that inform and influence the law on consent
- explain the basic legal rules on consent and how they are applied in practice
- compare and contrast the basic legal position with the rules relating to special groups such as mentally incapacitated patients and children
- assess whether the law on consent is adequate and effective, from the point of view both of the patient and of the medical practitioner.

Ethics

The main ethical argument underpinning this area of law is the age-old tug of war between autonomy, on the one hand, and paternalism, on the other. As discussed in Chapter 1, the principle of autonomy dictates that every person has a right to decide what happens to her body and this would include the right to make what others might think an unwise choice or a choice that results in harm to her. Autonomy requires that right to be respected and upheld in all circumstances, as long as the patient has the mental capacity to make that choice. By contrast, paternalism requires the patient to acknowledge that his level of knowledge and understanding of the medical situation he is faced with may not be as complete as that of the medical professional treating him or that his decision may be influenced by factors such as fear, anxiety, family pressure, religious conditioning etc. Paternalism would condone the medical practitioner making treatment decisions on behalf of the patient or proceeding with treatment that she deemed to be in that patient's best interests without first obtaining suitable consent, underpinned by a broadly utilitarian view that the end result of saving lives or improving the health of patients is a valid aim and that some infringement of autonomy along the way can be justified. Clearly, these two schools of thought are diametrically opposed and finding common ground can be virtually impossible. Depending on which argument persuades you, you will probably find that you either view the law in the UK as moving in the right direction or you think it is shirking its responsibility to act in the best interests of vulnerable patients.[4]

In order to further explore the ethical issues at play, some brief scenarios follow. Before reading the rest of the chapter and learning the law that applies to these scenarios, think first from an ethical standpoint, based on your own opinions about the options facing the medical practitioner in each situation, and make a note of what you think the practitioner should do. We will come back to these scenarios at the end of the chapter to see if knowledge of the legal rules changes your answers.

---

[4] For a fascinating in-depth discussion of the autonomy v paternalism argument, see McLean, S., *Autonomy, Consent and the Law*, 2011, Cambridge University Press.

Scenario 1

Amanda is a Jehovah's Witness. During childbirth she loses a lot of blood and requires a blood transfusion to save her life. She refuses to consent to the transfusion because her religion teaches that it is wrong to take blood from another person.

What should the doctor do? Can forcible treatment be justified in such a situation?

Scenario 2

Belinda is about to give birth but there is a problem with the labour and the foetus' heartbeat drops dangerously low. She is told that she needs to have an emergency caesarean or the foetus will die. She refuses to consent to the operation as she is absolutely committed to having a natural delivery.

What should the doctor do?

Scenario 3

Charles has contracted a highly contagious and potentially fatal illness. However, he is extremely claustrophobic and refuses to consent to being admitted to a quarantine facility so that he can be isolated and barrier nursed. There are 25 other patients on the ward in which Charles is currently being treated, some of whom are elderly and have compromised immune systems.

What should the doctor do?

Scenario 4

Delia refuses to consent to having her baby vaccinated against measles as she has read in the newspapers that scientists have found a link between the vaccine and autism. Delia used to work for the Vaccine Damage Tribunal before she had children and met many families dealing with the strain of caring for a child whom they believed was damaged by vaccination. She says she is not prepared to risk causing such damage to her child. Delia works three days per week and her baby attends a local nursery where she mixes with children between six weeks and five years of age.

What should the doctor do? Can she force Delia to have her baby vaccinated?

Scenario 5

Evie, aged 15, is anorexic and has now reached a dangerously low weight. Her doctor wants to admit her to hospital and force feed her to increase her weight as he is concerned that if she does not gain weight in the next few weeks she will die. Evie refuses to consent to being admitted to hospital as she does not want them to make her gain weight.

What should the doctor do?

Scenario 6

Felix is a drug addict. As a result of his addiction, he frequently behaves violently and commits robbery/burglary to feed his habit. He has been offered a detox programme by the court but is refusing to consent to being admitted into the unit.

What should the doctors (and/or the court) do?

Basic legal rules

If a doctor treats a patient without the requisite consent, various legal consequences may follow. First, it may constitute a battery, giving rise to a claim against the doctor in tort as well as a criminal prosecution.[5] It will almost certainly constitute clinical negligence (see Chapter 3) as it is likely that a body of responsible medical opinion would dictate the obtaining of consent before carrying out the treatment and, therefore, failure to do so would mean the doctor had fallen below the standard of care required and had breached his duty to the patient.[6] The doctor may also have breached the patient's human rights. For example, if he has attached the patient to a life support machine without consent, meaning others are responsible for feeding, cleaning, dressing and toileting the patient, it could be argued that the patient's right to freedom from inhuman and degrading treatment under Article 3 of the European Convention on Human Rights ('the Convention') has been breached. If the treatment entails the patient being detained in hospital without consent, this may infringe Article 5 which guarantees the right to liberty. Since the passing of the Human Rights Act 1998, all our public authorities (which includes NHS trusts) must ensure that the rights of individuals under the Convention are upheld and individuals now have redress in our domestic courts if their rights are infringed. In addition, treating a patient without consent will mean the doctor is in breach of professional guidance and codes of conduct issued by various regulatory and professional bodies (these will be discussed in more detail later in the chapter).

Despite all of this, it should not be assumed that obtaining consent is always the answer and as we will see there are circumstances in which a consent that has been obtained may be overridden or may not necessarily offer the doctor complete protection.

Common law

The following rather long but very useful quotation from Lord Donaldson sums up the basic position of the court in relation to consent to treatment:

> An adult who . . . suffers from no mental incapacity has an absolute right to choose whether to consent to treatment, to refuse it or to choose one rather than another treatment being offered . . . this right of choice is not limited to decisions which others might regard as sensible. It exists notwithstanding that the reasons for making the choice are

---

[5] See *Chatterton* v *Gerson* [1981] 1QB 432 and *R* v *Brown* [1994] 1 AC 212.
[6] See *Bolam* v *Friern HMC* [1957] 2 All ER 118 and *Bolitho* v *City and Hackney Health Authority* [1998] AC 232.

rational, irrational, unknown or even non-existent. The fact that, emergency situations apart, no medical treatment of an adult patient of full capacity can be undertaken without his consent, creates a situation in which the absence of consent has much the same effect as refusal.[7]

The most commonly cited case example of this principle in practice is the case of *Re C*.

KEY CASE

Re C (Adult: Refusal of Treatment) [1994] 1 WLR 290

C suffered from paranoid schizophrenia and was also suffering from gangrene. The infection was spreading rapidly and the view of those treating him was that he would die unless his leg were amputated. C refused to consent, stating that he would rather die with two legs than live with one. Despite his mental condition, he was assessed as having the requisite level of competence and understanding to make the decision (the assessment of mental capacity will be discussed in more detail later in the chapter) and therefore, a declaration was granted by the court that no amputation was to take place without his consent. C continued to refuse consent and died a short time later.

This case clearly demonstrates that, in these circumstances, the court is not interested in exercising any kind of best interests assessment or engaging in paternalistic or protective measures to keep the patient alive. Autonomy is to be respected in those who have capacity, regardless of the consequences, in a straightforward case involving an adult of sound mind. However, as we shall see later, in other patient groups the court takes a very different approach.

Form of consent

Consent can be either express or implied. In terms of express consent, this must be clear and evidenced but this does not necessarily mean that it must be in writing. However, the Department of Health issues standard consent forms that trusts can use[8] and there are others available for specific treatments: for example, the Human Fertilisation and Embryology Authority provides clinics with specific forms of consent for fertility treatments.[9] While having the consent written down on paper can

---

[7] *Re T* [1993] Fam 95 per Lord Donaldson at 112.
[8] The up-to-date guidance from the Department Health and the model consent forms is available at http://www.dh.gov.uk/en/Publicationsandstatistics/Publications/PublicationsPolicyAndGuidance/DH_103643.
[9] The consent forms and guidance on consent in fertility treatment were revised in April 2011 and are available at http://www.hfea.gov.uk/2504.html – see Chapter 7 for more detailed discussion.

be useful in terms of proving that consent was obtained, the court has stated clearly on a number of occasions that a mere signature on a form is not of itself enough to evidence that the patient adequately consented to the treatment. For example in *Chatterton* v *Gerson*,[10] although Miss Chatterton had signed a consent form for the operation to block a sensory nerve and alleviate her chronic back pain, she argued that because the surgeon had not adequately explained the detail of the procedure to her and the possible side-effects, including that it may lead to numbness and loss of muscle power, this vitiated her consent. The court stated that it must look beyond the existence of a signature and 'Look at all the circumstances and ask "Was there a real consent?". . . in my judgment, once the patient is informed in broad terms of the nature of the procedure which is intended and gives her consent, that consent is real.'[11] Of course, this inevitably leads to evidential difficulties of proving what a person may have said.

Consent does not necessarily have to be express, it can also be implied. For example, in *O'Brian* v *Cunard Steamship Co.*,[12] the mere holding out of an arm to the nurse who was administering the vaccinations was sufficient to amount to implied consent to the injection. If, for example, a GP asks a patient to remove items of clothing and get onto the bed so that he can examine her and that patient proceeds to do so, the patient will have validly consented to the examination, even though she has not expressly voiced that consent. Clearly, in many cases this will not be problematic as the consent of the patient is obvious by their conduct, but what if a person's actions are misinterpreted by the doctor? For this reason, it is clearly better for a medical professional to ensure they have express consent before proceeding to treat the patient.

Extent of consent

There is clearly an issue, primarily with implied consent but also sometimes where consent is express, with ensuring that the patient understands exactly what they are consenting to. This brings us back to the importance of having something written down. What if the patient extends their arm to a nurse, thus consenting to an injection (as in *O'Brian* v *Cunard Steamship Co.*, just examined), but thinks it is a flu jab when it is actually a rubella vaccination? Is this valid consent? A similar situation arose in a Canadian case,[13] in which the woman consented to an injection but she consented to it in the left arm and the doctor injected her right arm. Although this made no difference in terms of the effect of the injection, the court held that there

---

[10] [1981] QB 432 (QBD).
[11] Ibid. per Bristow J.
[12] (1891) 28 NE 288.
[13] *Allan* v *New Mount Sinai Hospital* (1980) 109 DLR (3d) 634.

had not been valid consent to inject the right arm and therefore, the doctor had committed a battery.

The standard Department of Health consent form contains specific sections that must be completed by the healthcare professional stating that they have explained the nature of the proposed treatment to the patient and there is also the option of attaching copies of any other information that has been provided, such as patient information leaflets, to the form. It also provides that by signing the form, the patient is consenting to further treatment of any type being undertaken if it becomes necessary to save their life or prevent serious harm to their health. For example, if something goes wrong during a routine operation and the patient bleeds profusely, urgent blood transfusions may be required or even the removal of a damaged organ. If the patient could die without the extra procedure being carried out there and then, the form envisages that they may consider they have consent to carry it out.

One issue that concerns some patients is exactly who will be carrying out the procedure. If a patient consents to an operation because they believe that a particular, highly qualified consultant will be carrying it out, but in fact he allows a junior doctor to do it under supervision, will the consent still be valid? If the patient has signed a standard consent form then it will remain valid. The form explicitly states that there is no guarantee of a particular person carrying out the procedure. It does, however, guarantee that the person who carries it out will be suitably qualified, so specific consent is required where the procedure will be done by a medical student or indeed a vet! In *R v Tabussum*,[14] the surgeon allowed his friend, a vet, to remove the patient's gall bladder. He did so very competently, but the court unsurprisingly held that the patient had not consented to this.

Validity of consent

When we look at the validity of a consent that has been given, we are effectively asking two things:

1 Whether the patient has consented of their own free will, without any undue pressure or influence from others.

2 Whether they have consented to that specific treatment, based on sufficient information about it.

A case that illustrates the court's insistence on free and independent consent of the patient himself is that of *Re T*.

---

[14] [2000] Lloyds Med Rep 404.

KEY CASE

Re T [1992] 4 All ER 649

T was 20 years old and 34 weeks pregnant. She was involved in a road traffic accident and sustained fairly serious injuries. The doctors treating her were concerned that her baby was at risk and in the evening of the day she was admitted, she consented to a caesarean section which was scheduled for the following morning. She was later visited by her mother, who was a devout Jehovah's Witness and believed that it was wrong to take blood from another person in the form of a transfusion. The next morning, T expressed her wish not to be given blood products. The consent form was amended and she signed to say that she would not consent to a transfusion and that the hospital was absolved of liability if it failed to provide such treatment. In the event, the child was stillborn and T suffered massive internal bleeding before slipping into a coma. A transfusion was needed to save her life but doctors did not have her consent to provide it. Her boyfriend and her father sought a declaration from the court allowing the doctors to give her the transfusion. The court looked at the extent of the consent that she had given and took a number of things into account, including:

- The fact that she had enquired about whether there were alternatives to blood products and was told that there were, but it was not made clear to her that they were of limited use and not as effective.

- Pressure from her mother may have played a part in T's decision, given the fact that T herself was not baptised a Jehovah's Witness and that she had not mentioned any aversion to transfusion until her mother had spoken to her, thus meaning the consent may not have been voluntary and independent.

- Her state of mind after the accident and the medications she had been given may have affected her mental capacity to make a decision.

In light of this, the Court of Appeal granted the declaration and allowed the doctors to disregard her refusal of blood products.

This case has been heavily criticised for highlighting the importance of autonomy and stating that a patient's decision should always be upheld even if that decision seems unwise and then completely disregarding that in favour of saving her life. However, when you read this case carefully it becomes apparent that on the facts, it was doubtful that T's refusal of blood was an independent and valid refusal.

As demonstrated in *Re T*, undue influence of another person can invalidate a patient's consent, but the court has made it clear that it will take a solid evidence base to do so. For example, in *Centre for Reproductive Medicine* v *U*,[15] the consent of the husband to posthumous use of his sperm in fertility treatment if he died was later withdrawn by him at the request of the nursing sister carrying out the couple's

[15] [2002] EWCA Civ 565.

treatment. She requested that he withdraw consent to posthumous use because the centre had a policy that such use was unethical and also because she herself had ethical objections. When he later died, his wife challenged the withdrawal of consent on the basis that he only did so because he felt their treatment may be suspended if he did not comply. However, the court held that there was no evidence to support this and in the absence of a valid consent, it was unlawful for the clinic to continue to store or use his sperm. Clearly, the court draws a distinction between a situation where a patient is persuaded to give or withdraw consent to something and where their free will is completely overridden, but where should the line be drawn? What about prisoners who are patients and who are persuaded to consent or refuse treatment by the prison doctor (who is often a prison officer)? Have they ever really had free and independent ability to make that decision, given the nature of their incarceration and the inequality in their relationship with the doctor? In *Freeman* v *Home Office*,[16] the court stated that, although it should be alert to the inequality in the relationship, it did not automatically render the decision of the patient invalid and that each case needed to be assessed on its individual facts. That said, Stephen Brown LJ did point out that in such a situation: 'A court must be alive to the risk that what may appear, on the face of it, to be real consent is not in fact so.'[17]

In addition to potential undue influence, a further factor that may invalidate a patient's consent or refusal of treatment is lack of information. Unlike, for example, the USA, where 'informed consent' is required before treatment is administered, the UK prefers a more generalised duty on doctors to give basic information. As stated in *Chatterton* v *Gerson* (discussed earlier): 'Once a patient is informed in broad terms of the nature of the procedure and has given consent, that consent is real.'[18] However, our courts have been keen to point out that a patient needs a certain amount of core information about the treatment being offered in order to render the decision they make valid[19]. This case also discussed the fact that although informing in such broad terms would constitute a defence against battery, the doctor may still be liable in negligence if the risks and implications are not also explained.

The main problem in this area is that there appears to be a conflict between what various professional bodies are advising as being best practice and what the courts are actually requiring doctors to divulge to patients. For example, in the latest GMC guidelines,[20] it states that 'patients have the right to information about their condition and the treatment options available to them.' It does acknowledge that

---

[16] *Freeman* v *Home Office (No. 2)* [1984] 1 All ER 1036.

[17] See n. 5 above.

[18] See n. 6 above.

[19] See, for example, *Davis* v *Barking, Havering and Brentwood Health Authority* [1993] 4 Med LR 85 and *Devi* v *West Midlands Regional Health Authority* [1980] CLY 687.

[20] 'Patients and Doctors Making Decisions Together' available at http://www.gmc-uk.org/guidance/ethical_guidance/consent_guidance_index.asp.

the amount of information they give to a particular patient may vary in light of factors such as:

- the nature of the condition
- the complexity of treatment
- the risks associated with the treatment or procedure
- the patient's wishes.

The point about the GMC guidelines is that they establish a basic right of the individual patient to information about their treatment options. However, it is then left to the courts to decide how much information doctors must give and this is where it gets a little less clear. The overall impression from case law is that courts generally set the standard fairly low in terms of how much information should be given to a patient. We looked at the case of *Sidaway* in Chapter 3 when discussing clinical negligence.[21] In that case, the patient argued that she had not been given enough information about the possible side-effects and long-term problems that she might encounter after the surgery to correct her back problem. The court was not prepared to say that the doctor should have given her more information. It noted that she was extremely distressed and in a lot of pain at the time this was being discussed and that all that was required was that the doctor had complied with the *Bolam* test, i.e. that he acted in accordance with a responsible body of medical opinion. As there were other doctors who said they would not have given her any more information than the defendant had provided, he was not negligent and the consent was valid. In the later case of *Pearce*,[22] the court expanded on this a little, stating that there was a duty on doctors to inform patients of a 'significant' risk, but note the cautious wording: 'If there is a *significant* risk which would affect the judgment of a *reasonable patient*, then *in the normal course* it is the responsibility of a doctor to inform a patient of that significant risk, *if the information is needed* so that the patient can determine for him or herself as to what course he or she should adopt.'[23] This is a far cry from the American idea that a patient has a right to make an informed choice and have all the information at her fingertips when she makes a medical decision. Those who argue that we are moving towards informed consent in this country perhaps need to read the wording of these judgments a little more carefully and note how, even where the rhetoric is fairly robust, the decision rarely follows it. Although in *Chester* v *Afshar*[24] mention was made of surgery without 'informed consent' being unlawful, this case is increasingly being seen as an

---

[21] *Sidaway* v *Board of Governors of the Bethlem Royal Hospital* [1985] AC 871 and see Chapter 3, pp. 37.
[22] *Pearce* v *United Bristol Healthcare NHS Trust* [1999] ECC 167 at para. 174.
[23] Ibid. per Lord Woolf at para. 174.
[24] [2004] UKHL 41.

anomaly in an otherwise rather paternalistic and heavily *Bolam*-influenced body of case law.

Mentally incapacitated patients

As detailed earlier, the idea of patient autonomy dictates that a person who has capacity may make any decision they wish in relation to their treatment, which should be upheld by the doctors treating them and by the courts in the event of a dispute. It is therefore vitally important to understand what is meant by 'capacity' and how it is assessed, as well as the various options for authorising treatment if a person is deemed not to have capacity to decide for himself.

In order fully to understand the legal position on mental capacity, it is necessary to examine a mixture of statute and common law. This is because, up until October 2007, the assessment of mental capacity was solely governed by common law principles with several key cases setting out the legal rules and how they should be applied. However, in October 2007, the Mental Capacity Act 2005 (MCA) came into force in England and Wales and it is this Act that now governs the assessment of mental capacity in anyone aged 16 years or over. Despite this change, the MCA in many instances merely puts the old common law rules on a statutory footing and, therefore, the case law is still useful as a guide to interpreting and understanding the rules.

Assessment of capacity

The MCA applies to all acts and decisions taken in relation to medical care by adults and by children aged 16 and over (except decisions involving advance decisions and lasting powers of attorney – see later). The basic premise of the Act, laid out in section 1, is that there is automatically a rebuttable presumption of capacity. In other words, doctors should assume that the patient has capacity unless there is clear evidence to the contrary. Capacity is decision specific, so a person may not have the capacity to consent to a complex heart operation with multiple potential risks, but may have capacity to consent to having blood taken for testing or to having a vaccination. Just because a person has been deemed to lack capacity to make a particular decision in relation to their healthcare, it should not be assumed that they are unable to consent to other treatments – an assessment must be made each time a treatment decision is required. Other fundamental principles of the Act set out in section 1 are:

- *All practicable steps must be taken to assist the person to make the decision* – for example, where a person suffers from dementia he may need to be asked to make the decision in the morning when he is more alert rather than later in the day when he can become more confused.

- *A person must be allowed to make unwise decisions* – just as in *Re C*,[25] it should not be presumed that because the decision being made by the patient seems unwise or reckless she does not have capacity to make that decision and this will extend to the person having a right to refuse life-saving treatment if she so chooses.

- *All acts done on behalf of a person lacking capacity must be the least restrictive action appropriate and must be in that patient's best interests* – this will be discussed in more detail later in the chapter.

Clearly, the Act has been drafted to ensure that while provision is made for proxy decision making where a person clearly lacks capacity, every chance must be given to that patient to make the decision herself and her rights must be protected at every step.

The test for capacity is set out in sections 2 and 3 of the MCA. Section 2(1) states that a person lacks capacity if, at the material time, 'he is unable to make a decision for himself in relation to the matter because of the impairment of or a disturbance in the functioning of the mind or brain'. Section 2 also makes clear that such impairment can be either permanent or temporary,[26] so a person brought into an accident and emergency department late on a Friday night, severely intoxicated, may well lack capacity to make treatment decisions in the few hours after he is admitted and gradually regains capacity as he sobers up. The assessment of capacity is made on the balance of probabilities and must not be made by reference to age, appearance or an aspect of a person's behaviour. Such protections are necessary but can make the assessment rather difficult.

ETHICS QUESTION

Should the assessment of capacity be made on the balance of probabilities or, given the important consequences that flow from a finding of incapacity, should a doctor need to show beyond reasonable doubt that the person lacks capacity before proceeding to treat him as incapable of consenting to or refusing treatment?

⬤ Understanding the capacity test

In order to further understand how an assessment of capacity is made, there are various sources of guidance available. Section 3 of the MCA elaborates on what is meant in section 2 by 'unable to make a decision'. It sets out the following factors that may lead to a finding of incapacity:

---

[25] *Re C (Adult: Refusal of Medical Treatment)* [1994] 1 All ER 819.
[26] Echoing the words of Wall LJ in *Re JT*: 'The patient may lack capacity for a number of reasons. It may be due to a permanent mental disorder or the short term effects of drink or drugs.'

- the person is unable to understand relevant information
- the person is unable to retain that information, even for a short period of time
- the person is unable to use or weigh up the information given
- the person is unable to communicate the decision.

Section 3 also states that relevant information includes information on the reasonably foreseeable consequences of either consenting to or refusing the treatment being discussed and this echoes sentiments expressed in another key source of guidance on the capacity test case law.

Re C, decided in 1994 and discussed in detail earlier, set out the seminal three-stage test that the MCA has effectively taken and put on a statutory footing. Here, the court stated that in order for a person to have capacity they must be able to:

- understand and retain information
- believe it
- weigh it up in the balance.

This case was also a classic example of the sentiments expressed in the MCA more than a decade later; you must not presume a person is incapable because he makes an unwise decision or his behaviour seems odd. C was a paranoid schizophrenic and believed that he was a world-class surgeon, but he was also capable of retaining information about his condition and believed that, if the infection spread, he would die. He weighed that up and decided that he would rather not have his leg amputated, in full awareness of the consequences. He passed the test of capacity and therefore the court had no choice but to allow his decision to stand.

The *Re C* test was affirmed a few years later in the case of *Re MB*.

KEY CASE

Re MB [1997] 2 FLR 426 CA

MB was in the later stages of pregnancy and was informed that it might be necessary to perform a caesarean section delivery. She initially consented to this, but then refused the necessary anaesthesia by injection because she had a phobia of needles. When she went into labour and complications arose, the hospital obtained a declaration from the court that they could carry out the operation and use the requisite anaesthesia, because she was incapable of consenting to or refusing treatment. MB appealed. Butler Sloss LJ reiterated the *Re C* test and also made it clear that any patient who has capacity, including a pregnant woman, can refuse treatment, even where it will lead to serious damage or death of the foetus or to her own death. However, she went on to explain that temporary factors, including panic brought on by extreme fear of something like needles, could completely erode capacity, so MB was temporarily rendered incapable by her extreme phobia of needles. Doctors could perform the operation and use needles if it was in her best interests and Butler Sloss was confident that MB would suffer more long-term harm if death or serious injury was caused to her baby than from having an injection. The appeal was dismissed.

This is a controversial case. Would you consider a needle phobia to constitute an impairment in the functioning of the mind or brain? Could it have been argued that the patient in *Re C* had such an impairment due to his schizophrenia and his belief that he was a top-class surgeon, thus overestimating his medical understanding of his condition? Do you think the decision in *Re MB* might have been different had the life of the foetus not been at stake? Although technically, as we will see in Chapters 8, 9 and 10, a foetus has no legal personality and therefore does not have a right to life under English law, case law does seem to reveal a tendency among judges to declare pregnant women incapable where their decision is such that it puts the life of the foetus at risk.[27]

The case of *Re B*[28] makes an important contribution to the meaning of 'understanding' in the capacity test, making it clear that a person need not necessarily have experienced elements of the treatment being refused in order to understand that treatment and have capacity to refuse it. B had been rendered tetraplegic after a blood vessel ruptured in her neck, but still retained normal mental capacity. She requested that doctors cease the artificial ventilation that was keeping her alive and doctors refused, given that this would certainly lead to her death. They argued that she was depressed and therefore her capacity to make the decision was compromised. They also argued that her ability to understand the consequences of her refusal of further treatment was invalid because she had never experienced the withdrawal of ventilation. Dame Butler Sloss stated: 'In assessing the competence of a patient, doctors should not allow the question of mental capacity to be confused with the consequences of the decision, however serious.' This woman had full capacity and the continued ventilation against her wishes amounted to an unlawful trespass. The issue of whether she had prior experience of the proposed treatment or situation was irrelevant.

Treating incapable patients

If a person is deemed to lack the necessary capacity to consent, there has to be a legal mechanism whereby essential treatment can still be given to that patient without doctors fearing that they are acting unlawfully. Up until the implementation of the MCA, there was no specific law permitting doctors to carry out any treatment when

---

[27] See *St George's Healthcare NHS Trust v S* [1998] 3 All ER 673 for an extreme example of this.
[28] *Re B (Consent to Treatment: Capacity)* [2002] EWHC Fam 429.

the patient lacked capacity. The only tool they had was the doctrine of necessity, which stated that they could provide the minimal amount of treatment that was absolutely necessary in order to keep the patient alive or prevent serious deterioration in their health but could do no more than that. For example, in *F v West Berkshire*,[29] a 36-year-old woman with severe mental handicap began a relationship with a man who suffered from similar disabilities. Her family was very concerned that, if she were to become pregnant, not only would she be unable to care for the child, but the pregnancy and birth would cause her severe trauma due to her lack of understanding. They therefore requested that doctors perform a sterilisation operation, as she could not be relied on to use other forms of contraception properly. Doctors were uncertain as to whether the doctrine of necessity would allow them to operate and sought a declaration from the court. The declaration was granted.

The area is now governed by the MCA. Replacing the common law doctrine of necessity is section 5, which states that a person may carry out 'acts in connection with care and treatment' on someone who lacks capacity as long as the person carrying out the act:

- takes reasonable steps to establish lack of capacity (i.e. applies the tests in sections 2 and 3 of the Act)
- reasonably believes the person lacks capacity and acts in the person's best interests.

In such a situation, the doctor may proceed as if the patient has capacity and has consented to the treatment being provided.

Further guidance is given on best interests in section 4, which states that consideration should be given to the likelihood of an improvement in the patient's mental condition, any previously expressed wishes, any known beliefs and values and the views of any family members, carers, proxy decision makers (more on this later) or anyone named by the patient as a person to be consulted. It should be noted, however, that there is only a requirement to take into account and consult 'if appropriate' such persons and their views are by no means binding.

ETHICS QUESTION

Is it right that in the event that my husband lost mental capacity to make treatment decisions, perhaps involving questions of life and death, doctors would not be compelled to take notice of my opinions on the best course of treatment for him? Is a medical professional, who may not have known him when lucid, the best person to decide what my husband would have wanted and what would be in his best interests? Perhaps it is better to prevent family members from making such decisions. We will revisit these issues when we look at euthanasia in Chapter 11.

---

[29] [1989] 2 All ER 545.

It should be noted that there are limitations to the protection offered to doctors by section 5. For example, section 6 states that a doctor must not carry out an act intended to restrain the patient unless it is reasonably believed to be necessary to prevent harm to the patient and it is a proportionate response given the likelihood and seriousness of the possible harm. The Code of Practice that accompanies the MCA also points out that some acts require what it calls 'careful consideration'. These include:

- withdrawal of artificial nutrition and hydration
- organ donation
- non-therapeutic sterilisation
- some termination of pregnancy cases
- cases where there is doubt as to what would be in the patient's best interests.

Although the Code is not clear on what it means by 'careful consideration', in practice, this is going to mean that in the situations listed, medical professionals are going to seek a declaration from the court before proceeding, rather than blindly relying on the protection afforded by section 5.

Proxy decision makers

The MCA provides for two further situations whereby medical professionals may treat a patient who is mentally incapacitated and who cannot give valid consent at the time. They are:

- where the patient has made a lasting power of attorney (LPA)
- where the patient has made an advance decision.

Lasting powers of attorney

The legal status of an LPA is set out in section 9 of the MCA. It is a document drawn up *before someone loses mental capacity* giving a particular person (known as the 'donee') the right to make decisions on their behalf should they ever become mentally incapacitated. These documents can be drafted to include decisions related to property and finances as well as those concerning personal care and welfare, so it is important to remember that not all LPAs will apply to medical decisions. It will not be sufficient for a doctor to simply be aware that the patient has an LPA and the identity of the donee; they will also need to make sure that it is not an LPA that is restricted to property or other issues. While LPAs have proved to be a major step forward in allowing those who lose capacity to have previously chosen the person who will make decisions on their behalf, giving the patient some control and peace of mind, it is important to note the large number of restrictions placed on the creation and application of these documents (see Table 6.1).

Table 6.1 Restrictions on LPAs

Restriction	Meaning
Only a person aged 18 years or over may create an LPA	While the majority of the MCA applies to those aged 16 years and over, the sections relating to LPAs specify the person must be 18 or over. Part of the reasoning behind this is that younger teenagers may be vulnerable to pressure from parents or others to nominate them under an LPA
Procedural restrictions	Simply writing something down on a piece of paper will not be sufficient. Section 10 of the MCA sets out various procedural requirements, including a prescribed form that must be used and that the LPA must be registered in order to be valid
Types of treatment	While an LPA can cover most forms of consent to or refusal of medical treatment, it will only apply to decisions relating to life-sustaining treatment if the document specifically provides for this
Advance decisions	The LPA is subject to a valid advance decision that has been made by the patient – see below
Conditions must be met	Although the donee of the LPA may make care and welfare decisions on behalf of the patient when she loses capacity, this is subject to various conditions. For example, the donee must show that he has a reasonable belief that the patient lacks capacity to make the particular decision and that the decision being made is in the patient's best interests (having regard to the section 4 checklist)
Does not extend to restraint	An LPA will not authorise a donee to consent to any treatment that amounts to restraint of the patient

The provisions relating to LPAs have been described as 'a significant change in the doctor patient relationship'[30] but clearly there are many situations in which, due to the number of restrictions placed on the application of LPAs, they will not be of use to a patient. Fortunately, there are other ways for someone to try to influence how treatment decisions will be made after they lose mental capacity.

Advance decisions

If a person feels that there are certain types of treatment that they would refuse if offered and they do not want such treatment given if they are not able to consent or refuse themselves, section 25 of the MCA allows them to make that decision in advance and it will be valid after they lose mental capacity. There are no specific procedural requirements laid down in the Act for a general refusal of most medical treatments. All that is required is that the person is aged 18 years or over and has capacity at the time they make the decision. However, there are two types of treatment that require further discussion. The first is basic care, such as washing and, arguably, feeding. These are not medical treatments per se but may be necessary to keep the patient well or to complement other treatments. According to the Code, such basic care *may not* be refused in advance. This clearly leads to difficult issues where a terminally ill patient wishes to refuse artificial nutrition and hydration

[30] Jones, M., *MCA Manual*, para. 9.39.

(ANH) and we will return to this difficult topic in the chapter on euthanasia. The second type of treatment is life-sustaining treatment. According to sections 25 and 26 of the Act, an advance decision refusing such treatment must be:

- verified in a statement by the patient and witnesses
- in writing
- signed by the patient
- signed by the witnesses.

As long as these formalities are dealt with properly, then an advance decision can refuse life-sustaining treatment, but there are various issues that a healthcare professional should bear in mind if he plans to treat a patient (or not) under the authority of such a document:

1 Is the document *valid*? This will involve checking if the patient had capacity when it was made, checking that they have not subsequently done an inconsistent act, such as making another one with a different decision, and that they have not subsequently granted the power to make the decision to a donee under an LPA.

2 Is the document *applicable*? This will be an issue where the treatment being discussed is not the same treatment specified in the document, where there are specific circumstances set out in the document that are not present at the time the decision needs to be made or where something happens that was not anticipated by the patient and which might affect the decision, such as a new treatment breakthrough.

Only if the document is both valid and applicable can medical staff rely on it, and if so, it will be as if the patient was capable and making the decision at the time the treatment is offered.

Court-appointed deputies

One final way in which decisions may sometimes be taken on behalf of a mentally incapacitated person is where a deputy is appointed by the Court of Protection (CoP). This situation is governed by sections 15–20 of the MCA, which sets out the powers of the new CoP that was created by the Act. Not only can the CoP make declarations as to the capacity of a person and to the lawfulness or otherwise of acts and omissions, it can also appoint a deputy to make all such decisions that may be necessary. Again, all such decisions that are taken must be in the person's best interests,[31] assessed using the section 4 checklist. However, guidance indicates that these provisions are unlikely to be used in relation to medical decisions, perhaps because there is no reason why the deputy would be in any better a position than

---

[31] Section 16 MCA 2005.

the doctors when it came to making such medical decisions and it would simply add a further layer of complexity to an already difficult situation.

As should be clear from these discussions, the MCA has had a significant impact on the provision of medical treatment to patients lacking mental capacity. Whereas at one time there was nobody who could give valid consent and doctors had to rely on the rather ill-defined and changeable common law doctrine of necessity to provide only the minimum treatment absolutely necessary, there are now several ways in which a person can provide for such decisions to be taken after they lose capacity. However, there were concerns in the early days, before the restrictions and safeguards had been fully explored, that perhaps this could lead to unscrupulous relatives or others taking decisions to withdraw treatment from terminally ill patients. It is perhaps telling of the inaccurate publicity surrounding the introduction of the Act that it was deemed necessary to address concerns over euthanasia in the Act itself. Section 62 states: 'For the avoidance of doubt, it is hereby declared that nothing in this Act is to be taken to affect the law relating to murder or manslaughter or the operation of section 2 Suicide Act 1961 (assisting suicide).' In actual fact, the Act better protects patients by allowing them a degree of control over decisions that may be made in the future after they are incapable of making them, either by expressing their wishes beforehand or by appointing somebody they trust to make those decisions for them. Arguably, euthanasia by the backdoor is now much less likely.

Children

So far we have considered the issue of consent when the patient is an adult, but very different issues can arise where the patient is a child. For one thing, there are parents involved who will often have an expectation that they can give consent to treatment and/or refuse treatment that is offered to their child. As we shall see, this is not always the case. Another key issue, especially since the introduction of the HRA, is that both the children and their parents have Article 8 rights that must be upheld. Difficulties arise for medical staff where these two sets of rights are in conflict.

Generally, the term 'child' applies to anyone under the age of 18 years, but we will look separately at the rather grey area in the law relating to those aged 16 and 17.

Can a child under 16 give valid consent?

The simple answer to this question is yes, in some circumstances. In 1985 the seminal case of *Gillick* set down the key principles relating to children and consent that are still the cornerstone of this area of law. As such, it is a case worth looking at in some detail.

KEY CASE

Gillick v West Norfolk and Wisbech Area Health Authority[32]

Mrs Gillick was a mother of five daughters. She became aware of a DHSS circular that had been sent around to GPs in her area giving them guidance on treating young people, especially teenagers under the age of 16. The guidance talked about the giving of contraceptive advice and treatment and made it clear that in such circumstances, the child should be urged to discuss such matters with their parents. However, the guidance also recognised that there would be circumstances in which this was not appropriate or in which the child could not be persuaded to involve the parents, and in such cases, GPs were advised that it was lawful for them to provide such treatment and advice without the consent of the parents. Mrs Gillick challenged the circular on the grounds that it was wrong in law because an under-16 could not legally give valid consent and that it infringed her legal rights as a parent. She wanted a declaration from the court that parents have the right to be informed whenever such treatment was proposed unless it was an absolute emergency.

The case had a rather convoluted path through the courts. It was dismissed at first hearing in the High Court, but Mrs Gillick was successful at the Court of Appeal on the grounds that it went to a parent's right of custody and the legal obligations that parents had to keep a child safe and well. The Court of Appeal held that doctors should obtain consent from the parents unless it was an emergency and stated that possible criminal consequences could flow if this was not done.

Unsurprisingly, the AHA appealed and the case ended up in the House of Lords where the Court of Appeal decision was overturned by a majority of 3:2. Lord Fraser gave one of the leading judgments, stating that it verged on the absurd to suggest that a 15-year-old could not validly consent to some treatment such as the setting of a broken arm. He disagreed about parental rights of custody requiring consent from them in relation to medical treatment, making the point that parental rights exist for the benefit of the child, not the parents, and that those rights dwindle as the child becomes able to make autonomous decisions. Lord Fraser therefore set out some guidelines on when it would be permissible for doctors to provide contraceptive advice and treatment to under-16s without the consent of the parents. They are where:

- the child will understand the advice
- the child cannot be persuaded to inform the parents
- the child is likely to begin to have or continue having sex
- unless the child is given contraceptive advice and/or treatment, their physical and/or mental health is likely to suffer
- the best interests of the child demand that such advice and/or treatment be given. ➡

---

[32] *Gillick v West Norfolk and Wisbech Area Health Authority & DHSS* [1986] 3 AC 112.

These 'Fraser Guidelines' have become very well known by health professionals and are used as a starting point in the assessment of whether under-16s can consent to all sorts of medical treatment, not just contraception. Lord Fraser was largely supported in the judgment by Lord Scarman, but Scarman did add a few key points. In relation to the child's level of understanding he made it clear that 'much' had to be understood in order for a child to be deemed capable[33] and made the point about dwindling parental rights in stronger terms than Fraser. Lord Scarman stated: 'The parental right to determine whether or not their minor child below the age of 18 will have medical treatment terminates if and when the child achieves a sufficient understanding and intelligence to enable him or her to understand fully what is proposed.'[34]

This is a hugely important case in medical law because it establishes that a child under 16 may give valid consent and a parent cannot veto that consent.

Refusal of treatment

Although *Gillick* clearly established that an under-16 could legally give consent to medical treatment, it did leave some questions unanswered. What happens in practice if the parents and the child disagree? Does the treatment on offer have to be in the child's best interests? Does *Gillick* put the child in the same legal position as a competent adult in relation to consent or are there further protections still in place because she is still a child? These issues came to be addressed largely in cases that came before the courts where children had refused treatment; in some cases, life-saving treatment. Would the courts be prepared to treat them in the same way as adults, as in *Re C*, and allow them to make even unwise decisions that may end their lives because they have capacity to make the decision and their autonomy is to be respected? One of the first cases to arise on this point was *Re E*,[35] which concerned a 15-year-old boy with leukaemia. E refused to consent to the blood transfusions that were necessary to save his life on the grounds that he and his family were Jehovah's Witnesses and did not believe in taking blood or blood products from another person. His parents supported his decision so doctors went to the court seeking a declaration that he did not have capacity to make the decision and the court agreed, citing the pressure from his devout parents and his lack of full appreciation of the serious nature of the consequences of the refusal as factors in their assessment of his capacity using the Fraser Guidelines. They particularly focused on Lord Scarman's comment that 'much must be understood' and felt that he did not pass that test, Ward J making the point that: 'The court should be very slow to allow an infant to martyr himself.' This clearly answered the question about whether children have the same rights as adults when it comes to consent . . . no. The court will set

---

[33] Ibid. per Lord Scarman at para. 189.
[34] Ibid.
[35] [1993] 1 FLR 1.

the bar higher, it appears, in order to be absolutely sure that children are protected either from pressure coming from parents or others or from their own limited experience and understanding. What *Re E* did not address, however, was what would happen if the parents disagreed with the child and were in a position to offer consent to the treatment. Could they do this, or would it be necessary to obtain a declaration from the court that treatment could be given without consent from the child? In *Re W*,[36] the court felt that when Lord Scarman talked of termination of parental rights to consent, he meant termination of their 'exclusive rights' to consent and this did not mean that they lost all power to give valid legal consent in relation to their child's treatment. Thus, if the child did not have capacity, the parents could still provide the necessary consent. *Re E* also concerned a child who was deemed not to have capacity to give valid consent and several other cases found children incompetent where they refused life-saving treatment[37], but what about if the child refusing treatment were capable? In *Re C*,[38] the court made the point that *Gillick* actually says nothing about refusal of treatment, only that a child may give valid consent, and therefore, there is nothing to stop either someone with parental responsibility or the court under its inherent jurisdiction vetoing that refusal, as the court did in this case when the teenage anorexic refused to remain on the ward in order to receive treatment. The court not only allowed the hospital to override her refusal but even authorised it to use reasonable force to ensure that she remained and received treatment, as this was in her best interests.

Best interests

A lot of this turns on an assessment of the best interests of the child. This assessment will be made where someone wants to override a child's refusal of treatment (or a parent's refusal where the child is too young to be 'Gillick competent') and, in practice, will mean that the court seeks information from the medical professionals and the parents as to what they think is in the child's best interests and then makes the decision on the basis of that information.

ETHICS QUESTION

Is it right that a court makes an assessment of what is in a child's best interests or is that a decision best left to the parents? How would you feel as a parent if a crucial decision regarding life-sustaining treatment was taken out of your hands and instead made by a judge who had never met you or your child? Does this respect the Article 8 rights of the parents?

---

[36] *Re W* [1993] Fam 64.
[37] See *Re R* [1992] Fam 11 and *Re W* [1993] Fam 64.
[38] [1998] 1 FLR 384.

The court has been called on to make such decisions on a whole raft of issues, including whether a child should have an MMR vaccination where the mother and father had differing opinions. In that case, the court decided that there was no rational or scientific basis for the mother's refusal and the vaccination was in the best interests of the child so the mother's refusal was overridden.[39] However, perhaps one of the best known cases where the court had to really dissect the concept of best interests is that of the Siamese twins, Mary and Jodie.

KEY CASE

Re A [2001][40]

Jodie and Mary were conjoined twins, born to parents from the island of Goma who came to the UK to receive specialist medical care when the problem with the twins was identified in utero. When the girls were born, it became clear that a decision as to whether or not to separate them was necessary and a conflict arose between the doctors and the parents. Jodie was the stronger of the girls, with most vital organs that she would need to survive and a good circulatory system. Mary was the smaller, weaker twin who shared virtually all her organs with her sister and relied on circulating blood from Jodie's body as she had no circulatory system of her own. Doctors were certain that Mary would die at some point, but perhaps not for several months. It was clear that, if the girls were separated, Mary would die immediately. However, if they were not separated, there was a risk that both would die as it was not clear how long Jodie's body could withstand the strain of supporting her sister.

Doctors felt it would be best to separate them immediately and give Jodie the better chance of survival, but the parents felt that it would be wrong to sacrifice one of their children for the other and said they would leave their fate up to God.

At the Court of Appeal, it was held that it would be lawful for the girls to be separated without their parents' consent as it was in the best interests of both Jodie and Mary, as Mary would be spared a painful and difficult existence attached to her increasingly mobile sister over the next few months. The parents appealed to the House of Lords, where the decision that it would be lawful to separate them was upheld. However, the Lords' reasoning on the best interests concept was interesting and they roundly condemned the Court of Appeal for avoiding the difficult issues. The Lords stated that a court could not get around the concept by arguing that the proposed treatment was also in Mary's best interests – it was clearly not in Mary's best interests to die, but it *was* in Jodie's best interests to separate them. There were two children and their respective best interests were in conflict. The court had to face up to that and weigh everything up in deciding which best interests were to be preferred. In the end, the best interest of Jodie outweighed the best interest of

[39] *Re C* [2003] EWCA Civ 1148.
[40] [2001] 1 FLR 1.

Mary because Jodie had a chance of survival and, if nothing were done, both girls would eventually die. The court felt it was better to save one than allow both to die. The operation was carried out without the consent of the parents and Mary died soon after. Jodie survived and went home with her parents several weeks after the operation.

The case of *Re A* raises some interesting legal and ethical questions regarding the role of the parents in giving consent to treatment or refusing treatment for their children. As a mother, this author feels that there is something inherently wrong in an emanation of the state, such as a court, making a decision that ended the life of a child, regardless of what the parents wanted. However, as an academic and lawyer, it is clear that, sometimes, the parents are not in the best position to make an objective assessment of what is in a child's best interests. Would it have been better to have respected the rights of the twins' parents to decide for themselves what treatment the girls should receive and allow Jodie to die because they were so emotionally conflicted that they were unable to sentence their other child to certain death? What is very clear is that there are no easy answers in a case like this, yet somehow the court must try to come up with one.

Article 8 issues

Article 8 of the European Convention on Human Rights requires respect to be had for a person's home, private and family life. When the HRA came into force, questions began to be asked about whether this would mean that the opinions of the parents had to be given more consideration in order to avoid breaching this Article – after all, there could be nothing more relevant to their private and family life than the health of their child. The case of *Glass* v *UK*[41] helped to clarify this issue. Mrs Glass' son had a terminal illness and his state of health was very changeable. During a particularly difficult period where he was not expected to survive, doctors treating him decided that it was in his best interests to place a 'do not resuscitate' (DNR) statement in his medical records so that if he was to develop further complications, such as pneumonia or heart failure, they would not take active steps to save him as this was merely prolonging his suffering with no hope of improvement in his condition. In the event, he did experience heart failure and after realising that hospital staff were not going to take any action, his mother pushed past them and resuscitated him herself. She complained to both English courts and, subsequently, the ECHR that the failure to inform her of the DNR instruction breached her Article 8 rights and the court agreed. It stated that although it was not unlawful to have taken

---

[41] 920040 30 EHRR 15.

such a decision and to record it in the notes without the mother's consent, they had an obligation under Article 8 to at least inform her that the decision had been made. This would have given her an opportunity to challenge it through the proper channels if appropriate.

The recent case of *Axon*[42] confirms that the Article 8 rights of parents are engaged where treatment decisions are being taken in relation to their child, but makes the point that where there is a conflict between the Article 8 rights of the parents and those of the child, those of the child must be considered the most important and interference with those of the parents will be justified in the best interests of the child.

16- and 17-year-olds

Young people of this age fall into a difficult category. On the one hand, they are clearly still technically minors and, in most cases, parents will still have parental responsibility for that child until he reaches 18. However, various statutes, such as the Family Law Reform Act 1969 (FLRA) and the MCA, treat those over 16 as adults for various specific purposes, including the assessment of mental capacity to consent.

Section 8 of the FLRA is worth recounting in full, both for the purpose of giving the reader the necessary information about what the Act says in relation to children aged 16 years and over and also for the purpose of illustrating how far we have come in terms of drafting since the 1960s when convoluted and difficult provisions such as this were the norm:

Section 8 FLRA 1969 states:

(1) The consent of a minor who has attained the age of 16 . . . to any surgical, medical or dental treatment which, in the absence of consent, would constitute a trespass . . . shall be as effective as it would be if he were of full age; and where a minor has, by virtue of this section, given an effective consent . . . it shall not be necessary to obtain any consent . . . from his parent.

(3) Nothing in this section shall be construed as making ineffective any consent which would have been effective if this section had not been enacted.

Essentially, this section says that a person aged 16 or over may give valid consent to medical treatment as if they were an adult. However, section 8(3) makes it clear that this is not intended to eliminate the ability of a parent to give valid legal consent on behalf of an under-18 for whom they still have parental responsibility. The question that arises is what then happens if the 17-year-old and the parents disagree over the best form of treatment. If the young person is consenting to treatment that

---

[42] R *(on the application of Axon)* v *Secretary of State for Health* [2006] EWHC 37 (Admin).

his parents do not wish him to have, it would appear there is nothing they can do about it as his valid consent will be sufficient for the doctors to lawfully provide that treatment. If the young person is refusing treatment, however, it may be that the parents can override him and provide the necessary consent if the treatment proposed can be shown to be in his best interests. Section 8 must now be read in conjunction with the MCA and capacity and issues of best interests would now be determined by sections 1–4 of that Act.

Back to ethics

At the beginning of this chapter, various scenarios were set out and the reader was asked to think about the ethical issues that might arise and what the right or wrong solution might have been, leaving aside any knowledge of the legal rules. We have now covered the legal rules and so need to go back to those scenarios to see what the legal answers would be and whether they accord with the ethical answers arrived at earlier.

Scenario 1

Amanda is a Jehovah's Witness. During childbirth she loses a lot of blood and requires a blood transfusion to save her life. She refuses to consent to the transfusion because her religion teaches that it is wrong to take blood from another person.

What should the doctor do? Can forcible treatment be justified in such a situation?

Legal answer

Presuming Amanda is an adult and has capacity to consent or refuse treatment, according to the tests laid out in the MCA, she may refuse even life-saving treatment if she so chooses (*Re C*). This is the case even if an onlooker would consider her decision to be unreasonable or immoral. The only way in which the doctors could forcefully administer the blood transfusion would be to establish that she lacked capacity or that she had come under some kind of undue influence, as was the case in *Re T*.

ETHICS QUESTION

Should the mother of a newborn baby, a young woman with a full life ahead of her, be allowed to refuse life-saving treatment because of a belief that others may not share? According to the principle of autonomy, she should absolutely be able to do this and to force treatment on her would be to violate the most basic and fundamental of her rights and to retreat to the paternalistic attitude of the medical profession in days gone by. A more pragmatic view might be to say that the courts would never openly authorise such a violation of a woman's autonomy, but they may be very open to an argument that she has come under undue influence or that she has lost so much blood that she has lost mental capacity to decide.

Scenario 2

Belinda is about to give birth but there is a problem with the labour and the foetus' heartbeat drops dangerously low. She is told that she needs to have an emergency caesarean or the foetus will die. She refuses to consent to the operation as she is absolutely committed to having a natural delivery.

What should the doctor do?

Legal answer

Assuming Belinda is an adult and has capacity, she has the right to refuse the caesarean, even where it puts her life and/or the life of her unborn child at risk. The life of the foetus is irrelevant as far as the law is concerned (at least officially) as it is not a legal person until after it is born.

ETHICS QUESTION

Should doctors be forced to stand by and allow a woman to make a decision that condemns an otherwise viable child to death? Is the unborn child inherently less worthy of protection when in the birth canal than when, mere seconds later, it emerges? Should there be situations where a woman accepts that one of the consequences of choosing to carry a child is that she temporarily gives up some of her autonomy over her body? Should the law intervene in such sensitive issues?

Scenario 3

Charles has contracted a highly contagious and potentially fatal illness. However, he is extremely claustrophobic and refuses to consent to being admitted to a quarantine facility so that he can be isolated and barrier nursed. There are 25 other patients on the ward in which Charles is currently being treated, some of whom are elderly and have compromised immune systems.

What should the doctor do?

Legal answer

The most likely legal solution to this scenario would be that doctors would go to court and argue that Charles lacks capacity to consent to or refuse treatment due to his extreme claustrophobia. This would then allow them to take actions necessary in connection with care and treatment under section 5 MCA, as long as it is in his best interests. Although to admit him to the quarantine facility would probably infringe his Article 8 rights and possibly his Article 5 rights, the infringement would be justified in order to protect the other vulnerable patients on the ward and would be authorised by law.

ETHICS QUESTION

Is it fair to force a situation on a person when he is clearly very afraid and is having his autonomy flouted? Can it ever be right to infringe one person's rights in order to safeguard the rights of someone else? Do the courts manipulate the law to reach the answer they feel is 'right'?

Scenario 4

Delia refuses to consent to having her baby vaccinated against measles as she has read in the newspapers that scientists have found a link between the vaccine and autism. Delia used to work for the Vaccine Damage Tribunal before she had children and met many families dealing with the strain of caring for a child that they believed was damaged by vaccination. She says she is not prepared to risk causing such damage to her child. Delia works three days per week and her baby attends a local nursery where she mixes with children between six weeks and five years of age.

What should the doctor do? Can she force Delia to have her baby vaccinated?

Legal answer

As the baby's mother, Delia will have parental responsibility and can therefore validly consent to or refuse treatment on her child's behalf. However, this is subject to the caveat that decisions made must be in the child's best interests. If there is a dispute between Delia and the doctors or Delia and the child's father, the court will authorise the vaccination *if and only if* it is in the child's best interests. In similar cases, the court has ruled that medical evidence on the safety of vaccines and the public health advantages far outweigh the risks and that it is in the child's best interests to have the vaccine. Remember that the court will look at best interests in a broad sense, so it may take into account things like the likelihood of the child's being excluded from the nursery if she is not vaccinated and the resulting social and other consequences of that (*Re A*).

ETHICS QUESTIONS

Should a mother have the final say in healthcare decisions regarding her child, presuming the mother has capacity? Is it right that a court can override the wishes of the parents? What would be the ethical (and legal) situation if the child had the vaccination as a result of a declaration from the court and were damaged by it?

Scenario 5

Evie, aged 15, is anorexic and has now reached a dangerously low weight. Her doctor wants to admit her to hospital and force feed her to increase her weight as he is concerned that if she does not gain weight in the next few weeks she will die. Evie refuses to consent to being admitted to hospital as she does not want them to make her gain weight.

What should the doctor do?

Legal answer

Evie is a minor, but can give valid consent to treatment if she is deemed to be *Gillick* competent. It is likely, looking at cases such as *Re C*, that a court would find her anorexia to have rendered her incompetent to make the decision, given that a symptom of the disease is fear of recovery. However, whether or not she was *Gillick* competent, cases such as *Re R* and *Re W* make it clear that a refusal of treatment by a minor can be overridden, either by parents or by the court, if it is in the child's best interests.

ETHICS QUESTION

Most anorexics are intelligent and capable of passing the *Gillick* test for competence, so is finding her incompetent really justified? If the law is going to allow children to legally consent to treatment, including perhaps sometimes risky surgery or other life-threatening treatment, is it logical to then state that they do not have the same legal power to refuse treatment? Is a paternalistic reluctance to 'allow an infant to martyr themselves' justified?

Scenario 6

Felix is a drug addict. As a result of his addiction, he frequently behaves violently and commits robbery/burglary to feed his habit. He has been offered a detox programme by the court but is refusing to consent to being admitted into the unit.

What should the doctors (and/or the court) do?

Legal answer

Assuming Felix is an adult, the presumption under the MCA is that he has capacity unless there is evidence to the contrary. The assessment is decision specific and the fact that he is a drug addict does not automatically mean that he lacks capacity (*Re C*). If he understands the consequences of his refusal and is deemed competent, doctors will not be legally able to treat him and to do so would constitute a battery. Only if his drug use were so severe that it could be shown to have rendered him incapacitated under sections 2 and 3 of the MCA would they be able to treat him under the legal protection of section 5.

ETHICS QUESTION

Should a doctor be placed in a situation in which he has to stand back and watch some-one die when he could save them? Is it always right to respect a person's autonomy, even if it means they harm themselves? Is it right that, if Felix has capacity, doctors are unable to detain him, even to protect the public?

Summary

As stated at the beginning of the chapter, the rules on consent to treatment underpin all medical law. It is one of the most difficult and controversial legal issues and is yet another example of the law desperately trying to balance the rights of individuals to control what happens to their bodies and the responsibility of the medical profession to do what is best for the patient. Even the most straightforward legal situation, with a person of adult years and sound mind, can be hugely controversial if that person refuses life-saving treatment. The layers of legal and ethical questions involved in more complex situations, such as those who lack capacity and children, are many and cause us to question our most basic values and ethical views. Yet despite its difficulties, consent is an area that every student of medical law must endeavour to understand, for it is a necessary backdrop to many other topics, including confidentiality, euthanasia, organ donation, abortion and fertility treatment. Ultimately, the question that must be asked is whether the law as it stands provides a clear and fair framework that balances all the competing rights and responsibilities in relation to all patient groups.

Self-test questions

1 Has the MCA 2005 resulted in better protection for mentally incapacitated patients?

2 What is the test of capacity and where is it found?

3 What guidance is there for medical professionals trying to assess the best interests of a mentally incapacitated patient?

4 What mechanisms exist to allow a person to specify what treatments they may or may not want if and when they become mentally incapacitated in the future?

5 Can anyone act as a proxy decision maker for a mentally incapacitated patient?

6 What is implied consent and is it legally valid?

7 What is meant by 'autonomy'?

8 Is it necessary to use a particular type of consent form in order for the consent to be valid?

9 Is a doctor required to inform the patient of all the possible risks and side-effects of a proposed treatment in order for the consent of the patient to be valid?

10 What legal principle was established in the *Gillick* case?

11 In what circumstances do parents cease to have the right to make treatment decisions for their child?

12 Do doctors have to respect the Article 8 rights of a child and what happens if they conflict with the Article 8 rights of the parents?

13 Does a child have the same rights to consent to and refuse treatment as an adult?

14 What are the key differences in law between the rights of those under 16 and those between 16 and 18 to consent to treatment?

Practice essay question

Speaking about the case of *Re L (Patient: Non-consensual Treatment)* [1997] 8 Med LR 217, where a woman refused a caesarean section due to a phobia of needles, putting her own life and the life of her much wanted baby at risk, and was declared to lack capacity to make the decision by the court, Charles Foster states: 'The court's response was compassionate, wholly just and analytically wholly indefensible.'

Discuss the approach of the courts to the assessment of capacity in adult patients in light of this statement.

Practice problem question

Kara (aged 33) is in the accident and emergency department of Greytown Hospital (A&E). She has taken a substantial overdose of paracetamol. She requires treatment as a matter of urgency, otherwise she will die. The treatment needs to be commenced as soon as possible, in order to maximise its effectiveness.

Advise the doctors treating Kara in the following scenarios:

1 Kara has been brought to hospital by ambulance. Although she called for the ambulance herself, saying that she had taken an overdose and needed help, once the ambulance arrived she would not open the door to let the paramedics in. It was only after she had collapsed that her husband, Kevin, arrived home and let the paramedics in so that Kara could be put into the ambulance and taken to hospital. Kevin is begging the doctors to save his wife. At hospital it is discovered that Kara is approximately 14 weeks' pregnant.

2 Kara has been brought to hospital by ambulance, which she called for herself. On arrival in A&E she informs the doctors that she has just been told that she has a

terminal illness. She cannot face the prospects of dying slowly and in pain over the next few months and just wants to die peacefully in hospital now. She has drawn up a document setting out her wishes, which include a refusal of any care or treatment in respect of the overdose. This is a document that has been signed by Kara and witnessed. Kara begins to lose consciousness. Kevin, Kara's husband, arrives at the hospital having just been informed about Kara's condition. He is adamant that she should be treated to save her life, that she is still in shock at the news of her illness and that, since he has a lasting power of attorney, he has the right to consent to treatment on Kara's behalf.

Confidentiality

In this chapter, we will cover:

- the common law duty of confidence
- situations in which the duty may be legally overridden
- protection afforded by the HRA
- the role and effect of the Data Protection Act 1998
- remedies if information is erroneously disclosed.

Introduction

The duty of a health professional to keep confidential information disclosed to him in the course of his interaction with a patient is arguably the obligation that causes the most confusion in terms of disentangling the legal position from the ethical, professional and other guidance. The duty sits within a complex and overlapping legal framework that encompasses common law, statute, codes of practice, professional guidance documents, internal trust policies and human rights considerations. As Lord Coleridge CJ has noted: 'A legal common law duty is nothing else than the enforcing by law of that which is a moral obligation without legal enforcement.'[1] Between establishing what the legal duties are, addressing key ethical concerns and ensuring they are staying within the guidance issued by their professional body, it is understandable that doctors find this to be one of the most daunting areas of medical law they have to tackle. In the interests of finding a coherent path through the wealth of material to be covered, it is worth bearing in mind that, in general, all issues involving the potential disclosure of medical information give rise to the following questions:

[1] *R v Instan* [1893] 1 QB 450.

Is the information confidential?

Is there a *power* to share the information?

Is there a *duty* to share the information?

To whom can the information be disclosed?

Are there any prerequisite steps, e.g. consent, information, application, court order etc?

Common law

The obligation of confidentiality

The Hippocratic Oath states: 'all that may come to my knowledge in the exercise of my profession or in daily commerce with men, which ought not to be spread abroad, I will keep secret and never reveal.' The General Medical Council (GMC) confirms this in its guidance to doctors[2] and the British Medical Association (BMA) refers to the 'moral duty of confidentiality' as an 'essential requirement for the preservation of trust between patients and health professionals'.[3] Clearly, if a doctor could freely disclose any information about a patient and his medical problems, it is likely that some patients would feel less inclined to confide in their doctor, with potentially catastrophic public health consequences. The duty will apply not only to the doctor, but to all those working within the NHS and private healthcare organisations, and will almost always be reinforced by strict terms in their contract of employment.

What constitutes confidential information?

There has been difficulty over the years in obtaining a precise definition of what will actually constitute confidential information. For many years, we were left to grapple with, frankly, inadequate and unhelpful judicial comments, such as the statement made in the *Saltman* case,[4] that confidential information was any information which has the 'necessary quality of confidence about it'. Further cases clarified what common sense had already told us, such as that information which had been anonymised would not be classed as confidential[5] and that to establish a claim for breach of confidentiality, information must have been imparted in circumstances importing an obligation of confidence and used in an unauthorised manner.[6] However, pinning

---

[2] See 'Confidentiality', GMC, October 2009.
[3] BMA, 'Confidentiality and Disclosure of Health Information', 1999.
[4] *Saltman Engineering Company* v *Campbell Engineering Company Limited* (1948) 65 RPC 203.
[5] *Ex parte Source Informatics Limited* [2000] All ER 786.
[6] *Attorney General* v *Guardian Newspapers* [1990] 1 AC 101.

down exactly what sort of information was covered in a general, rather than a medical context, was extremely difficult. Fortunately, clarification was provided in relation specifically to medical information by the case of *Stevens* v *Plymouth*.

KEY CASE

Stevens v *Plymouth City Council* [2002] EWCA Civ 388

This case involved a social care record but the court made it clear that its comments applied to all forms of care record including medical records. The claimant's adult son had special needs and had a social care record that contained information about his medical condition, his social worker and his general care and well-being. The claimant became unhappy about the progress of a guardianship application over her son and wished to access his records as a means of gathering information in support of her application. The local authority refused to disclose the file. The court stated:

> Some of the information will indeed be confidential to C: the most obvious examples are the medical reports and recommendations but social workers and other professionals also owe him a duty to respect his confidences. Some of the information may be confidential to other people: opinions shared at professionals' meetings could fall within this category. But some of it may not be confidential at all: straightforward descriptions of everyday life are not normally thought confidential.[7]

Despite this, the court said it was 'content to assume that most, if not all of the information sought is covered by a common law obligation of confidence'.

Key point
The case is helpful for our purposes because, although it recognised that parts of the records would inevitably include 'straightforward descriptions of everyday life' and other information that could not strictly be defined as confidential, it also stated that, as a matter of law, a health record would as a whole be classed as a confidential document, avoiding the need to separate out of the record confidential and non-confidential information. This makes life a little easier for the medical lawyer in this field.

Overriding the duty

There are basically three situations in which the common law duty of confidentiality may be overridden. They are:

- where the person holding the information has consent, either express or implied, to disclose the information

---

[7] Ibid. at para. 33.

- where the person holding the information can show that there is an overriding public interest in disclosing it

- where there is a court order or a statutory obligation to disclose.

Consent

Implied consent

This applies where you have medical information being shared between members of the medical team: for example, within a GP practice or between a GP and a hospital consultant. As Mason and Laurie have noted: 'It is obvious that such technical breaches must be, and generally are, accepted in practice – a modern hospital cannot function except as a team effort.'[8] So, for example, when our GP says that he is referring us to a consultant at the local hospital and we agree to that being done, we are held to have impliedly consented to that GP sharing as much information as is necessary with that consultant. However, there are three issues to consider here. First, how much information are we consenting to being disclosed? If a patient is being referred for a skin complaint and the GP mentions a previous problem the patient has had with depression, would that be covered by the implied consent? Second, are patients aware of just how many people may legitimately have access to their medical information during the course of that referral? Research conducted by Gillon suggests that with a standard referral, at least 25 and possibly as many as 100 health professionals and administrative personnel could have access to the record, all of whom have a professional responsibility to open and use the record.[9] If patients have no idea that so many people may have access to their information, there is surely an argument that the consent is not valid. Third, even if you do consider that implied consent would cover such disclosures, what about the situation where information is disclosed outside of the medical team: for example, to the community mental health team or to social services? Is there implied consent for this or is this completely beyond the contemplation of the patient when they agree to a referral?

Express consent

Express consent is often more straightforward in that a person of sound mind can give her consent to her medical information being used and usually sign something so that the health professional has a record of that consent. This gives the professional a legitimate justification for breaching the common law duty of confidence. (For more detailed discussion of consent, see Chapter 6.) However, they can run into difficulty when the patient is not a capable adult.

[8] Mason K. and Lawile G., 'Law and Medical Ethics' 7th ed, 2009 OUP, p. 258.
[9] See Stauch M. and Wheat K. 'Text, Cases and Materials on Medical Law and Ethics', 4th ed, 2011, Routledge, p. 252.

Children

If a child is deemed to be *Gillick* competent[10] then clearly they can consent to disclosure of their medical information to specific people such as other medical professionals and parents. As the *Axon* case made clear, children are accorded the same right to confidentiality as adults – the right is in no way diminished by their young age.[11] However, a conflict can clearly arise with a child if there is deemed to be a child protection issue at stake. Most often, where children refuse to consent to disclosure of information, another justification must be sought for overriding the obligation of confidence, such as the Children Act (see later). In the absence of such concerns, the doctor's duty is to the patient herself, not the patient's parents or anybody else, and a child should be able to expect the same degree of confidentiality as an adult.

Mental incapacity

We have already looked at the Mental Capacity Act (MCA) 2005 in detail in Chapter 6 when we talked about consent. You will remember that under section 5, a healthcare professional may carry out 'acts in connection with care and treatment' without that person's consent if that person lacks capacity under the tests set out in sections 2 and 3 of the Act. Although the Act does not specifically refer to confidentiality, it can be assumed that disclosure of information could be an 'act in connection with care and treatment' for these purposes. Section 5 offers protection from liability, but only where the person carrying out the act: (a) takes reasonable steps to establish lack of capacity; and (b) reasonably believes the patient lacks capacity and acts in the patient's best interests (taking into account things such as previously known views of the patient, chance of their reacquiring capacity, views of relatives etc).[12] In this situation, the legal position is the same as if the person was capable and consenting. Bear in mind also that all such decisions must be taken in accordance with the general principles of the MCA, which are set out on page 108. Note in particular the last principle, which states that regard must be had to the least restrictive option. There is an argument that this requires disclosures made under section 5 to be made only to the extent absolutely necessary to protect the patient's best interests, so for example, to the community nurse who will be going in every day to care for the patient but not necessarily to the patient's family if they are not carers and the patient does not want them to be given the information. Section 5 should not be seen as carte blanche to reveal information about a patient more widely than is necessary.

---

[10] For a discussion of assessment of *Gillick* competence, see p. 117.
[11] *Axon v Secretary of State for Health & Anor* [2006] EWHC (Admin).
[12] Section 4 MCA 2005.

Overriding public interest

As we discussed in the introduction, there is a strong public interest in maintaining doctor–patient confidentiality and encouraging a patient to trust that they can divulge information to a doctor safe in the knowledge that the information will not be disclosed. Therefore, when we talk about 'overriding public interest' allowing disclosure, we are talking about something that outweighs that inherent interest in maintaining confidentiality – this is clearly a high threshold. Thus, the term has been interpreted very specifically by the courts. They have stressed, for example, that the concept of public interest should be clearly distinguished from simply things that are of interest to the public[13] and that it is ultimately up to the court to conduct this difficult balancing exercise, weighing up the competing interests and deciding effectively which interest is more important. Mr Justice Rose summed up the problem in *X* v *Y* in relation to patients suffering from AIDS, stating:

> In the long run, preservation of confidentiality is the only way of securing public health; otherwise doctors will be discredited as a source of education, for future individual patients will not come forward if doctors are going to squeal on them. Consequently, confidentiality is vital to secure public as well as private health, for unless those affected come forward they cannot be counselled and self treatment does not provide the best care.[14]

KEY CASE

W v *Egdell* [1990] 1 All ER 835

W was detained in a secure hospital, having gone on a rampage with what he called 'fireworks' but which were actually extremely powerful homemade explosive devices and killing several people. He had applied to the Mental Health Review Tribunal (MHRT), with the ultimate goal of being moved to a less secure facility and eventually rehabilitated into the community. Dr Egdell, a psychiatrist, was instructed by W to prepare a report for the MHRT hearing. In doing so, Dr Egdell became concerned that those caring for W had underestimated the danger he still posed to society and the level of his continued fascination with his 'fireworks'. The report was ultimately unfavourable and W's solicitors declined to disclose the report and withdrew his application to the MHRT. Dr Egdell, concerned that a future application might still be made, decided to disclose the report to the person running the secure facility and the government minister who would ultimately have responsibility for deciding whether W should be released. He did so without W's consent.

The Court of Appeal made it clear that the decision was not between W's private interest in confidentiality and the public interest in disclosure but between the ➡

---

[13] *Campbell* v *MGN Limited* [2004] UKHL 22.
[14] *X* v *Y* [1988] 1 All ER.

public interest in maintaining doctor–patient confidentiality and the public interest in disclosing for the protection of the public. On the facts, they decided that the balance came own 'decisively' in favour of disclosure. The danger to the public that this patient posed if he were ever released was more important.

Key point

The case is a good illustration of the sort of interest that might be sufficient to override the public interest in maintaining doctor–patient confidentiality. However, the case is not without its critics. Mason and Laurie call it 'a serious intrusion into the relationship of trust between a doctor and a patient'[15] and it is perhaps more controversial because it involves a psychiatrist – if there is any doctor that a patient needs to feel he can bare his soul to in complete confidence, it is surely a psychiatrist. The court was clear that the fact that Dr Egdell had been extremely discerning about the level of disclosure and had specifically targeted individuals who were also bound by duties of confidentiality, thus ensuring as far as possible that the information was not disclosed any more widely than was absolutely necessary, counted in his favour and we should be careful not to draw sweeping conclusions about the kind of disclosure that will be tolerated. If he had informed the press or the patient's family, the outcome might have been different.

Statutory authorities and court orders

Information may have to be shared with certain persons or organisations in certain circumstances – in other words, a statute or a court order may impose a duty on a health carer to reveal certain confidential information. Statutory examples include where they have diagnosed a notifiable disease such as cholera or smallpox[16] and where the information is identifying information for the purposes of investigating a road traffic accident.[17] More recently, the Children Act requires disclosure when there is a child protection issue at stake.[18]

A court may order disclosure of information in the context of a civil claim, such as clinical negligence litigation or in the case of criminal or child protection proceedings.[19] In such cases, it is worth noting that the holder of the information can apply for what is called a public interest immunity (PII) certificate, which effectively challenges the court order to disclose on the basis that divulging the information is not in the public interest. This is more common in cases involving, for example, the government where disclosure may present a risk to national security, but nevertheless will apply in other areas. Apart from this exception, if the court orders disclosure,

---

[15] 7th edn, p. 262.
[16] Public Health (Control of Diseases) Act 1984.
[17] Road Traffic Act 1988 s. 172(2).
[18] See Children Act 2004 s.12.
[19] For example, see Supreme Court Act 1981 and the Civil Procedure Rules.

then the information will have to be released but it will usually only be required to be divulged to the court or certain specified and limited persons who will often in turn be bound by duties of confidentiality.

Human Rights Act 1998

As we have discussed, the Human Rights Act 1998 (HRA) incorporates the European Convention on Human Rights into our domestic law and allows us as individuals to rely on the Convention rights in our domestic courts. We therefore need to examine the effect that this has had on the area of confidentiality of medical information and whether, as some suggest, we now have a separate action for breach of privacy under Article 8 of the Convention.

Article 8

Article 8 protects our right to a private life. It states:

(1) Everyone has the right to respect for his private and family life, his home and his correspondence.

(2) There shall be no interference by a public authority with the existence of this right except such as is in accordance with the law and is necessary in a democratic society in the interests of national security, public safety or the economic well-being of the country, for the prevention of disorder or crime, for the protection of health or morals, or for the protection of the rights and freedoms of others.

It has long been established in the European Court of Human Rights that Article 8 applies to medical records. For example, in *Z v Finland*, the state was investigating Z's husband for allegedly deliberately infecting women with the HIV virus and was trying to establish whether sexual contact with these women had occurred after he discovered his HIV status. It wished to access his wife's medical records as it felt that they may contain clues as to when he had discovered his condition but Z refused to allow access. The court acknowledged that to release the information was a breach of her Article 8 rights, but held that the breach was justified under Article 8(2) – the state was investigating a crime and trying to protect other women.[20]

Conflicting rights

Essentially, then, protecting privacy under Article 8 is about balancing often competing rights and interests, very like the balancing exercise that we talked about at common law. One of the most interesting situations that arises is where the Article 8 rights of parents come into conflict with the Article 8 rights of a child patient.

---

[20] *Z v Finland* (1998) 25 EHRR 371.

The approach of the courts has been that where the Article 8 rights of a child conflict with the Article 8 rights of the parents, the rights of child will prevail. For example, where a GP suspects possible abuse, he is not under an obligation to share information about his suspicions or his examination of the child with the parents, even if they are also his patients.[21]

KEY CASE

Glass v *UK* [2004] EHRR 104

The teenage son of Mrs Glass had been born with severe disabilities and a shortened life expectancy. He was admitted to hospital numerous times throughout his childhood and Mrs Glass had always made it very clear to hospital staff that she wanted all steps taken to prolong his life for as long as possible. On the occasion in question, he was admitted for respiratory problems and a decision was taken by the medical staff that a 'do not resuscitate' (DNR) order should be placed in his notes, effectively stating that if he were to deteriorate, they would not take measures to revive him. Crucially, Mrs Glass was not informed about this decision and the information that had been placed in his notes.

Soon after, his respiratory condition did indeed deteriorate and medical staff did not take any action. After a physical scuffle between members of the family and various medical staff, Mrs Glass resuscitated him herself. Among other claims and actions against the hospital, she argued that the failure to inform her of the medical decision that had been taken was a breach of her Article 8 rights.

The European Court of Human Rights agreed with her. Although under English law the hospital was not required to have the consent of Mrs Glass to take such a decision and need only be concerned with the best interests of the child (see Chapter 6), it was required by virtue of Article 8 to respect her right to private family life by informing her that such a decision had been taken, thus allowing her to process that information and come to terms with the possible consequences.

Key point

This case perfectly illustrates one of the crucial differences between a common law action for confidentiality and an action under Article 8, which is that under common law, the duty of confidentiality arises out of the relationship between the parties, e.g. doctor–patient, lawyer–client etc., whereas here, there was no doctor–patient relationship between the medical staff and Mrs Glass, yet they were still held to have a duty to uphold her Article 8 rights. Thus, a right to privacy under Article 8 is a more general right personal to the individual the information relates to, rather than something that arises because of the relationship with the person who receives the information.

---

[21] *JD* v *East Berkshire Community NHS Trust* [2005] 2 AC 373.

Article 8 v Article 10

Article 8 often comes into conflict with Article 10, which states:

(1) Everyone has the right to freedom of expression. This right shall include freedom to hold opinions and to receive and impart information and ideas without interference by a public authority and regardless of frontiers.

(2) The exercise of these freedoms, since it carries with it duties and responsibilities, may be subject to such formalities, restrictions, conditions or penalties as are prescribed by law and necessary in a democratic society, in the interests of national security, territorial integrity of public safety, for the prevention of disorder or crime, for the protection of health or morals, for the protection of the reputation or rights of others, for preventing the disclosure of information received in confidence, or for maintaining the authority and impartiality of the judiciary.

The leading case on this is *Campbell* v *MGN*.[22] The supermodel Naomi Campbell, who had previously been quoted in the press stating that she had never used drugs, was photographed leaving a Narcotics Anonymous meeting. The photograph, accompanied by an article describing the length of time she had been attending the meetings and the type of treatment she was receiving there, was published in a leading newspaper. She complained that the publication breached her Article 8 rights to privacy, while the newspaper argued that, under Article 10, it was entitled to publish the information in the public interest, to correct the record about her drug use. Two key principles were set out in the House of Lords judgment. First, in order to establish whether the information concerned should be protected under Article 8, there is a two-stage test:

1 Is the information obviously private?

2 Where it is not, is the information of a nature where its disclosure would be likely to give substantial offence to the subject of the information?

On this assessment, the information published by the newspaper did attract the protection of Article 8 and, by a narrow majority, the Lords overturned the Court of Appeal decision and found in favour of Ms Campbell. Second, in relation to the public interest argument put forward by the newspaper, the Lords were keen to draw a distinction between information that it was genuinely in the public interest to reveal and information that was simply of interest to the public. In this case, any potential benefit in the disclosure was outweighed by the harm done by interfering with her privacy.

According to the House of Lords in subsequent cases,[23] Campbell establishes that neither Article 8 nor Article 10 will have precedence and, in each case, the focus will

---

[22] *Campbell* v *MGN Ltd* [2004] UKHL 22.
[23] See *Re S* [2005] 1 AC 593.

be on the comparative importance of the two specific rights being claimed, looking at any justifications for disclosure and whether it is proportionate to a legitimate aim being pursued.

In conclusion, there is still debate among academics and judges about whether in fact there is now a separate action for breach of privacy or whether the rules on Article 8 simply inform and influence the way we approach confidentiality at common law. It seems to the author that there are sufficient differences at the moment between the two concepts to treat them as two distinct actions. However, as time goes on and the influence of the HRA continues to have a bearing on how judges interpret our common law confidentiality cases, there may be sufficient coming together of ideas to justify one overarching action for disclosure of confidential or private information.

Data Protection Act 1998 (DPA)

The DPA is a piece of legislation that aims to protect the security of data that are held about individuals. It is a complex and comprehensive statutory scheme, but its relevance in the medical sphere is fortunately relatively straightforward. The Act prescribes how a person or organisation that holds 'personal data' (meaning any information that contains identifying information such as name, address, age, sex etc.) must process those data in accordance with eight principles and in accordance with the detailed rules set out in the Act. Processing relates to any dealings with the data, so not just disclosure but updating, storing, moving, reorganising etc..[24] The Act clearly applies to medical information and, in actual fact, such information falls within the definition of 'sensitive personal data' and is therefore accorded more protection.[25] The data controller for the purposes of the Act will, in most medical cases, be the trust.

Disclosure by the trust

The first principle of the DPA is that all data must be processed 'fairly and lawfully'.[26] This effectively means that in order for the processing to be in accordance with the DPA, it must be done in accordance with the common law and Article 8 rules that we have already discussed. For this reason, it makes sense to look at those regimes first before moving on to consider whether the DPA also applies.

If an NHS trust wishes to disclose medical information, it will have to do so in accordance with the procedure set out in the DPA for processing sensitive personal

---

[24] See Data Protection Act s. 1.
[25] Data Protection Act s. 2.
[26] Data Protection Act Sch 1 Pt 1.

data. The Act sets out two lists of criteria in Schedules 2 and 3 and requires that one criterion from each list be met in order to lawfully process the data. The criteria directly relevant to medical information are set out in the following box.

Schedule 2:

- consent
- compliance with a legal obligation
- necessary to protect the vital interests of the data subject (see further later)
- necessary for the exercise of a statutory or public function
- pursuance of legitimate interests.

Schedule 3:

- express consent
- necessary to protect the vital interests of the data subject
- necessary for medical reasons
- necessary in the substantial public interest for the purpose of detecting or preventing an unlawful act or failure to act.

There are several important observations to note about these two schedules. Possibly the most striking thing is their similarity to the types of consideration articulated by judges in the sphere of common law confidentiality and Article 8 arguments – it is about balancing the same competing interests. Note that 'express' consent appears on only one list so it is perfectly possible to disclose information under the DPA either without consent at all or with only implied consent, if other alternative criteria are met.

In relation to the protection of the vital interests of the data subject, which appears on both lists, the Act goes on to specify that if you are relying on this option in Schedule 3, this will only apply where consent either cannot be obtained (or cannot reasonably be obtained) or is being unreasonably withheld and the vital interests of another are at stake.[27] In other words, the Act is saying that it is better to obtain consent if possible and this criterion should only be relied on as a last resort.

Access to information by the patient

Clearly, there are situations then where the Act permits disclosure of medical information to other people or organisations. However, the Act also sets out a process whereby the patient herself has an albeit limited right to access any data that are

---

[27] Data Protection Act 1998 Sch 3 para. 3.

held about them. This may be simply to check that they are accurate and up to date, or to see whether they exist at all, or it may be that she is contemplating something such as a clinical negligence claim and needs to gather information about the medical treatment that she received. Section 7 allows what is called a subject access request. If a person requests the information from the data controller in writing, the data controller must reply within 40 days. There may be a fee charged to cover administrative expenses such as photocopying costs and staff time. Despite the fact that this can be a very useful provision for those wishing to access their own medical information, there are two key exemptions to this general right of access that limit its effectiveness.

The first exemption is where the information requested also contains information relating to a third party. This is common in social work and mental health records, where details regarding the patient's relationships with family members, friends and/or other patients may be crucial to the overall assessment of their well-being and therefore an integral part of the records being held. If such information is going to be disclosed, it has to be shown either that the relevant third party has consented to the disclosure or that disclosure is reasonable in the circumstances (this will not apply if the third party is a medical professional involved in the care of that patient unless the disclosure would cause serious harm to the physical or mental health of that professional).[28] This provision is intended to protect other vulnerable parties such as other patients and as such, in this author's opinion, it is a necessary provision. However, there is no escaping the fact that due to the manner in which care is provided, particularly to vulnerable groups such as mental health patients, the side-effect is that there are a wealth of pieces of data and situations in which a patient may legitimately be denied access to information that is held about her.

There is another exemption that causes perhaps far more concerns than the professional exemption detailed and that is the one contained in the subject access modification order.[29] This permits information to be withheld from the patient where the release of the information is likely to cause serious harm to the physical or mental health or condition of the data subject or another person. This clearly begs the question 'in whose opinion?'. The order states that where the data are not held by a medical professional, then such a professional must be consulted before access to data is denied on this basis, but despite this meagre attempt at protection of the rights of the data subject, this provision effectively allows a doctor (who may not even be the patient's physician or have had anything to do with the patient before the subject access request) to determine that the patient is too fragile or not emotionally equipped to deal with the information that she is requesting. There is no framework or further guidance on how this should be assessed and in an age

[28] See s. 10 DPA 1998.
[29] Data Protection (Subject Access Modification) (Health) Order 2000, SI 2000/413 Art 5(1).

when the medical profession insists that it has left behind the paternalistic approach previously adopted and now puts patients' rights at the forefront of care, this seems to hark back to the bad old days when 'doctor knew best' and decisions were taken without the patient's full knowledge in the interests of protecting them. Given all the other developments towards openness and attempts to rebalance power between doctor and patient, this author wonders whether, after 10 years, it is perhaps time that the order were revised to bring it more in line with current thinking on access to information and patient care.

Vulnerable groups

Subject access requests under section 7 can also be made on behalf of a child or a mentally incapacitated adult but only in very limited circumstances. With adults, only someone who has effectively stepped into the shoes of the patient, in other words, a proxy decision maker such as someone appointed under an LPA or a court deputy, may make a request for the release of the information. In the case of a child, a person with PR can make the request, unless one of three exemptions applies:

- The child provided the information in the expectation that it would not be disclosed to the person making the request.
- The data were obtained from an examination or investigation that the child consented to in expectation that the information would not be disclosed.
- The child expressly indicates that he does not wish the information to be disclosed.

If any of these criteria is met, the person with PR will not be able to access the information. The courts have been very clear that a child has just as much right to confidentiality as an adult and where that child is *Gillick* competent (see Chapter 6) the wishes of that child will take precedence over the request of the parent or other person making the request.

Remedies

One of the fundamental problems with the law on confidentiality of any sort of information, let alone sensitive medical information, is the inadequacy of any potential remedies. Unless the patient finds himself in the unusual position of knowing in advance that someone is going to illegally disclose information about him, the reality is that these situations do not come to court until the damage has effectively been done – the information has been disclosed. Therefore, any remedy is going to fall a long way short of putting the patient back in the position he would have been in before the breach, which is the normal aim of the civil courts in providing a remedy. The most common available remedies are now set out.

Damages

In what circumstances may damages be sought? At the outset we need to distinguish between damages sought for breach of contract (frequently an implied term – see, e.g., *W* v *Egdell*), and a claim in equity.

Mason and McCall Smith have commented:[30]

> For many years the law was unclear as to the remedies for breach of confidentiality in spite of its recognition of such breaches as a proper basis for legal action. This latter was considerably clarified and its requirements set out in the House of Lords decision in *AG* v *Guardian Newspapers (No. 2)*. It is likely that a patient would be able to claim damages for improper disclosure of information about his health, even if it was said that 'No one has suggested that damages would be an adequate remedy in this case' – the implication being that they were there for the taking in the absence of a better solution. They might of course only be nominal; on the other hand, they might be considerable were it possible to show loss of society, severe injury to feelings, job loss, interference with prospects of promotion or the like. However a distinction has to be made between actions in contract and in tort. Thus, in the trial stage of *W* v *Egdell*, Scott J discarded the possibility of damages for shock and distress – other than nominal – largely on the particular facts of the case but also because it was based on breach of an implied contractual term; the decision had no relevance to an action in tort.

Where damages are awarded, they may be minimal if no actual financial loss can be established (see *Douglas* case later).

We also need to consider the impact of the HRA, and, in particular, Article 8, on any claims for damages. In *Cornelius* v *De Taranto*[31] was a case concerning the transmission of a medico-legal report to a third party without the express consent of the patient. On finding that express consent had not been given, the claimant was awarded damages in the sum of £45,000 at first instance, representing around one-third of her total loss. However, a major part of the action was concerned with lack of consent to a referral, an aspect of the case that she lost as the court found that her evidence was not credible. On that basis, her damages were reduced on appeal.

Other high-profile claimants have had success in their claim for breach of confidence but have not necessarily come out with large amounts of damages. In *Douglas* v *Hello!*,[32] the claimants had entered into a commercial agreement with a particular magazine regarding publication of authorised photographs of their wedding. The defendant obtained unauthorised photographs and published them. The High Court awarded damages of £1 million to the authorised magazine in respect of loss of sales attributable to the publication of the unauthorised photographs but, note, only £14,750 to the claimants for distress and inconvenience. Naomi Campbell's damages were similarly modest.

---

[30] Mason J.K. and McCall Smith, *Medical Ethics and the Law*, 2007, Oxford University Press, 8.72.
[31] *Cornelius* v *De Taranto* [2001] EWCA Civ 1511.
[32] *Douglas* v *Hello! Ltd and others* [2005] EWCA Civ 595.

Injunction

As noted already, it may be possible to prevent the disclosure in the first instance, by obtaining a court injunction. Breach of such an injunction will be punishable as contempt of court. It is noted by Mason and McCall Smith that this is a 'common remedy in this area – and one which has been extended considerably in recent years' (8.76).[33] The problem with this remedy is that it requires that the possibility of breach be known in advance, which is not often the case. One well-known example is the application by the killers of Jamie Bulger for the press to be prevented from disclosing details about their release dates, their new identities and their locations after release.[34] Their application was unusual in that they were requesting open-ended injunctions with a worldwide geographical scope. The injunctions were granted, partly on the basis that such information was confidential and private under Article 8 but possibly more on the practical ground that they had successfully argued the injunction was necessary to protect their Article 2 rights (right to life) as they would be in grave danger from members of the public if the information were disclosed.

Duty to disclose

We have already touched on the possibility of there being a duty to disclose in certain circumstances. For example, what should happen when a child is at risk, or injury is sustained by a third party that could have been (at least arguably) prevented by a timely disclosure of information? Generally, such liability falls to be considered in terms of negligence and is limited by duty of care considerations, so that where a third party is harmed, for example, by a psychiatric patient, generally, no duty is owed to that third party. (For considerations of such a liability see Chapter 3.)

There are, however, various other situations in which a medical practitioner will be under a statutory duty to disclose certain information about a patient to specific persons or organisations. These include:

- Abortion Act 1967 – requires name and address and other information to be supplied to the Department of Health.
- Misuse of Drugs (Notification of Supply to Addicts) Regulations 1973 – Home Office must be informed of name, address, sex, date of birth, NHS number and what drugs the patient is addicted to within seven days.
- Children Act 1989 – local authority must be informed if a child is accommodated in a residential care home, nursing home or mental health nursing home or by a health authority for more than three months.

[33] See n. 30, 8.76.
[34] *Venables and Others* v *NGI and Others* – *The Times* 7 December 2001.

In these situations, a failure to disclose the information will be a statutory breach and the various remedies set out in those statutes will apply. These range from fines at various levels to custodial sentences in severe cases.

■ Rights under the DPA

The right to object

Section 10 prevents processing of personal data where such processing is likely to cause damage or distress. The person must object in writing, stating the reasons why (a) processing of those data or processing for that purpose or in that manner is likely to cause substantial damage or distress to him or another; and (b) that the damage or distress is or would be unwarranted. The data controller must respond within 21 days, stating if and to what extent he intends to comply and any issues he takes with the objection. An application can be made to the court if a justifiable request to cease processing on this basis is not complied with. It is important to note that the damage or distress does not need to relate to the data subject himself.

The right to compensation

Section 13 provides that if a data controller breaches the Act and a person suffers damage as a result, they are entitled to compensation for that damage from the data controller. If the consequence is *distress* rather than damage, compensation may still be claimed under the section if either the person has also suffered damage or if contravention relates to processing of data for one of the special purposes (journalism, artistic or literary purposes). Once again, this remedy is available to persons other than the data subject.

Rectification

Section 14 applies where the court is satisfied *on the application of the data subject* that data held are inaccurate. It has the power to order the data controller to rectify, block, erase or destroy the data and anything containing opinion based on the data. Unlike those under sections 10 and 13, this remedy is not available to people other than the data subject.

Less draconian orders may be made if the following criteria are satisfied:

1 data were obtained from the data subject or a third party

2 data controller took all reasonable steps to ensure the accuracy of the data

3 data subject has notified the data controller of the inaccuracy and this is noted in the data.

In such circumstances, the court may order that the data be supplemented with a statement of the true facts, such statement to be approved by the court (section

14(2)(a)). Alternatively, if the data were obtained from the data subject or a third party but the other criteria are not met, the court may make an order to ensure compliance with those criteria. It is common in these circumstances for the court to require the data controller to notify any affected third parties.

An order under section 14 may be made in circumstances where the data subject has suffered damage that entitles him to compensation under section 13 and there is a substantial risk of further contravention.

Offences

There are various criminal offences under the Act, such as:

- failure to comply with the notification requirements in section 17
- failure to comply with any regulations made under section 20 (unless the data controller can show that he exercised all due diligence to comply)
- failure to comply with an enforcement notice (see later)
- complying with an enforcement notice by knowingly or recklessly giving false information
- carrying out of assessable processing (processing likely to cause substantial damage or substantial distress to data subjects or otherwise prejudice their rights and freedoms) without a notice from the information commissioner stating that in his opinion the processing is compliant with the Act or the passage of 28 days from notification to the information controller (IC)
- failure to provide certain non-notifiable data within 21 days of a written request by any person unless it can be shown that all due diligence was exercised to comply.

In most cases, the sanction for committing one of these offences under the Act will be a fine and the forfeit, destruction or erasure of the material in question.

Enforcement

There are various methods available to the information commissioner and to the courts to enforce sanctions against anyone who is found to be in breach of the Act, some more effective than others.

Notice

If a data controller is contravening any of the data protection principles, the IC may serve a notice requiring him to take or not take certain steps within a specified time or to refrain from processing personal data or particular personal data or processing for a certain purpose or in a specified manner after a specified time. The IC will take into account any damage or distress caused or likely to be caused. The notice must contain a statement of the data protection principles contravened and reasons for the decision, as well as details of the data controller's right to appeal under section 48. Note that if an appeal is launched, the notice need not be complied with until that appeal has been resolved unless there is an urgent need for compliance and the reasons for the urgency are clearly stated in the notice. Compliance will never be required before the expiry of seven days from the date of the notice.

The IC may cancel the notice either of his own volition or on application in writing by the data controller on the grounds of change in circumstances that mean the action required in the notice is no longer necessary to comply with the data protection principles.

Information notices and special information notices

Persons affected by the processing of data may request an assessment by the IC of whether the processing is compliant under section 42. Where such a request is made, the IC may serve an information notice on the data controller requiring him to provide certain information necessary in order to make such an assessment. Where the IC suspects that data are not being used for the special purposes as claimed, he may serve a special information notice (s.44). Notices must contain a statement that a section 42 request has been made or that the IC suspects data are not being processed for special purposes and the grounds for that suspicion.

If, as a result of receiving the information requested, the IC concludes that data are not being processed for the special purposes, he may issue a determination to that effect. This can be followed by an enforcement notice, but only with leave of the court. The court will grant leave if (a) the contravention appears to the IC to be of substantial public importance; and (b) the data controller has been given notice of the IC's application for leave (except in urgent cases) (section 46).

If a notice is served, the data controller can appeal to the information tribunal. He can also appeal against a refusal to cancel or vary a notice or against a statement of urgency contained in the notice.

Powers of entry and inspection

The wide-ranging powers of entry and inspection contained in Schedule 9 are also important when it comes to enforcing the law. As long as there are reasonable grounds for suspecting that the Act is being contravened and that evidence may be found on certain premises, warrants can be issued for entry, search and seizure of many types of material. This greatly assists the IC and the court in gathering enough information to establish whether a breach has occurred.

Summary

We have looked at common law remedies for breach of confidentiality and noted that the focus of these actions has been greatly influenced by the HRA and is now essentially a balancing exercise between Article 8 and Article 10. Damages are available but the damage may already be done. Injunctions are possible only if the person has advance warning of the possibility of publication. We have also looked at rights and remedies under the DPA and what provision the Act makes for enforcement of its provisions. (Table 7.1 contains a summary.)

It should be noted that there is also the possibility of a complaint being made to professional bodies, such as the GMC, but again, although action may be taken against an individual medical professional who has disclosed information when he should not have, the damage has already been done and no specific remedy would be available to the patient.

Confidentiality of their medical information is probably one of the most important aspects of patient care as far as the patients themselves are concerned. When divulging details of their ailments to their doctor, they are rendering themselves extremely vulnerable and the unauthorised disclosure of that information is possibly one of the

Table 7.1 Summary of remedies available

Remedy	Description	Advantages/disadvantages
Damages	Usually for direct harm or loss caused by the disclosure, or sometimes for distress	Tend to be low level for distress caused, even though in medical cases, such distress may be considerable
Injunction	An order from the court that information should not be disclosed for a certain period of time and/or to certain people	You must know in advance that a disclosure is going to be made to take advantage of this remedy. However, there is a clear legal consequence if such an order is breached
Breach of duty	Common law or statutory remedy where a person has been under a duty to disclose information and has failed to do so	Only applies in the very limited circumstances where a person is under a positive duty to disclose information
		Damage will already be done so disclosure after the event may be pointless
Rights under the DPA	Various rights for data subjects to ensure information held about them is correct, up to date, accurate and processed appropriately	Useful in terms of how medical information is held, but not particularly helpful where the information has been improperly disclosed
		Although the IC has several important powers to investigate and rectify and the data controller may be subject to certain sanctions, the benefits to the individual patient are minimal

most severe breaches of trust a medical professional can commit. That said, there are times when it may genuinely be in the patient's best interests to disclose the information to a particular person or organisation and that balance between respect for the duty of confidentiality and the patient's right to privacy, on the one hand, and the slightly paternalistic but nevertheless sometimes necessary task of acting in that patient's best interests, on the other, is one of the most difficult that a medical professional faces.

Self-test questions

1 What are the three situations at common law in which the duty of confidentiality may legitimately be breached?

2 How do the courts define overriding public interest?

3 What are the key differences between breach of confidentiality at common law and breach of Article 8?

4 What is the Data Protection (Subject Access Modification) (Health) Order 2000?

5 In what circumstances may a person be entitled to damages where information has been wrongly disclosed?

Practice essay question

'The doctor's overriding duty to society represents what is arguably the most controversial permissible exception to the rule of confidentiality' (Mason and McCall Smith, *Law and Medical Ethics*)

Discuss the extent to which the overriding public interest exception potentially undermines the effectiveness of the law on confidentiality of medical records in the UK.

Practice problem question

Brenda is 71 years old and suffers from Alzheimer's. Because of her illness, Brenda is described as frequently confused and unable to make basic decisions. She has been cared for at home by her daughter, Mary. However, Mary is finding it increasingly difficult to cope with Brenda's needs and disturbed behaviour. Mary has repeatedly tried to contact her GP, social services, and the consultant psychiatrist in charge of Brenda's care, to explore care options for Brenda in the future. Brenda has now been admitted to hospital for respite care, but Mary is insistent that Brenda cannot come home until a proper care package has been put in place, with appropriate health/social services support. She is threatening legal proceedings and has requested copies of all Mary's health and social care records, to enable her to 'take advice'.

Advise the trust as to whether it may disclose the information Mary has requested.

8 Beginning of life I: fertility and conception

The following three chapters will look at the various issues and challenges facing lawmakers when it comes to the creation of new life. The chapters examine the various forms of legal and moral protection afforded to a foetus and how the law deals with issues as diverse as contraception and surrogacy, fertility treatment and abortion.

Clearly, these are all highly emotional subjects in which people generally hold very strong points of view depending on their own values or beliefs. As such, it is not surprising to see that ethical issues play a huge part in shaping how the law develops, but so do other influences such as politics, media and economics.

The aims of the following three chapters are to explain and critically analyse the ethical and legal issues relating to these three 'beginning of life' areas and will examine when (legally speaking) life begins; the regulation of various forms of contraception; how the law operates in providing appropriate protection for embryos and establishing the purposes for which they can legally be created and destroyed; the regulation of the controversial practice of surrogacy as a 'treatment' for infertility; and the rules and ethical debates surrounding the regulation of abortion.

Introduction

Fertility treatment is big business in the United Kingdom, with one cycle of IVF costing in the region of £5000 if NHS funding cannot be obtained.[1] Rapid scientific development has presented great opportunities for infertile couples and for embryo research to find new treatments for diseases, but has also presented legal and ethical dilemmas. Should scientists (for research purposes) be allowed to create embryos using a human nucleus in a rabbit or cow egg? Should women be allowed to donate their eggs for fertility treatment or research? If so, should they be paid? Should a woman be allowed to receive fertility treatment in order to have a child for an infertile couple? The fundamental problem with trying to legislate in this area was highlighted recently in the

[1] See http://www.nhs.uk/chq/Pages/889.aspx?CategoryID=54&SubCategoryID=127.

Irish case of *Roche v Roche*.[2] The case centred on whether the protections afforded to citizens by the Irish Constitution applied to Mr and Mrs Roche's preimplantation embryos and, while holding that they did not, the court stressed that because of their ability to become life in the future, human embryos have a 'moral status' and ought to be treated with 'respect'.[3] Translating this non-legal but nevertheless special status into meaningful regulation is an extremely difficult yet necessary task facing governments around the world, as science continues apace.

The aims of this chapter are to explain and critically analyse the ethical and legal issues relating to:

- deciding when (legally) life begins
- regulating various forms of contraception
- providing appropriate protection for embryos and establishing the purposes for which they can legally be created and destroyed.

Before going any further, some terminology requires definition and clarification:

- 'embryo' describes a fertilised egg for the first eight weeks of development
- 'foetus' describes the fertilised egg after eight weeks of development
- 'blastocyst' relates to the fertilised egg around four–five days after fertilisation, at which point it contains somewhere between 50 and 100 cells.

When does life begin?

There are various options open to legislators when deciding at what point legal protection should be awarded to a developing foetus. Some religious bodies, such as the Roman Catholic Church, would argue that life begins at the moment of conception, when egg and sperm have combined and an independent process has begun that will ultimately lead to the birth of a baby.[4] Another possibility is that life begins at the moment the fertilised egg implants into the wall of the uterus (usually around day 10 post-fertilisation) as up until that point, there is no viable pregnancy and the fertilised egg has no means of nourishment to enable it to develop. Determining whether life is going to be held to begin before or after implantation is hugely important when it comes to regulating contraception, as will become clear later in this chapter.

Another popular choice for the point at which life begins is around day 15 or 16 post-fertilisation, at the appearance of the 'primitive streak'. This is the beginnings

---

[2] *Roche v Roche and Ors* [2009] IESC 82.
[3] For an excellent discussion of this case and the contrasting positions in Ireland and the UK, see Gomez, D. 'The Special Status of the Human Embryo in the Regulation of Assisted Conception in the United Kingdom', MLJI 2011, vol. 7, no. 1, pp. 6–18.
[4] See Catechism of the Catholic Church 2270.

of what will become the brain and central nervous system of the foetus and is the first sign that rather than being a collection of randomly multiplying cells, the entity is beginning to become a structured organism. Again, deciding whether life begins and is therefore afforded legal protection before or after the appearance of the primitive streak is important, as embryos of less than 14 days' gestation are required for use in stem cell and other embryo-related research.

There is then a whole raft of possibilities as the pregnancy progresses – different points at which one could decide that the foetus has reached a stage where life has begun and legal protection should be afforded. Should it be at week 10, when the foetus is recognisably 'human', having a face, arms, legs, fingers, toes, eyelashes? Should it be at week 24, when the foetus is officially 'viable' in the sense that it is medically recognised to be capable of independent life outside the mother's body? Should it be the moment of birth when it actually does survive outside the mother? The decision as to what protection should be awarded at what stage of development is crucial to a coherent and effective system of regulating abortion and selective reduction of multiple pregnancy (see Chapter 7 for a full discussion of these issues).

In England and Wales, the fact that no comprehensive decision has been reached on when a life begins, in the sense of its being worthy of legal protection, means that lots of different legal provisions apply and different levels of protection are available to an embryo and a foetus in various situations. For example, the Human Fertilisation and Embryology Act[5] restricts the circumstances in which an embryo can be legally created in vitro (outside the woman's body) and what can be done with such an embryo, including that it may not be kept beyond 14 days or the appearance of the primitive streak, if earlier.[6] However, despite this protection, the law also permits abortion, in some cases, right up until the moment of birth.[7] It is a legal and ethical maze that legislators, medical professionals and patients must navigate with extreme caution.

Contraception

Although some religions do not permit followers to practise any form of contraception, it is now widely accepted throughout the western world that people may seek to limit the number of children they have and to seek to choose the timing of any pregnancy. As Douglas states: 'Methods, effective or not for avoiding conception or childbirth are probably as old as civilisation itself.'[8] Some methods of contraception,

---

[5] 1990 (as amended by the HFE Act 2008).
[6] Section 3(3) HFE Act.
[7] Section 1 Abortion Act 1967.
[8] Douglas, G., *Law, Fertility and Reproduction*, 1991. Sweet and Maxwell.

Table 8.1 Forms of contraception

Method	Description
Condoms	Barrier method, preventing the sperm from reaching the egg so no fertilisation can take place
Intra-uterine device (commonly known as an IUD or 'coil')	A device placed inside the woman's uterus that prevents a fertilised egg from implanting
Long-acting, injectable contraceptive (depo-provera)	A hormone-based method that prevents the woman from releasing an egg each month, making fertilisation impossible. The woman has the injection once every three months and does not then have to remember to take a pill each day
The pill	A pill containing a combination of chemicals that prevent an egg being released each month and therefore, prevents fertilisation
	The woman must take the pill correctly (i.e. on the correct days and, with some kinds of pill, at the same time of day) in order for it to be effective
Post-coital birth control (commonly referred to as the 'morning-after pill')	This is another hormone-based pill that acts on the lining of the uterus and causes it to be shed. Thus, if an egg has been fertilised, it cannot implant in the uterus and will come away with the rest of the uterine lining, preventing further development
Sterilisation	Males and females can undergo surgical procedures to render them sterile. Clearly this is the most extreme form of contraception and is usually irreversible

such as sterilisation, are very clear examples of medical treatment and as such, the usual rules will apply on things like consent (see Chapter 5) and clinical negligence if something goes wrong (see Chapter 4). However, other methods do not fall quite so clearly into the definition of medical treatment, which begs the question of whether they should be regulated at all.

Methods of contraception

When discussing legal issues surrounding contraception, it is important that the reader understands the processes that are being referred to. Set out in Table 8.1 are the various forms of contraception available and a brief definition of each.

The chosen method of contraception is clearly an important factor as each type raises different ethical and legal issues. There has been particular controversy over the post-coital methods, with some arguing that rather than being a method of contraception, the morning-after pill is, in fact, a form of early abortion. It was very important to address this issue as, clearly, if it were a form of abortion, it would be regulated by the Abortion Act 1967 and the various legal requirements contained therein. As it happened, this question was addressed in the case of *Smeaton*.

> **KEY CASE**
>
> ## *R v Secretary of State ex parte Smeaton* [2002] EWHC 610
>
> This case was a challenge to the decision taken by the Secretary of State to allow the morning-after pill to be available over the counter in pharmacies. Previously, it had been necessary to see a doctor to obtain a prescription for it. The rationale behind this policy change was that extending access to the morning-after pill would help to reduce the high number of teenage pregnancies in England and Wales. However, Smeaton argued that because the pill effectively removes a fertilised egg from the woman's uterus, this constituted an offence under the Offences Against the Persons Act 1858 (which makes it unlawful for anyone to procure a miscarriage in a woman). On this basis, it should be dealt with like any other form of abortion, meaning that, in order to be legal, it would have to be carried out in accordance with the Abortion Act 1967 (see Chapter 10) and should certainly not be sold over the counter.
>
> On the technical point about whether the loss of a fertilised egg before implantation can be termed a 'miscarriage' for the purpose of the 1858 Act, Munby J was clear that: 'There is no miscarriage if a fertilised egg is lost prior to implantation. Current medical understanding . . . excludes the result brought about by the mini-pill, the pill, or the morning-after pill.'[9] Thus, providing the morning-after pill over the counter in pharmacies would not breach the 1858 Act and no criminal liability would attach to the pharmacist. However, the court also made it clear that it was not making a judgment about when life begins. It was stated that it is not the role of the court to make moral or religious judgments, merely to decide on the law that applies in a given situation.

◼ Enforced contraception

Before moving on to other issues relating to conception, it should be noted that, thus far, it has been assumed that the contraception in question has been consented to by the patient. However, there are situations in which various forms of contraception have been forced on patients who lack mental capacity to consent, in cases where such action has been deemed to be in their best interests. For example, in *Re B*,[10] the court granted a declaration that a sterilisation operation could be performed on a 17-year-old girl who was mentally handicapped. The girl was becoming sexually aware but could not understand that intercourse caused pregnancy. She was in the care of the local authority, which argued that she would be unable to deal with the physical and emotional stresses of pregnancy and childbirth

---

[9] [2002] EWHC 610 (point 17 in original transcript).
[10] *Re B (A Minor)* [1987] 2 All ER 206.

and would not be able to function as a mother. The evidence before the court also suggested that she would be unable to use other methods of contraception given her lack of understanding of the causes of conception and therefore, as a last resort, the declaration was granted.

ETHICS QUESTIONS

Does everyone have the right to have a family if they so choose? Is a mentally handi-capped person less entitled to procreate? Should the local authority and the doctors treating her have opted for something less extreme, such as three-monthly contraceptive injections instead? That way, the option of having children would have been preserved for her should her mental condition improve in the future. Should doctors and/or the court have the right to permanently take away someone's ability to have a child or is this an example of paternalism at its most dangerous?

Regulating the creation of embryos

Infertility is defined by the National Institute for Clinical Excellence as 'failing to get pregnant after two years of regular, unprotected sex' or having three or more miscar-riages or stillbirths, and it is estimated to affect one in every seven couples in the UK.[11] There are many factors that can contribute to infertility, such as obesity, smoking, excessive consumption of alcohol and delaying the age at which couples begin to try to get pregnant, but in 24% of cases, infertility is completely unexplained.

Since the birth of the first 'testtube' baby, Louise Brown, in 1978, fertility treat-ment has advanced quickly and science has provided infertile patients with all sorts of options and possible solutions to the problem. Recent innovations available include:

- AID – artificial insemination using donor sperm
- AIH – artificial insemination by the husband
- IVF – in-vitro fertilisation – the embryo is created outside the woman's body and is then implanted in her uterus in the hope that a viable pregnancy will result
- GIFT – gamete intra-fallopian transfer – gametes are introduced into the fallopian tube of the woman in the hope that a 'natural' conception will take place
- cryopreservation – the freezing of gametes or embryos for future use

---

[11] See NICE guidelines 'Fertility – Assessment and Guidance for People with Fertility Problems', February 2004, available at http://guidance.nice.org.uk/CG11.

- egg donation – for a woman who does not produce eggs or has eggs that are deficient in some way, eggs from a donor can be used, often alongside the patient's husband's sperm, to create an embryo

- ICSI – intra-cytoplasmic sperm injection – the sperm are injected into the egg in the laboratory and the fertilised egg is then placed in the woman in the hope that it will implant.

Clearly, such procedures have the potential to change lives, but there is also potential for unscrupulous clinics to charge huge amounts of money for treatments that have a very low success rate (even standard IVF, which has been practised for more than 30 years, still has a less than 25% chance of success per cycle).[12] From its beginning, there was a recognition that fertility treatment needed to be regulated in some way, but there was also much debate about the form such regulation should take. Before looking at the regulation in detail, the sheer number and complexity of the ethical issues involved must be outlined.

ETHICS QUESTIONS

If fertility treatment is regulated and people have to establish certain criteria in order to access it, is this discriminatory? John Harris has observed, 'It seems invidious to require that people who need assistance with procreation meet tests to which those who need no such assistance are not subjected.'[13] There is also the issue of Article 12 of the ECHR, which states: 'Men and women of marriageable age have the right to marry and to found a family, subject to the national laws governing the exercise of this right.' Should fertility treatment be restricted on the grounds of age? Numerous cases have been reported where people have received treatment and become parents in their sixties[14] but is this ethical? Not according to Professor Robert Winston, who stated: 'Children should reasonably expect that their parents should be young enough to indulge in the pursuits which are all part of growing up with their family.' Should there be other grounds on which treatment could be refused? In the case of *Harriott*,[15] an infertile woman applied to adopt a child but was rejected on the basis that she had been pro-secuted for a prostitution-related offence 20 years earlier. Later she decided to try IVF treatment but when the hospital checked her records and discovered the reason for the failure of the adoption, the ethical advisory committee refused to approve the provision of treatment. Ms Harriott sought judicial review of the decision but was refused leave on the basis that the committee's decision was neither illegal nor discriminatory! ➡

---

[12] 2008 figures – see http://www.hfea.gov.uk/fertility-clinics-success-rates.html, which shows the latest figures broken down into individual clinics as compared to the national average.

[13] Harris, J., 'No Sex Selection Please – We're British', *Journal of Medical Ethics*, 2005, vol. 31, no. 5.

[14] For example, Dr Patricia Rashbrook became the oldest UK mother to give birth after IVF treatment when she gave birth to her son at the age of 62 (she had to travel to the former Soviet Union for the treatment as she was refused in the UK).

[15] *R v Ethical Advisory Committee of St Mary's Hospital ex parte Harriott* [1988] 1 FLR 512.

> The reader should bear in mind the following crucial ethical questions as this chapter progresses:
>
> - Should we use all the technology that is available?
> - Should everyone have access to such technology?
> - Are doctors 'playing God'?
> - Is it right that 'spare' embryos are simply thrown away?[16]
> - Do considerations about the best interests of the resulting child justify restricting treatment on the basis of age, previous convictions, marital status, sexual orientation etc?
> - Should we instead be encouraging infertile couples to adopt the thousands of children already in existence in England and Wales and in need of families?
> - Should the cost of treatment be restricted so that everyone can access the same types of treatment nationwide?

The legal background

In the early 1980s, during the aftermath of the birth of Louise Brown, then Dame (now Baroness) Warnock was commissioned to produce a report into this new area of fertility treatment. The remit of her committee was to consider the social, ethical and legal implications of the developments that had been made in the field. The Warnock Report was published in 1984 and led to the passing of the Human Fertilisation and Embryology Act 1990 (the '1990 Act'), which regulates the creation, keeping and use of embryos outside the human body and the use of gametes to create embryos. Section 5 of the 1990 Act established the Human Fertilisation and Embryology Authority (the HFEA), a regulatory body responsible for overseeing implementation of the Act. The members of the HFEA are a mixture of medical and laypersons and they report annually to the Secretary of State for Health. The HFEA grants and revokes licences for the various providers of fertility treatments and issues a code of practice, giving further guidance on how to implement the requirements set out in the legislation.[17]

The 1990 Act remained largely un-amended until the passing of the Human Fertilisation and Embryology Act 2008 (the '2008 Act'). This was a response to the huge amount of scientific development that had taken place since the original 1990 Act was passed, in both treatment services and embryo research. Part 1 of the 2008

---

[16] As Gomez observes: 'The common practice within the fertility sector is for embryos to be immersed in water or alcohol and then disposed of in the clinical waste. Anecdotal evidence suggests that on occasion, embryos have been scored through with a pipette and disposed of in the clinical waste, and that straws containing embryos have simply been put in the sharps bin' – see n. 3 above.

[17] Currently in force is the 8th Code of Practice, dated April 2009, available at http://www.hfea.gov.uk/code.html.

Act makes amendments to the 1990 Act and in the main, references in this chapter will be to the 1990 Act as amended. Part 2 of the 2008 Act makes specific provisions relating to legal parenthood of resulting children and will be discussed in more detail later.

Legal provisions

Any centre creating, using or storing embryos and/or storing and using gametes to create embryos must have one or more of four types of licence set out in the 1990 Act (as amended). These are:

- to provide treatment services[18]
- to provide non-medical treatment services[19]
- to store gametes[20]
- to carry out research.[21]

It should also be noted that certain activities cannot be licensed, including:

- keeping or using an embryo after the appearance of the primitive streak
- placing an embryo in an animal
- placing in a woman any embryo other than a 'permitted embryo', i.e. one that is not a human admixed embryo (see later for more on these) and has not had its DNA altered in any way.

Licences provide that one person in each treatment centre must be designated as the 'person responsible' and this person has a duty to ensure that activities are carried out at the centre in accordance with the conditions of the licence. This includes onerous record-keeping requirements, as well as restrictions on when and how treatment may be given. For example, section 13(5) of the 1990 Act provided that 'a woman shall not be provided with treatment services unless account has been taken of the welfare of any child who may be born as a result of the treatment (including the need of that child for a father) and of any other child who may be affected by the birth'. This was always a controversial section and as time went by became increasingly out of date as more single women and same-sex couples were provided with fertility treatment. Thus, the 2008 Act replaced the 'need for a father' with a need for 'supportive parenting' and a 'commitment to the health, well-being and development of the child'.[22] The Act does not define 'welfare' but the code of practice gives guidance on the sort of factors that a treatment provider should take into

[18] See section 11 and section 13 HFE Act 1990 as amended and Sch. 2 para. 2.
[19] See section 11(1)(a).
[20] See section 11(1)(b), section 14 and Sch. 1 para. 2.
[21] See section 11(1) and Sch. 2 para. 3.
[22] See section 14(2).

account when assessing the welfare of any child born from the treatment, including child protection issues and alcohol abuse. However, the code also states that all licensed activities should be carried out in a non-discriminatory way.

ETHICS QUESTIONS

Are treatment services being carried out in a non-discriminatory way if someone like Ms Harriott is denied IVF on the basis of a minor criminal conviction 20 years earlier? Is such a conviction really likely to have an adverse impact on the welfare of the resulting child? Should a couple be denied fertility treatment because one of them had a problem with alcohol years before they met and decided to start a family? Or does the possibility of relapse and the danger that may pose to a child override that person's Article 12 right to found a family?

Consent

A central tenet of the legislation is the requirement for what it calls 'effective consent'. This is required for the creation of the embryo in the first place and any future storage or use of the embryo.[23] Consent must be obtained from both the woman being treated and her partner if they are receiving treatment together and both must have the opportunity to have access to counselling about the implications of the services that are being provided.[24] The consent should also provide for the length of time both parties want the embryos stored (up to the statutory maximum of 10 years) and what is to happen if one of them dies or becomes mentally incapacitated. If one of the gamete providers withdraws consent then the gametes or embryos may no longer be stored and if no consents exist, they must be 'allowed to perish'. These consent provisions were thoroughly examined and tested in the well-known case of *Evans*.

KEY CASE

Evans v Amicus Healthcare Ltd [2004] EWCA Civ 727

Natalie Evans and her partner, Howard Johnson, embarked on fertility treatment when Ms Evans was diagnosed with ovarian cancer. Her eggs were removed and mixed with Mr Johnson's sperm and the resulting embryos were stored until they could later be used. Ms Evans' ovaries were then removed and she underwent chemotherapy. Her treatment was successful but, unfortunately, the relationship

---

[23] See section 13(6) and Sch. 3.

[24] Code of Practice section 3 provides further guidance on the kind of counselling that should be made available.

broke down. She wished to have the embryos implanted in an attempt to have her own genetic child but Johnson withdrew his consent to their use and to their future storage. The case went through our domestic courts and eventually to the Grand Chamber of the European Court of Human Rights,[25] with Ms Evans arguing that destroying the embryos would breach her Article 8 right to a private and family life. The court agreed that her Article 8 rights were invoked, but so were the Article 8 rights of Mr Johnson and the two competing rights were entirely irreconcilable. To uphold the rights of one would automatically be to frustrate the rights of the other. In the end, in line with all the domestic courts before it, the Grand Chamber did not consider that 'the applicant's right to respect for the decision to become a parent in the genetic sense should be accorded greater weight than J's right to respect for his decision not to have a genetically-related child with her'. The court decided that the requirement to have valid consent from both parties was acceptable, even though it would lead to situations such as this where viable and much wanted embryos would have to be destroyed.

The *Evans* case was hugely controversial at the time and all the judges who heard the case expressed enormous sympathy for Ms Evans' situation. It is viewed by some as a waste of valuable embryos and, clearly, those who view life as beginning at conception will be of the opinion that these embryos were 'killed' simply because the father did not want them implanted. In a way, you could argue that Evans lost out because the embryos were created in the context of a loving relationship and, as such, there was always a chance that one party could withdraw consent. This is incredibly difficult to reconcile with the fact that fertility treatment is regularly provided to single women and that, had she been single and used donor sperm to create her embryos, Evans could have had them implanted.

Legal parentage

Another problematic area has been the legal status of those receiving treatment and those donating gametes. Who exactly is to be treated as the legal mother and the legal father of the resulting child? In terms of motherhood, this is legally (if not ethically) very straightforward under the legislation. Section 33 of the 2008 Act reiterates the old section 27 of the 1990 Act, providing that the woman who carries the child will be the legal mother. This is so whether or not she has used her own egg: in other words, whether or not she is the biological mother. The egg donor is not legally recognised as the mother.

Legal fatherhood is a little more complicated. Section 35 of the 2008 Act (again mirroring earlier provisions in the 1990 Act) provides that where the woman being

[25] *Evans v UK*, app. no. 6339/05 (2007).

treated is married, her husband will be the legal father unless he can show that he did not consent to the treatment. Again, this is regardless of the biological parentage of the child. The importance of this provision was illustrated by the difficult case of *Leeds Teaching Hospitals NHS Trust* v *A*.[26] In this case, two couples were undergoing fertility treatment at the defendant's hospital, with each husband consenting to his respective wife's treatment. Unfortunately, there was an error and Mrs A's egg was mixed with Mr B's sperm. Mr and Mrs B's treatment was unsuccessful but Mrs A became pregnant with twins. The error was only discovered when the twins were born and were found to be of mixed race. Clearly, Mrs A was the legal (and biological) mother. The issue for the court was whether Mr A was the legal father of the twins. The court held that he had consented to his wife's egg being fertilised with his own sperm; he had not consented to the treatment that was actually carried out, so he was not the legal father. However, with the permission of Mr B, Mr A was granted parental responsibility and custody of the twins. The case highlights the importance of consent being detailed and explicit.

Where the couple are unmarried, things are even more complex. Sections 36 and 37 of the 2008 Act deem that, in order for the mother's partner to be treated as the legal father of the child, the following conditions must be satisfied:

- She must have received IVF or donor insemination (DI).
- The sperm is not that of her male partner.
- Her partner is alive at the time of treatment.
- They must both have consented in writing to his being treated as the legal father.[27]

This may seem fairly straightforward at first glance, but then consider the provisions of section 37, which allows for consent to be withdrawn. The man or the woman can withdraw their consent to treatment at any time before the embryo or gametes are transferred into the woman. Imagine a scenario in which an unmarried couple are being treated using IVF and both consent to the man being treated as the father. Embryos are created and are ready for transfer but the strain of the treatment has had an adverse impact on the relationship and the couple split up. The woman decides she no longer wants her ex-partner to be the legal father and withdraws her consent to him being considered as such. He has a right to be informed but has no right to stop her proceeding with the treatment and having the embryos implanted, as it was not his sperm used to fertilise them. When the child is born, he will not be the legal father.

[26] [2003] EWHC 259.
[27] See the agreed fatherhood conditions set out in section 37(1) HFE Act 2008.

> **ETHICS QUESTION**
>
> Compare the scenario just recounted to that of Natalie Evans and Howard Johnson. In *Evans*, the court felt that Ms Evans' rights under Article 8 to found a family and have the embryos implanted did not outweigh Mr Johnson's right to decide not to father children with her. However, had donor sperm been used, he would not have been able to withdraw consent to storage and not only would she have been able to proceed with the treatment, she would also have been able to withdraw her consent to his being the legal father and thus deprive him of any legal rights in relation to the child who was born.
>
> Does the biological connection or lack thereof justify such a different legal position for the man in the two scenarios?

The other thing to be noted is that these provisions only apply where the pregnancy has been brought about in a licensed clinic using IVF or DI. Thus, private arrangements whereby a friend or acquaintance provides an infertile couple with donated sperm and the woman inseminates herself will not be covered and in such situations, the donor is the legal father of child.[28]

One of the main reasons for the passing of the 2008 Act was to update regulation of fertility treatment in light of changes in society since the original 1990 Act was devised. For example, the Civil Partnerships Act 2005 provides that any provision of law that refers to a 'spouse', 'husband' or 'wife' must now be read as including a civil partner. With increasing numbers of lesbian couples opting to undergo fertility treatment with donor sperm to have a family, it was not acceptable to leave the female second parent with no legal status. This was addressed in the 2008 Act[29] which sets out provisions mirroring those applying to men in heterosexual relationships. If the couple are in a civil partnership and the female partner has consented to the treatment, she will be the legal second parent. If they are not in a civil partnership, she can still be treated as the legal second parent if the 'agreed female parenthood conditions' apply (these are the same as those set out earlier for a male partner).[30] This provoked controversy when the Bill was going through Parliament, with many voicing concerns about whether it was right to allow the creation of children who would have no legal father. However, given the continued erosion of prejudice towards same-sex couples in general and in particular of same-sex couples using fertility services to create their families, the controversy has subsided fairly quickly since the introduction of the Act.

---

[28] *See Leeds Teaching Hospitals NHS Trust v A* [2003] EWHC 259 QB for an example of a situation where the court had to decide whether a sperm donor in such a situation could have a contact order in respect of the child after the lesbian couple tried to sever contact.

[29] Sections 42–44.

[30] Section 44(1).

Another category of legal parent to be considered is that of the posthumous father. This issue achieved a huge amount of publicity in the 1990s with the case of Diane Blood.

KEY CASE

R v Human Fertilisation and Embryology Authority ex parte Blood[31]

Diane Blood had been married for several years when her husband Steven contracted meningitis. He spent several weeks in a coma before he died and, during this time, Mrs Blood asked for his sperm to be taken and stored so that she would be able to conceive after his death. Hospital staff removed sperm from Steven and stored it. Later, Mrs Blood applied to the HFEA to use the sperm and was denied on the basis that her husband could not consent to either the storage or use of his sperm and to do so without consent was illegal under the 1990 Act.[32] Mrs Blood argued that she and her husband had discussed such issues before he died and that he would have wanted her to use his sperm to have his children.

The court expressed great sympathy for her but reluctantly accepted that under the 1990 Act, the initial collection and storage of his sperm had been illegal as there was no effective consent. It was also clear that such illegally obtained sperm could not legally be used in treatment in the UK. However, the 1990 Act did provide for the HFEA to authorise export of sperm in various circumstances and under Articles 59 and 60 of the Treaty of Rome, European Union citizens have the right to receive various services, including medical services, anywhere in the Union. Other countries would legally be able to provide Mrs Blood with treatment and there was no objective justification for the HFEA to fail to authorise the export of Mr Blood's sperm. As a result of the ruling, Mrs Blood travelled to a clinic in Belgium and received treatment that led to the birth of a healthy son. She repeated the process a few years later and had a second son. However, under English law, her husband could not be registered as the legal father on the birth certificate.

The *Blood* case left open the question of whether treatment could have gone ahead in the UK had the sperm been collected and stored legally, i.e. with Mr Blood's consent before he became ill. The situation regarding posthumous fathers is now governed by section 39 of the 2008 Act. This provides that where an embryo or sperm are transferred to a woman after the death of the man, he can be registered as the legal father if:

---

[31] [1997] 2 All ER 687.
[32] Schedule 3 1990 Act.

- He consented to the use of the sperm or embryos after his death and to being treated as the legal father after his death for registration purposes.

- He did not withdraw that consent.

- No one else is to be treated as the legal father or second parent (for example, the mother has not entered into a marriage/civil partnership or into a relationship where the new partner satisfies the parenthood conditions in the Act).

ETHICS QUESTION

Is it acceptable to create a child after the death of a husband or partner? Should a man be able to father a child after he is dead or should that capability and potential die with him?

Information

The issue of whether children conceived as a result of gamete donation should be able to access information about the donor has been a difficult one for the law to deal with. On the one hand, people may be reluctant to donate gametes if they fear contact from children many years later or any kind of legal or moral obligation that may arise as a result. Gamete donation is critical to the provision of fertility services and clinics have traditionally been very reluctant to see such information become available. On the other hand, in a post-HRA culture and an increasingly rights-based society, it was becoming untenable to deny people who had been conceived this way access to some information.

The 1990 Act gave a very limited right of access to information about a gamete donor.[33] It provided that anyone over the age of 16 years who had been conceived using donor gametes could make a request to the HFEA for non-identifying information. However, the HFEA had discretion to refuse such a request. The provisions were mainly used where someone was getting married or entering into a sexual relationship and wanted confirmation that they were not genetically related to their proposed partner. The law was amended by the HFEA (Disclosure of Information) Regulations 2004, which gives gamete-conceived people the following rights:

- to access non-identifying information provided by donors before 1 April 2005

- to access both non-identifying and identifying information provided by donors after 1 April 2005

- to access information about genetic half-siblings.

---

[33] Section 31, as amended.

Donors may also access certain information under the Regulations, such as:

● the number, sex and year of birth of their children
● whether anyone has made an application for information about them
● what, if any information has been provided to an applicant.

However, information regarding donors is still exempt from the provisions of section 7 of the Data Protection Act 1987, which allows someone access to all personal data held about them by a public authority in order to maintain some restrictions. It appears such safeguards have prevented the anticipated fall in numbers of donors. The HFEA has reported that according to their figures, the rates of donation have actually slightly increased since 2005.[34]

Embryos in research

Increasingly there is a demand for embryos to be used in research. This includes research into treatments for disease, such as stem cell therapies, as well as research into fertility treatment itself. From an ethical perspective, there are many who feel that the creation, use and ultimate destruction of an embryo for such purposes is never justified.[35] By the same taken, scientists have fought very hard in recent years (especially during the passage of the Bill that became the 2008 Act) to have the regulation relaxed to allow them to carry out more research of this nature. They argue that it is immoral to have such a potentially potent resource for curing disease and not to make full use of it.

Pre-implantation genetic diagnosis (PGD)

This is a technique whereby IVF treatment is begun in the usual way, but before any embryos are implanted into the woman, they are screened to establish their genetic profile. Those that display a profile indicating a genetic disease are destroyed and only healthy embryos are transferred.

The 2008 Act states that PGD may be used to:

● test for a chromosome, gene or mitochondrial abnormality
● where there is a risk that the embryo has such an abnormality, establish whether it has that abnormality or any other
● establish the sex of the embryo if there is a gender-related physical or mental disability; serious illness; or serious medical condition potentially present (for example, haemophilia only presents in males).

---

[34] See press release from the HFEA dated 3 May 2007, available at http://www.hfea.gov.uk/465.html.
[35] For example, see Comment on Reproductive Ethics (CORE), a group that opposes such use of embryos – discussed in more detail later in the chapter.

The 2008 Act does place some restrictions on this controversial practice. For example, the HFEA must be satisfied that a person with the abnormality will have or develop a serious physical or mental disability, a serious illness or any other serious medical condition and the code of practice states that 'the centre should consider the circumstances of those seeking treatment, rather than the particular inheritable condition'.[37] However, the problem is the lack of definition of 'serious physical or mental disability'. As we know from cases such as *Jepson* (see Chapter 10),[38] the definition of 'serious foetal abnormality' in the Abortion Act 1967 has become wide enough over the years to incorporate an uncomplicated cleft palate. What to some may constitute a disability serious enough to justify destruction of an embryo may to others seem like a manageable condition. There are also other issues to consider, such as whether PGD should be used to screen for disabilities present at the time or should also be used for adult onset conditions such as Huntingdon's disease and breast cancer. Is 30 years of life followed by an early death due to one of these diseases not worth embarking on in the first place? Perhaps the real question is whether any or all of the HFEA, doctors, parents and politicians should be making such decisions at all? In relation to positively screening in such embryos, this is expressly prohibited under the 2008 Act[39] and the standard licence conditions issued to clinics by the HFEA.

Saviour siblings

PGD has many uses, some of which have been discussed already. Perhaps one of the most controversial is where cells from an early stage embryo, created using IVF, are tested to see if they are a good tissue match for a sick sibling. Only embryos that are a good match are transferred to the woman and those that are not are either stored for future use or destroyed. For example, in the case of the Hashmi family, their eldest child, Zane, was suffering from a genetic disease called beta thallasaemia, which would be fatal if a tissue match could not be found.

---

[36] McDougall, 1938. *British Journal of Psychology*, vol. 28, pp. 321–345.
[37] Code of Practice, paras 10.4 and 10.5.
[38] *Jepson v Chief Constable West Mercia Police Constabulary* [2003] EWHC 2218.
[39] Section 14.

KEY CASE

R (on the application of Quintavalle) v *Human Fertilisation and Embryology Authority*[40]

The Hashmis received permission from the HFEA not only to screen their embryos for the condition but also to actively seek to select embryos that would be a good tissue match for Zane. This was challenged by representatives of the pressure group Comment on Reproductive Ethics (CORE), a group promoting the integrity of the human embryo, on the basis that this was little different from selecting an embryo with blue eyes and blonde hair or sex selection for social reasons and that it was not permitted under the 1990 Act. However, Lord Hoffman felt that the ethical issues raised by this case were for the HFEA to grapple with rather than the court and on a sensible interpretation of the legislation, 'determining the genetic characteristics of the embryo by way of PGD . . . would be "in the course of" providing the mother with IVF services'.[41] On the issue of whether this should extend to positive selection of an embryo that was tissue matched to Zane, Lord Brown stated: 'The fact is that once the concession is made (as necessarily it had to be) that PGD itself is licensable to produce not just a viable foetus but a genetically healthy child, there can be no logical basis for construing the authority's power to end at that point . . . the limits of permissible embryo selection are for the authority.'

As a result of the treatment, Mrs Hashmi gave birth to a healthy baby boy and cells from his umbilical cord blood were used successfully to treat Zane.

The *Hashmi* case raises general questions about how far we allow judges to exercise creative interpretation of such legislation and how much flexibility and power we devolve to the HFEA. At the time of writing, proposals are being considered by the government to abolish the HFEA and have its functions absorbed by the Care Quality Commission. Would we still be happy to allow such flexibility if the organisation policing the legislation were not a dedicated, specialist body but a general healthcare regulator?

Human admixed embryos

The 2008 Act permits the creation of what it calls 'human admixed embryos'.[42] The nucleus of a human cell is placed within an empty animal egg, resulting in an embryo that is 99.9% human. The embryo is allowed to develop to the blastocyst stage, at which point cells are extracted and developed into a stem cell line that can

---

[40] [2005] 2 ALL ER 555, HL.
[41] Ibid. at 570.
[42] Section 4A.

be used in various research projects. Scientists see this as a way of getting around the acute shortage of human eggs available for embryonic stem cell research. Most eggs that are left over from fertility treatment are the poorer quality ones that were not selected for treatment and this inevitably leads to poorer quality stem cell lines. Using admixed embryos also avoids the woman having to incur the health risks associated with egg donation. However, the proposal and the subsequent inclusion of such embryos as permitted embryos in the Act has caused great concern. The day after the first licence was granted to Newcastle University permitting the creation of such embryos, the tabloid newspaper *The Sun* ran an article with a picture of a child with a human body and a cow head, warning of the Frankenstein-like practices authorised by this new Act. Despite such sensationalist neaction from some quanters of the media, the potential treatment possibilities stemming from the research being carried out was sufficient to persuade Parliament to allow the creation of such embryos despite public concerns.

Summary

This chapter has outlined the very difficult task facing legislators in regulating scientific procedures that develop extremely quickly and often leave the law lagging way behind. English law steadfastly refuses to attribute full legal personhood to an embryo on the basis that this would compromise the autonomy of a pregnant woman and would make lawful abortion impossible. However, there is recognition in the law that an embryo/foetus is deserving of some limited legal protection. Difficulties persist, particularly where protecting such entities directly conflicts with the needs of science to use them in research projects and treatment of disease. These are the issues at the frontier of developing law, where there is not necessarily a 'right' and a 'wrong' answer and the law must tread a cautious path, balancing the rights of women, embryos and those suffering from diseases that stem cell therapies and other treatments could alleviate.

Self-test questions

1 What is a 'permitted embryo'?

2 If a child is conceived through IVF with a donor egg, who is the legal mother of the child?

3 In what circumstances will an unmarried partner be the legal father of a child conceived through IVF?

4 Can sperm from a dead man be used in fertility treatment?

5 Is sex selection of embryos ever permitted?

6 Up to what stage of development can an embryo be used in research before it must be destroyed?

7 How long can embryos be stored for treatment purposes before they must be destroyed?

Practice essay question

Herring writes: 'A woman aged 62 went to Los Angeles and used IVF to become pregnant with her brother's sperm. Apparently this was an attempt to win a dispute over an inheritance with other members of her family' (Warnock 2002).

Does this indicate that any claim to reproductive autonomy must have some limits? To what extent do you consider that UK law has put in place 'acceptable limits'?

Practice problem question

Lisa, aged 38, and David, aged 40, have been in a relationship for five years and have been trying to start a family for the past three. After consulting their GP and undergoing various tests, it is discovered that Lisa is not producing eggs and therefore the only option for them to conceive a child will be to undergo IVF treatment using donor eggs.

The treatment is commenced and a cycle of IVF is carried out. Two embryos are implanted in Lisa and the remaining three embryos are stored for future use. The cycle fails and Lisa does not become pregnant. This puts a huge strain on Lisa and David's relationship and they ultimately separate. Lisa is very keen to use the three remaining embryos as she is 'not getting any younger' and the longer she leaves it, the lower her chances of success. David is now in a new relationship and is adamant he does not want children with Lisa. He wants the embryos destroyed.

Advise David and Lisa as to their legal rights in this scenario.

9 Beginning of life II: surrogacy

Introduction

Chapter 8 looked at the basic legal status of the embryo and discussed the legal and ethical issues involved in fertility treatment in general. We will now focus our attention on a particular use of fertility treatment that causes yet more controversy – the surrogacy arrangement. In this chapter, we will look at:

- the nature of a surrogacy arrangement
- the legal framework governing these arrangements
- ethical arguments for and against surrogacy
- the effect of payments
- the human rights implications for those involved.

The nature of a surrogacy arrangement

Surrogacy arrangements arise because, for one reason or another, a person is unable to have her own biological child and so she seeks the services of a surrogate mother to carry a child for her. In a surrogacy arrangement, a woman will agree to carry a child for a commissioning couple on the understanding that she then surrenders the child to them after birth and relinquishes all her parental rights. Before we look at the specific types of arrangement that exist and the legal and ethical issues involved, it is necessary to think about some fundamental concepts underpinning the practice. Essentially, surrogacy is used in the United Kingdom as a solution for infertility. In Chapter 8 (see pp. 156–160) we talked about whether or not people have a right to found a family and whether infertility is an illness demanding treatment at all. Your views on these issues will no doubt have a profound effect on the way in which you view the practice of surrogacy, as it is generally recognised to be one of the most extreme methods of addressing fertility problems. It is fair to say that the courts have tolerated, rather than actively encouraged, such arrangements, largely motivated by a desire to do what is best for the child born as a result of the actions of the adults involved. As the then Lady Justice Hale pointed out: 'The issue [of surrogacy arrangements] is a difficult one, upon which opinions are divided. If there is a trend it is towards acceptance and regulation as a last resort rather than prohibition.'[1] As you read through this chapter, you will see that the issue of surrogacy is both emotional and complex. The response of the law to this thorny topic has been far from satisfactory given the implications for all parties concerned.

As stated already, a surrogacy arrangement is an arrangement made before the child is conceived whereby a woman agrees to carry the child and hand it over to another person or persons after the birth, relinquishing her parental rights.[2] The arrangement can take one of two forms. The first is known as partial surrogacy. This is where the surrogate mother has one of her own eggs fertilised with the sperm of the commissioning father or a donor, so the resulting child is the biological child of the surrogate. The second form is known as full surrogacy or, rather more crudely, 'womb leasing' and involves a child being created with the egg and sperm of the commissioning couple (or donor(s) where appropriate) and implanted into the surrogate. Here there is no genetic link between the child and the woman who carries it. As we will see, while the law does not generally distinguish between the two forms of surrogacy, the distinction can make a profound difference when it comes to the ethical and moral arguments, particularly where the relationship between the parties breaks down.

The legal framework

Background

Prior to 1985, and in the absence of any legislation on surrogacy, the only legal guidance for anyone entering into a surrogacy arrangement was that they had to be careful not to fall foul of other legislation relating to, for example, adoption. Under the Adoption Act 1976, there were provisions prohibiting payments for adoptions, which those involved in surrogacy arrangements could easily contravene. For example, as we will see later, the law permits a commissioning couple to recompense the surrogate for expenses reasonably incurred. In practice, this can amount to thousands of pounds and if the parties are not very careful to attribute such payments very specifically to named and identifiable expenses, they run the risk of being held to have paid for an adoption if they then subsequently go down that route to obtain legal parental rights over the child. The surrogacy contract itself was deemed unenforceable at common law for public policy reasons but even if it

---

[1] *Briody v St Helens and Knowsley Health Authority* [2001] EWCA 1010.
[2] See section 1 Surrogacy Arrangements Act 1985 c. 49.

had not been, there are clearly terms contained within such a contract that would always be unenforceable. For example, many contain terms requiring the surrogate to eat healthily, attend all ante-natal appointments, refrain from smoking or drinking alcohol etc. which would be impossible to police (how could you ever check that she had not had a sneaky cigarette or glass of wine?) and would require too great an infringement of the woman's autonomy for the court to enforce.

It was during the 1980s that the *Kim Cotton* case brought the issue of surrogacy into the public eye and forced the courts to try to clarify its position.[3] Ms Cotton was an English woman who acted as a surrogate for an American couple. The commissioning couple flew to England when they were notified of the birth of the baby girl. Ms Cotton left the hospital shortly after the birth, leaving the baby in the care of medical staff until the commissioning couple could come and collect her a few hours later. However, a concerned member of staff at the hospital informed the local authority and an emergency hearing was called to determine whether custody should be given to the commissioning couple, allowing them to take her back to America, or whether she should be taken into the care of the local authority. Reading other contemporaneous judgments gives one a feel for the level of animosity felt among the judiciary and society in general for the practice of surrogacy at this particular time. For example, in *A v C*[4] (an earlier case involving a surrogacy arrangement) Ormrod LJ stated: 'This was a wholly artificial situation from the very beginning which should never have happened and which no responsible adult should ever have allowed to happen.'[5] Elsewhere in that judgment, the arrangement was described as akin to 'baby farming' and called an 'ugly little drama'. Indeed, the Warnock Report, commissioned to look into regulation of fertility treatment and published in 1984 said of surrogacy: 'It is inconsistent with human dignity that a woman should use her uterus for financial payment and treat it as an incubator for someone else's child.'[6] The court in the *Kim Cotton* case took a very pragmatic approach and, instead of condemning the adults involved as previous cases had done, looked at the issue purely from the perspective of what was in the best interests of the child. Further, the court specifically stated that the adults' participation in such an arrangement would have no bearing on the court's assessment of their ability to parent the child. In the opinion of the court, given that Ms Cotton had voluntarily relinquished her parental rights and the commissioning couple were fully willing and able to offer a stable and loving home, the best interests of the child were served by granting the couple parental responsibility and allowing them to take her back to the United States. This was a landmark case, which came to define the approach taken by the law in relation to surrogacy in general: neither

---

[3] *Re C (A Minor) (Wardship: Surrogacy)* [1985] FLR 846.
[4] [1985] FLR 445 (the case was decided in 1978 but not reported until 1985).
[5] See n. 4 above.
[6] Warnock Report, para. 8.10.

criminalising the practice nor championing it as a sensible solution to infertility. Arguably, this 'betwixt and between' thinking is still at the root of the many problems that persist with surrogacy.

Statute

The Surrogacy Arrangements Act 1985 was passed in the aftermath of the *Baby Cotton* case and the publication of the Warnock Report. This was a report by Dame Mary Warnock into fertility treatment in general, rather than surrogacy in particular. She was asked to look at what were considered at the time to be fairly worrying developments in this area of science and at whether any regulatory changes were needed. As we will discuss in greater detail later when we look at proposals for reform, the Warnock Report made many interesting recommendations in relation to fertility treatment and, specifically, the practice of surrogacy, but these were largely rejected by the government. In fact, not a single one of the Warnock recommendations was incorporated into the Surrogacy Arrangements Act. The Act is, in fact, rather an ineffectual piece of legislation that neither prohibits nor expressly encourages or regulates surrogacy arrangements. The Act does make it a criminal offence to set up a *commercial* surrogacy arrangement, but this liability does not attach to the surrogate herself or to the commissioning couple, but rather to any third party or agency that facilitates the arrangement for commercial gain.[7] There is also a ban on the advertising of surrogacy services, though the HFE Act 2008 inserted a proviso that this ban will not apply to advertisements placed by or on behalf of a non-profit-making body advertising services that do not contravene section 2.[8]

One of the key provisions of the 1985 Act was actually added by the HFE Act 1990 and states categorically: 'No surrogacy arrangement is enforceable by or against any of the persons making it.'[9] This reflects the position in the United States, where high-profile cases such as *Baby M*[10] have established the position that surrogacy contracts will not be held legally enforceable and where the relationship between the parties breaks down the decision about the future of the child will rest solely on a best interests assessment. In the *Baby M* case, although the contract was not enforceable per se, the court did end up deciding that it was in the best interests of the child, by then aged 18 months, to stay with the commissioning couple who had raised her since her birth. Arguably, this decision effectively enforced the contract. However, the birth mother was allowed regular contact with the child.[11] Pattinson argues that the legal vulnerability of all parties to the arrangement that results from this lack of

---

[7] See section 2, especially 2(2).
[8] See section 3(1)(A).
[9] Section 1A Surrogacy Arrangements Act 1985.
[10] *In the Matter of Baby M* (1988) 537 A. 2d. 1277.
[11] See also *Johnson v Calvert* 851 P 2d 776 (Cal 1993).

enforceability is intended to discourage surrogacy arrangements[12] but if this was the intention, there is little evidence that it has been achieved.

Legal parenthood

The thorny issue of the legal parentage of children born as a result of surrogacy arrangements is, strangely, not covered in the Surrogacy Arrangements Act 1985 but has been addressed by both the 1990 and 2008 HFE Acts. When it comes to the identity of the legal mother, English law is very clear that the woman who carries and gives birth to the child is the mother in the eyes of the law.[13] This is in contrast to the position in America where it is up to the parties to show they have a claim to legal maternity. So, for example, in *Johnson* v *Calvert*,[14] both the birth mother and the commissioning woman were found to have a valid claim to being the legal mother of the child and the court in that case made its decision to grant legal rights to the commissioning woman based on intention, i.e. the birth mother had never intended to retain legal rights over the child, whereas the commissioning woman had intended all along to assume those rights and responsibilities. In the UK, the birth mother is the legal mother until those rights are transferred to the commissioning woman either by way of a parental order[15] or by adoption.[16]

The position regarding the legal father is more complicated. Section 35 of the 2008 Act states that if the surrogate is married, her husband is the legal father of the child unless he has not consented to the treatment. This was also the position under the 1990 Act and had to be examined in the *Leeds Teaching Hospitals* case.[17]

KEY CASE

Leeds Teaching Hospitals NHS Trust v *A*

Mr and Mrs A and Mr and Mrs B were both undergoing fertility treatment at the defendant's hospital. An error occurred and Mrs A was accidentally inseminated with the sperm of Mr B. Mrs B's fertility treatment was unsuccessful but Mrs A did become pregnant and subsequently gave birth to twins. The error was discovered because the twins were mixed race (Mr and Mrs A both being white British) and the court was asked to establish legal parentage of the children. In terms of legal motherhood, the court was very clear that under what was then section 27 of the ➡

---

[12] Pattinson, S. D., *Medical Law and Ethics*, 2nd edn, 2009, Sweet & Maxwell, at p. 300.
[13] Section 33(1) HFE Act 2008.
[14] See n. 12.
[15] Section 54 HFE Act 2008.
[16] Section 33(2) HFE Act 2008.
[17] *Leeds Teaching Hospitals NHS Trust* v *A* [2003] EWHC 259.

1990 Act, Mrs A was the legal mother because she had carried and given birth to them and that would be the case whether or not they were conceived using her eggs. In terms of the father, the Act stated that where the mother was married, the legal father would be her husband unless he had not consented to the treatment, so Mr A argued that he should be their legal father. However, the court came to the conclusion that although Mr A had consented to his wife receiving fertility treatment, he had not consented to the use of Mr B's sperm. In other words, he had not consented to the specific actions that the clinic had taken and therefore he could not rely on section 28 of the Act to establish legal parentage. Here it should be noted the difference between the strict legal position and the pragmatic approach usually taken by the courts when it comes to resolving such sensitive and difficult cases. Mr and Mrs A had by the time of the case been raising the twins for some time and they had a strong bond with Mr A. Although they were bound by the legal position to come to the conclusion that Mr A was not the legal father, the court granted his application for parental responsibility, thus effectively getting around the strict legal situation to allow the family to continue to function as a unit and to give him the necessary legal powers to raise the children with his wife.

Where the birth mother is not married, the 1990 Act provided that a man could be the legal father if he was receiving 'treatment together' with the mother[18] but in practice this provision proved extremely problematic. In one case,[19] an unmarried couple received fertility treatment together that failed and their relationship subsequently broke down. Some of the embryos created had been stored for future use and some time later, the woman and her new partner approached the clinic for treatment to have the embryos implanted. The clinic was unaware that the woman was now with a different partner, the treatment was carried out and a child was born. Was the biological father the legal father? Was the new partner receiving 'treatment together' with the mother and therefore the legal father? The court ultimately decided that the assessment of treatment together must be made at the time the embryos are implanted and therefore the ex-partner was not the legal father, but it was clear that the provision was not adequately addressing the issue of unmarried fathers.

The 2008 Act has attempted to remove the ambiguity around the legal father and section 37 sets out the 'agreed fatherhood conditions' which outline the requirements which allow a man to be classed as the legal father.

---

[18] Section 28(3).
[19] *Re R* [2005] UKHL 33.

37 The agreed fatherhood conditions

(1) The agreed fatherhood conditions referred to in section 36(b) are met in relation to a man ('M') in relation to treatment provided to W under a licence if, but only if, –

    (a) M has given the person responsible a notice stating that he consents to being treated as the father of any child resulting from treatment provided to W under the licence,

    (b) W has given the person responsible a notice stating that she consents to M being so treated,

    (c) neither M nor W has, since giving notice under paragraph (a) or (b), given the person responsible notice of the withdrawal of M's or W's consent to M being so treated,

    (d) W has not, since the giving of the notice under paragraph (b), given the person responsible –

        (i) a further notice under that paragraph stating that she consents to another man being treated as the father of any resulting child, or

        (ii) a notice under section 44(1)(b) stating that she consents to a woman being treated as a parent of any resulting child, and

    (e) W and M are not within prohibited degrees of relationship in relation to each other.

(2) A notice under subsection (1)(a), (b) or (c) must be in writing and must be signed by the person giving it.

(3) A notice under subsection (1)(a), (b) or (c) by a person ('S') who is unable to sign because of illness, injury or physical disability is to be taken to comply with the requirement of subsection (2) as to signature if it is signed at the direction of S, in the presence of S and in the presence of at least one witness who attests the signature.

The provisions require the man to have expressly consented in writing to being treated as the legal father and the mother to have expressly consented in writing to his being so treated. They also require that neither of these consents has been subsequently withdrawn. This, theoretically, addresses the issue of relationship breakdown as either party can expressly revoke the consent in order to avoid confusion. However, there is still the chance that the parties do not get around to doing this. There is also an argument that it is unfair to allow the woman to revoke her consent to her ex-partner being treated as the father and then to go on and use the embryos to give birth to his genetic child. One crucial point to note is that these provisions only apply where the child is born as a result of treatment carried out in the UK in a licensed clinic. Many surrogacy arrangements are, in fact, the result of sexual intercourse between the surrogate and the commissioning man or by way of the surrogate using donated sperm from the commissioning man to inseminate herself at home. These situations are not covered by the parentage provisions in the Act and under common law rules, the genetic father will be the legal father in such cases.

In addition to the changes made to the rules governing fatherhood where the surrogate is unmarried, the 2008 Act has also made provision for a child to have a second female parent instead of a legal father. Where the surrogate is in a recognised civil partnership, the position is exactly the same as if she were married and her female partner will be the legal second parent of the resulting child as long as she consented to the treatment.[20] Where there is no civil partnership, the surrogate's female partner can be the legal second parent where the 'agreed female parenthood conditions' are met and these are exactly the same as the agreed fatherhood conditions.[21]

In a 'straightforward' surrogacy arrangement, the legal mother is the surrogate and the legal father is either her husband, civil partner or current partner if they both consent in writing to this. After the baby is born, the easiest scenario is that a parental order is sought under section 54 of the 2008 Act, transferring legal parental responsibility for the child to the commissioning couple, although there are strict criteria that must be met for this to go through and it cannot happen without the consent of both the surrogate and any other legal parent of the child. However, parental orders are more widely available now than they used to be under the 1990 Act which required the commissioning couple to be married. They are now available to married couples, civil partners and unmarried couples in what it refers to as an 'enduring family relationship'.[22] A parental order is generally preferable to going through the adoption process, particularly where there have been payments made to the surrogate, as there is then a risk of falling foul of the rules on payments for adoptions.[23] We will return to the issue of payments later in the chapter.

Ethical arguments

We have looked at what the law says about surrogacy (which is arguably surprisingly little considering the potential implications of the practice on those involved) but we now need to consider the complex ethical arguments involved. For convenience, we will look at each of the parties to a surrogacy arrangement in turn.

The surrogate

Ethical arguments relating to the surrogate form the most controversial and interesting debates in this area. On the one hand, taking a utilitarian approach and adhering to the key notion of autonomy, one can argue that a surrogate is simply providing a much needed service to an infertile couple. The end result is that a need is met, a problem is solved and the couple have a child that is genetically linked to one or both of them. If we believe that a person of sound mind can make any use of their body that they choose, whether or not it is risky or wise, we must therefore

---

[20] Section 42 HFE Act 2008.
[21] Section 43.
[22] Section 54(2).
[23] See section 95 Adoption and Children Act 2002.

conclude that a woman may use her body in this manner if she sees fit. This would also fit with feminist notions of a woman's complete right to control her own body. On the other hand, even today with excellent healthcare and facilities, pregnancy and childbirth are by no means free of risk and apart from the general discomfort and inconvenience, there is a real risk of long-term health problems or even death as a result of a woman acting as a surrogate. This makes some uneasy with the law permitting surrogacy in the UK, but, of course, the counter-argument is that we permit people to do other dangerous things. Are you also going to ban skydiving or bungee jumping? What is the justification for letting someone jump off a cliff for fun but prohibiting a woman acting altruistically to give a childless couple the one thing they long for? Such an approach would clearly be extremely paternalistic and fly in the face of the sacrosanct notion of autonomy.

The ethical concerns also extend to the surrogate's mental and emotional well-being. Motivation to become a surrogate may be complex and made up of several different factors but what if the commissioning couple are known to the surrogate, as either friends or relatives? Does this put her under emotional pressure to agree to participate? You will have noted that there is no legal requirement to provide counselling, although the HFEA Code of Practice recommends it. It is therefore difficult to ensure that the surrogate is fully aware of the potential emotional impact of giving the child up at the end of the process, which may be different depending on whether or not the commissioning couple are known to her. There may also be differing emotional consequences depending on whether she is involved in a full or partial surrogacy arrangement, as with partial surrogacy there is the genetic link with the child to take into account.

Another interesting idea is whether one can use a virtue ethics argument to support the actions of the surrogate, pointing to the incredibly selfless, altruistic act of putting her body through the strain and trauma of pregnancy and birth and then enduring the emotional pain of handing over the child. The validity of such an argument would depend on the definition of 'virtue' in that many would argue you cannot comply with the virtue ethics idea if the act you are engaging in is not inherently virtuous. Can the act of carrying a child who may or may not be genetically linked to you, then giving it up to a childless couple be considered virtuous or is it rendered selfish by the possible adverse emotional impact on the child?

The child

When it comes to the impact on the child, several key ethical issues need to be examined. First, the emotional and psychological impact of knowing he or she was created with the express intent of being handed over to another couple has not been fully assessed, although Wallbank quotes research among children who have been adopted that shows certain adverse effects, including feelings of rejection and low self-esteem.[24] There is also the impact of the legal complexity surrounding parentage. When the 2008 Act was going through Parliament, there was much debate, particularly among the Lords, that the then Bill was creating a situation in which you could effectively create a child with no legal father and the possibility of never having a legal father.[25] While the expansion of the parentage provisions to allow civil partners and other same-sex partners to have legal rights over children in their family was generally supported and considered to be a positive step, the spectre of the erosion of the traditional family unit was never far away during the unfolding debate. In addition in relation to parentage, writers such as Wallbank[26] argue that the real potential for psychological trauma to the child comes from lack of knowledge about the circumstances of their conception and their origins. She argues for openness to be required by law, but this could prove extremely impractical. As a mother of three, the author knows only too well that each child has a different emotional and psychological makeup and to ask the law to require certain amounts of information to be given in certain timescales would severely intrude on the relationship between the child and the parents who are raising him. It is respectfully argued that the extent and timing of disclosures about the circumstances of their birth should be left to the discretion of the parents.

There is also, as always with fertility-related issues, the well-rehearsed argument about whether we are 'playing God' and treating babies as commodities to be created and traded at will. Are we allowing respect for human life to be diminished by allowing childless couples to effectively go shopping for a woman who is prepared to carry a child for them and to provide her with incentives (financial or otherwise) for her services? Is this going a step too far in seeking solutions to infertility? Of course, it could be argued that it is a positive thing for a child to know that he was so wanted that his parents went to such lengths to create him. Society's traditional view of womanhood and motherhood and the nature of the mother–child relationship may well contribute to the general unease that seems to be felt about the practice and the concerns we have as a society for the welfare of children born as a result of surrogacy. Are we really worried about the impact of the arrangement on the child per se or is it that we find it inherently distasteful or unnatural for a woman to seemingly abandon the child she has carried and delivered?

The commissioning couple

Finally, we need to consider some moral and ethical arguments relating to the commissioning couple. As noted earlier, many people will feel that although infertility

---

[24] Wallbank, J., 'Too Many Mothers? Surrogacy, Kinship and the Welfare of the Child', *Med L Rev* 2002, 10(3), 271–294.

[25] Sections 33(1), 38(1) and 45(1) HFE Act 2008.

[26] See n. 25.

is a sad situation, worthy of sympathy and perhaps a couple of cycles of IVF on the NHS, surrogacy is going one step too far in seeking a solution to the problem because it crosses too many ethical 'red lines': a birth mother giving up her child, the apparent 'buying' of a baby, commoditisation of the whole creation process and so on. However, couples who find themselves facing fertility issues may well feel that the ethical concerns are outweighed by the sheer suffering that their infertile state causes and the debilitating emotional impact it has on them and their relationships. To procreate is a basic human function that most people expect to be able to achieve and if they can achieve it with the assistance of a surrogate, so be it. Could it not be argued that if we resolve the ethical debate over fertility treatment itself in favour of providing it, then we should also logically permit infertile couples to engage in surrogacy arrangements, as they are merely another form of infertility treatment?

One key issue that must not be overlooked, however, is the legal vacuum in which these couples are operating. We rather blithely state that the contract is unenforceable, but let us think about what that may actually mean for the commissioning couple. After perhaps many years of infertility and trying other means such as regular fertility treatment, they embark on the long and complex process of finding a surrogate and undergoing treatment to produce a pregnancy. What happens if after all that (and possibly thousands of pounds in expenses) the surrogate decides she does not want to give the baby up? In that scenario, the surrogate is the legal mother and if she is married, her husband is the legal father, even if the sperm came from the commissioning husband. The commissioning couple are left in the tragic position of having no baby and also, potentially, the knowledge that a child who is genetically linked to at least one of them is out there being raised by someone else. In all the ethical debate over the welfare of the child and the potential exploitation of the surrogate, the vulnerability of commissioning couples is sometimes overlooked, yet they are arguably the parties with the least protection and the most to lose in the venture. One final important point to note is that nothing in the law requires that the commissioning couple be infertile and it is theoretically possible for them to engage the services of a surrogate for other reasons, such as a desire by the woman not to interrupt her career. No such cases have been reported but the reader should think about all the possible justifications this allows someone to use to employ a surrogate, whether and in what way, as yet, these might affect their views on the acceptability of the practice.

The effect of payment

Under section 54(8) of the Surrogacy Arrangements Act, a parental order may not be made where any money has been paid to the surrogate other than 'expenses reasonably incurred'. The law envisages things such as medical expenses, maternity clothing and lost earnings being valid expenses but, in practice, surrogates are regularly paid sums in the region of £25,000 or more during the course of the arrangement. In some cases, it is plain that the rules are being stretched, such as one case in which a surrogate who was not working and was claiming unemployment benefits received £12,000 from the commissioning couple, ostensibly for lost earnings.[27] However, the court does have the power to retrospectively authorise illegal payments that have been made and it will almost always be in the best interests of the child to do so and allow the parental order to proceed. This may well be why the Brazier Committee was unable to find a single example of an order being refused on the grounds that illegal payments had been made.[28]

Of course, the whole issue of payments complicates the already difficult ethical debate and adds fuel to the fiery allegations that surrogacy amounts to the commoditisation of babies – that essentially couples are buying a baby. It also adds significantly to concerns over the potential exploitation of the surrogate. Specifically, could women from poor backgrounds and experiencing financial difficulties be tempted to become surrogates because of the financial incentive and then suffer long-term emotional and psychological damage as a result? This concern is compounded by cases such as *Re X & Y*,[29] in which a British couple had employed the services of a Ukrainian woman to act as a surrogate. She was paid €235 per month during the pregnancy and then a lump sum of €25,000 on the birth of healthy twins. She used the money to put down a deposit on a flat. Although the case revolved around authorisation of the payment so that a parental order could be made, it clearly raises at least the possibility that this woman was influenced in her decision to become a surrogate by financial reward. Is this acceptable? Perhaps under the principle of autonomy it is no different to a person choosing to do any kind of risky work for suitable remuneration. However, given that the surrogate is engaged in potentially life-threatening work, 24 hours a day, seven days per week for nine months, and then enduring hours of pain and perhaps years of emotional distress afterwards, it could be argued that such an amount seems exploitatively meagre.

Human rights implications

There are clearly some issues regarding Convention rights to address when it comes to surrogacy. The Article 2 arguments about the rights of a foetus will not be rehearsed here as they are covered in detail elsewhere in this volume. However, Article 8, which guarantees respect for private and family life and Article 12

---

[27] *Re C (application by Mr and Mrs X under s. 30 of the Human Fertilisation and Embryology Act 1990)* [2002] EWHC 157 (Fam).

[28] Margaret Brazier, Alistair Campbell and Susan Golombok, 'Surrogacy: Review for Health Ministers of Current Arrangements for Payments and Regulation', HMSO, London, 1998, Cm 4068 para 5.3.

[29] *Re X & Y (Foreign Surrogacy)* [2008] EWHC 3030 (Fam).

governing the right to marry and found a family, are clearly central to the debate. Could either the commissioning couple or the surrogate argue that their rights are inadequately protected because the contract is legally unenforceable? It would be difficult in relation to Article 8 as this usually requires some interference by the state in the affairs of the family and, if anything, here you would be arguing complete lack of interference. Article 12 could possibly be invoked on the basis that the surrogate has backed out of the arrangement and the state's failure to enforce the contract is preventing the commissioning couple from founding a family.

A better argument may well be that there is potentially a breach of Article 13 that requires states to have effective remedies for breaches of a person's rights. If the parties have no legal redress when one or the other backs out, potentially leaving them without legal rights over their genetic child, it could well be argued that this breaches Article 13.

Reform

As would be expected with such a controversial and ethically complex issue, proposals for reform have come thick and fast in the years since the Surrogacy Arrangements Act was passed. Of particular note is the report by Margaret Brazier in 1997, commissioned specifically to address the question of whether there was a need for reform of the law on surrogacy.[30] The key issues examined in the Brazier Report were:

- whether payments, including expenses, to surrogate mothers should continue to be allowed
- whether there was a case for regulation of surrogacy through a recognised body
- whether changes were needed to the Surrogacy Arrangements Act 1985.

On the issue of expenses, the Brazier Report recommended that genuine expenses should continue to be allowed, but that any additional expenses should be prohibited and a recognised system for establishing what would be genuine expenses should be created by legislation. On regulation, it proposed that all surrogacy agencies should be registered with the Department of Health and governed by a code of practice. Acknowledging that the creation of such a code would be a lengthy process involving consultation with a wide range of organisations, the report suggested as an interim measure that agencies should sign up to a voluntary code governing their conduct and should also voluntarily register with the Department of Health. It proposed the full-scale repeal of the Surrogacy Arrangements Act 1985

---

[30] Brazier and ors, 'Surrogacy: Review for Health Ministers of Current Arrangements for Payments and Regulation', 1998 Cm 4068.

and the drafting of a new piece of legislation that would keep the ban on commercial surrogacy and maintain the position that the contract was unenforceable (treating it instead as a memorandum of understanding), but would include new provisions on payment and parental orders and would set out the new code of practice.

The Brazier Report has come in for much criticism. The surrogacy support group COTS (Childlessness Overcome Through Surrogacy) set up by Kim Cotton vehemently opposed the prohibition on payments, stating that failure to adequately recompense a surrogate is exploitative, in that she is then performing a risky service without appropriate remuneration. Michael Freeman agrees with this criticism, reminding us that women using their bodies to earn money is not uncommon and nobody suggests that fashion models should go unpaid.[31] He points out that further weakening the strength of an agreement between the parties by calling it a memorandum of understanding rather than a contract merely reinforces the vulnerability of all parties concerned and has no useful practical effect in law. Freeman continues to rebut the Brazier proposals, arguing that the last thing needed in this area is another regulatory authority and that it would be much better to allow the HFEA to regulate surrogacy in the same way in which it regulates other forms of fertility treatment. He also queries how a code of practice would work and how the content would be decided. Would it set age limits for surrogates or for commissioning couples? Would it specify marital status or that the surrogate must have completed her own family first? Would post-menopausal women be allowed access to surrogacy services or would this be confined to women suffering fertility problems during their natural reproductive years? In defence of the report, it must be pointed out that these questions are the same ones that arise in the area of general fertility treatment such as IVF and they are ones that the HFEA and the individual clinics manage to address on a case-by-case or area-by-area basis, largely dictated by costs and resources available. The fact that difficult questions need to be addressed does not mean that a practice should not be regulated.

None of the recommendations made in the Brazier Report were implemented, although it remained the subject of much academic debate and discussion. It was briefly revisited during the passage of the Human Fertilisation and Embryology Bill (now the 2008 Act) but ultimately the new Act focused on updating parentage provisions and ensuring the law had moved with the pace of the science in the area of assisted conception. It stayed well clear of addressing the fundamental issue of the permissibility of surrogacy and made no attempt to regulate it further.

---

[31] Freeman, M., 'Does Surrogacy have a Future after Brazier?', 1999, *Med L Rev*, 7(1), p. 2.

Summary

The real problem with critically analysing the law in relation to surrogacy is that there is very little law to evaluate. The approach taken has very much been one of turning a blind eye and not criminalising the conduct of those involved, but not providing legal protection or encouragement in the process. The problem with this approach (and one that is echoed in Chapter 10 when we discuss the middle-ground approach taken to abortion) is that in attempting to please everyone it actually pleases no one. It allows people to embark on surrogacy arrangements without the necessary legal protections and leaves them in a legal lacuna that can have devastating practical and emotional consequences in the albeit relatively small number of cases where things go wrong and the agreement breaks down. The absence of proper statutory regulation leads to judges having to be very creative when it comes to dealing with the real situations and children before them, so they are forced to take sensitive and practical steps such as retrospectively authorising illegal payments and separating strict legal parenthood from custody arrangements. Jackson is highly critical of this lack of guidance and statute and comments of judges such as Macfarlane J and Hedley J:[32] 'Their sensitive and non-judgmental attempts to safeguard the interests of children and their parents with wholly inadequate legal tools should be required reading for ministers.'[33]

Self-test questions

1 Before 1985, was a surrogacy arrangement legal?

2 Define 'legal mother' in a surrogacy arrangement.

3 If the surrogate is unmarried, who is the legal father of the child?

4 Are any payments made by the commissioning couple to the surrogate legal?

Practice essay question

'English law seems more interested in regulating the commercialisation of surrogacy than in dealing with the real legal and ethical issues surrounding the subject'.

What are those 'real legal and ethical issues' and how does English law deal with them?

---

[32] In *Re G (Surrogacy: Foreign Domicile)* [2007] EWHC 2814 (Fam) and *Re X&Y (Foreign Surrogacy)* [2008] EWHC 3030 respectively.

[33] Jackson, E., *Medical Law: Text, Cases and Materials*, 2009, Oxford University Press, p. 854.

Practice problem question

Ellie and Flo are in a lesbian relationship and wish to have a child. However, unfortunately, neither woman can carry a child to full term. Niamh, Ellie's sister, agrees to act as a surrogate mother using Ellie's eggs and Conor, Niamh's husband, agrees to father the child. Discuss the legal and/or ethical issues arising out of the following alternative scenarios:

1 Ellie and Flo approach their GP for advice and to recommend a clinic at which Ellie could undergo egg collection and then in-vitro fertilisation treatment. Their GP refuses to give any advice on the grounds that he does not consider Ellie and Flo to be in a suitable relationship and he disapproves of the practice of surrogacy involving a sibling.

2 Niamh is paid £6000 for bearing the child. Two weeks after handing the child over to Ellie and Flo she begins to regret the decision and wants the child back.

10 Beginning of life III: abortion

Introduction

As Montgomery points out, abortion 'must be one of the most controversial areas of healthcare law'.[1] This is something of an understatement. The abortion debate polarises opinion like virtually no other with any kind of middle ground being nigh on impossible to find. There are several key reasons that opinions on the law and ethics surrounding abortion tend to be at the extreme ends of the spectrum. First, there is an innate sense within our society that the vulnerable must be protected and there are few things more vulnerable than a foetus. It has long been held in special esteem, because it represents the possibility of new life and that is something to which human beings are programmed to respond. There is also, as we mentioned in Chapter 9, the long-held view that the mother–child relationship is sacrosanct and therefore anything that challenges that view or involves a mother behaving in a way that is not nurturing or 'motherly' tends to invoke strongly negative reactions. Then there is the issue of advancing science and increasing knowledge among the general public about develop-ment of a foetus during a pregnancy. It is difficult to reconcile the image of a tiny pre-mature newborn born at 23 weeks' gestation with the idea that we permit abortion in some cases up to 24 weeks and, in other cases, beyond that up to the very moment of birth. Running through all the arguments and varying degrees of acceptance of abortion is a crucial question: when exactly does life begin? How a person responds to that question will largely determine not only whether they feel that abortion should be permitted, but in what circumstances and how it should be regulated or controlled.

In this chapter, we look at the following:

- the basics – how a pregnancy progresses and what types and methods of abortion exist
- statistics – numbers of abortions at various stages of pregnancy
- the law – why it was necessary to legislate and the potential difference between what the Act says and how abortion is regulated in practice
- procedural issues.

[1] Montgomery J., 'Health Case Law' 2nd ed, 2002, OUP, p. 379.

Woven through the discussion is an evaluation of the interaction between law and ethics in this area and the impact of the wider debate on the law and any proposals for reform.

The basics

Pregnancy

A pregnancy is dated from the first day of the woman's last menstrual period (LMP) and lasts for 40 weeks from this date. When talking about abortion limits, one should bear in mind that, for example, if we say the abortion pill is available up to 12 weeks, this means 12 weeks from the first day of the LMP and, in reality, most women do not discover they are pregnant until they are officially around six weeks into the pregnancy. A pregnancy is divided into three trimesters, the first lasting until 13 weeks, the second lasting from week 14 to week 28 and the third lasting from week 29 to week 40. Almost all development of vital organs and parts is completed in the first trimester, so, for example, the heart starts beating at around six weeks, all recognisable organs have appeared by around 10 weeks and the foetus will begin moving around at about 12 weeks, though the mother may not feel this until week 18 or later.

Methods of abortion

An abortion is the termination of a pregnancy due to the loss or destruction of the embryo or foetus before birth. They can be either spontaneous (i.e. they happen by chance without any action by the woman or another person to cause it, what we generally call a miscarriage) or induced, where some process is undergone in order to cause the termination to happen. The latter is the type of abortion we are focusing on in this section.

There are essentially three types of abortion widely available in England and Wales. They are:

1 The *abortion pill* (RU-486) – this is available during the first 12 or so weeks of the pregnancy and acts on the uterus, causing it to shed its lining and, with it, any fertilised egg that may have implanted. For the woman, it is like having a very severe and heavy menstrual period and she will experience pain as the uterus contracts and continuous bleeding for several days. This is the simplest method of abortion available and does not need to be carried out in a medical environment, so once the woman has obtained the pill, the rest of the process can happen at home.

2 *Surgical abortion* (also known as a dilation and cutterage or 'D&C') – this is necessary where the pregnancy has advanced to a stage where the chemical method is

no longer appropriate. The lining of the uterus is scraped away by the surgeon to ensure that all the products of conception are removed. A general anaesthetic is usually required and the woman will experience pain, discomfort and bleeding for several days afterwards. As with any surgery there is also the added risk of infection with this method.

3 *Late abortions* – where the foetus is too large and the pregnancy too established for the surgical method to be appropriate, the woman will effectively have to give birth in order to terminate the pregnancy. This will be a vaginal delivery as the added risks of a caesarean section are considered too great to be justified in such circumstances unless there are pressing medical reasons for it. Clearly, this method is extremely traumatic for the woman, both physically and emotionally. She will normally be on or close to the labour ward in which women are giving birth to live babies. An injection of potassium chloride is injected into the heart of the foetus to ensure that it will be born dead and then a drip is set up containing chemicals to induce labour.

Clearly, none of these methods is without distress for the woman, but the late abortion is generally considered to be by far the most problematic. It accounts for a very small percentage of the total number of abortions each year[2] but one of the main concerns reported by those working in the field is the situation in which, despite the procedure being carried out correctly, the foetus is actually born alive. Nadine Morris, an MP and ex-nurse who has campaigned for better regulation of abortion has said:

> A little boy was aborted into a cardboard bedpan, which was thrust into my arms. When I looked into the cardboard bedpan, the little boy was gasping for breath through the mucous and amniotic fluid. I stood by the sluice with him in my arms, in the bedpan, for seven minutes while he gasped for breath. A botched abortion became a live birth and then, seven minutes later, a death.[3]

This situation is, fortunately, very rare but anecdotal evidence suggests that it does still happen occasionally. If and when it does, it thrusts the medical professionals involved into an extremely difficult legal black hole between the rules on abortion and the rules on neonaticide, which we consider in more detail in Chapter 8. It clearly also inflames the ethical debate on whether such late abortions should be permitted at all.

---

[2] According to DH statistics, just 1% were carried out at or after 20 weeks' gestation during 2010; http://www.dh.gov.uk/en/Publicationsandstatistics/Publications/PublicationsStatistics/DH_126769.
[3] Morris, N. Quoted in The Christian Institute, 21 May 2008 and available at www.christian.org.uk/issues/2007/hte_bill/commons_21May68.htm

Statistics

Before we get into the detailed debate about whether or not abortion should be regulated by law and, if so, whether the current law is appropriate, it is important to understand how common abortion is so that we have a context in which to assess the law. Have a look at the following statistics[4] and before we get into the ethical debate, ask yourself as you are reading what your initial reaction is to the numbers. Do you instinctively feel there are too many, about the right amount in a country of this size or are you surprised by how few there are? Do you think the numbers suggest a need for tighter or lighter regulation?

- A total of 189,574 abortions were performed in 2010. This was a rise of 20% in 10 years and was up 2.5% on 2006 figures.
- 92% of those abortions were carried out at under 13 weeks' gestation.
- 77% were carried out at under 10 weeks' gestation.
- Only 1% were carried out on the basis that the foetus had a serious foetal abnormality.
- 34% of women having abortions have had one or more previous abortions.

The law

The main piece of legislation on abortion in England and Wales is the Abortion Act 1967 but the development of legal regulation of the practice can be traced back as far as 1861. Section 58 of the Offences Against the Person Act (OAPA) 1861 states that anyone who unlawfully procures a miscarriage in a woman is guilty of a criminal offence.[5] Note that criminal liability does not attach to the woman herself but to the medical professional or other person who carries out the abortion.[6] This section continues in force and in reality, all that the Abortion Act does is provide statutory defences against this offence. The prima facie legal position is still that abortion is illegal.[7] In 1929, the Infant Life Preservation Act extended this protection of the foetus to make it illegal to take the life of the child as it was actually being born.

---

[4] Abortion statistics, England and Wales: 2010, published May 2001 DH 126769.

[5] Section 58 Offences Against the Person Act 1861.

[6] This means a person who physically acts to procure the miscarriage, so in September 2010, Noreen Akhtar was acquitted after he told his pregnant wife, who spoke no English, that she needed to go into hospital to have a cyst removed when, in actual fact, he had arranged a late abortion. Staff became suspicious and called an interpreter who discovered that the woman knew nothing of the planned abortion. Her husband could not be prosecuted because he had not actually used a poison, instrument or other thing to procure a miscarriage.

[7] See *Gil Magoria* case – *The Times*, 1 March 2008 – doctor sentenced to three years and nine months for trying to procure his wife's miscarriage.

In 1939 an important case came before the courts concerning the interpretation of section 58 of the OAPA. *R v Bourne*[8] concerned a 14-year-old girl who had suffered a very violent rape and was pregnant as a result. Dr Bourne carried out the abortion at the request of the girl and her parents on the basis that he was preventing further psychological damage to the girl that would be caused if she had to proceed with the pregnancy and give birth to her rapist's child at such a young age. Criminal proceedings were brought but the court took a rather pragmatic view given the circumstances and, in particular, looked at the interpretation of the word 'unlawful' in section 58. It was decided that where the abortion was carried out to save the mother's life or prevent damage to her health, the miscarriage would not have been 'unlawfully' procured and therefore the offence was not made out. This was the only dent in the armour of section 58 until the Abortion Act was passed 28 years later. The following key points should be noted about the Abortion Act (as amended by the Human Fertilisation and Embryology Act 1990):

- It does not permit abortion on demand (see later for discussion of whether that is effectively the way it is interpreted). The situation must fall within one of the four statutory grounds set out in the Act that provide defences to the section 58 OAPA offence.[9]
- Two doctors must independently and in good faith conclude that one of the grounds set out in the Abortion Act is satisfied (section 1).
- The abortion must be carried out at an approved place (section 1(3)).
- The chief medical officer must be notified within seven days that the abortion has been carried out, but he is not informed of the details or the reasons for the abortion (section 2).

The requirement for two doctors to separately and in good faith assess the situation as falling within one of the four statutory grounds has been described as something of an illusory concept.[10]

(1) Subject to the provisions of this section, a person shall not be guilty of an offence under the law relating to abortion when a pregnancy is terminated by a registered medical practitioner if two registered medical practitioners are of the opinion, formed in good faith.

---

[8] *R v Bourne* [1939] 1 KB 697.
[9] Supra.
[10] See, for example, Pattinson, S., *Medical Law and Ethics*, 2nd edn, 2009, Sweet & Maxwell, p. 243.

The only successful prosecution to date was brought in 1974[11] and was a rather extreme case where the second doctor had not examined the patient, had not asked for any information about the reasons for the abortion and then went on to perform the procedure to an inadequate standard. The problem is largely that a jury is being asked to assess whether a doctor acted in good faith and, in the absence of actions or words that expressly point to bad faith, it ends up being a rather *Bolam*-like assessment, i.e. they acted in good faith because they say they acted in good faith (see Chapter 3 for in-depth discussion of the *Bolam* case). The Human Fertilisation and Embryology Bill suggested reforming this area and abolishing the requirement for two doctors to approve the procedure but that provision was not included in the resulting Act.[12]

The grounds

There are four grounds on which an abortion may be carried out legally and these are set out in section 1 of the Act:

- That the pregnancy has not exceeded its 24th week and that the continuation of the pregnancy would involve risk, greater than if the pregnancy were terminated, of injury to the physical or mental health of the pregnant woman or any existing children of her family (section 1(1)(a)).

- That the termination is necessary to prevent grave permanent injury to the physical or mental health of the pregnant woman (section 1(1)(b)).

- That the continuance of the pregnancy would involve risk to the life of the pregnant woman, greater than if the pregnancy were terminated (section 1(1)(c)).

- That there is a substantial risk that if the child were born it would suffer from such physical or mental abnormalities as to be seriously handicapped (section 1(1)(d)).

The 24-week limit

There are several issues that jump out on a cursory reading of these grounds. The first ground in section 1(1)(a) is often referred to as the 'social ground'. This is the only ground to which the 24-week limit applies, which means that if the woman is relying on any of the other three grounds, the abortion may be carried out at any time before the child is born, even up to 40 weeks and beyond (see p. 193 for more on the time limit). Clearly, the breadth of section 1(1)(a) depends on the interpretation of 'injury to the physical or mental health of the woman or any existing children'. The World Health Organisation has advocated an approach that

---

[11] *R v Smith* [1974] 1 All ER 376.
[12] See HL Bill 6 2007–8, 17.

looks at the overall health of the woman and/or any children of the family in terms of a 'state of physical or mental well-being, not merely an absence of disease or infirmity',[13] which would indicate that the bar is set fairly low. It is easy to imagine that in a family on a very low income, where a woman feels she cannot financially support another child, the stress it would cause and the impact on the existing children may be sufficient to pass the section 1(1)(a) test – does this equate to a right to abortion on economic grounds? If it does, should the law be more specific and simply grant women a right to abortion in such circumstances, instead of arguably cloaking such a right in a criminal defence?

The father

It is striking that the section refers to the welfare of other children of the family but makes no mention of the father. A common question asked by students of medical law is what rights does the father have when it comes to abortion law? The short answer is virtually none. The key case of *Paton* v *UK*[14] makes it clear that not only does the foetus itself not have any legal rights prior to live birth, but the father has none in his own right either. Mr Paton had tried to argue that even if he could not bring a claim under article 2 on behalf of the child (see elsewhere in this chapter for a detailed analysis of the rights of a foetus prior to birth), his Article 8 rights were breached when his partner was allowed to obtain an abortion without his knowledge. The court, while sympathetic to an extent, acknowledged that there was an argument that his Article 8 rights had been infringed but that such infringement was necessary in order to protect the Article 8 rights, not to mention the right to autonomy, of the pregnant woman. In practice, it would simply be unfeasible to uphold the father's rights in such a situation. Either the court would have to try to force a woman to continue with an unwanted pregnancy (leading to all sorts of potential breaches of Article 8, Article 3 etc.) or the woman would simply resort to the kind of backstreet abortion practitioners whom the Act was brought in to eradicate. The inalienable biological fact that it is the woman who carries the child necessitates the father being left out of the legal picture when it comes to termination of pregnancy.[15]

Time limit

In relation to the 24-week limit, several attempts have been made over the years to reduce it to 20 weeks or even earlier, most recently during the debates over the then Human Fertilisation and Embryology Bill during 2007 and 2008. Despite detailed

---

[13] See WHO publication 'Abortion Laws' 1971, available at http://whqlibdoc.who.int/publications/1971/a53898_eng.pdf.

[14] *Paton* v *UK* [1980] EHRR 408.

[15] See also *C* v *S* [1987] QB 135; *Kelly* v *Kelly* [1997] SLT 896 and *Vo* v *France* (2004) 2 FCR 577.

arguments taking place on the floor of the House and investigations by the Science and Technology Select Committee,[16] it was concluded that there was not enough compelling evidence to justify lowering the limit. The Committee stated:

> While survival rates at 24 weeks (the current upper limit for abortion) and over have improved since 1990, survival rates (viability) have not done so below that gestational point. The Committee concludes that there is no scientific basis – on the grounds of viability – to reduce the upper time limit.[17]

While the Committee was unequivocal that the evidence was simply not compelling enough to justify any amendment, the numerous media stories about babies born before 24 weeks' gestation and surviving[18] have contributed to growing unrest among many and a feeling that the limit may no longer be appropriate.

◼ Serious abnormality

The other issue that causes much academic and public debate is the definition of serious abnormality or handicap as required under section 1(1)(d).

> (1) Subject to the provisions of this section, a person shall not be guilty of an offence under the law relating to abortion when a pregnancy is terminated by a registered medical practitioner if two registered medical practitioners are of the opinion, formed in good faith . . .
>
>   (d) that there is a substantial risk that if the child were born it would suffer from such physical or mental abnormalities as to be seriously handicapped.

Who decides what constitutes a serious abnormality? There is surprisingly little in the way of guidance on this, given that, under this ground, an abortion may take place up to and beyond 40 weeks, but the Royal College of Obstetricians and Gynaecologists have said that doctors should take into account things such as:

- the availability of effective treatment
- the probable degree of self-awareness and ability to communicate
- the degree of suffering that would be experienced
- the extent to which that person would be dependent on others.[19]

---

[16] Science and Technology Committee Press Release No. 66 of Session 2006–07, 'Scientific Developments Relating to the Abortion Act 1967', 31 October 2007.

[17] See n. 14.

[18] See, for example, http://www.dailymail.co.uk/health/article-437236/Born-just-22-weeks-Amilla-allowed-home.html and http://www.telegraph.co.uk/health/healthnews/7901876/Twin-born-after-23-week-pregnancy-becomes-most-premature-baby-to-survive.html.

[19] See the RCOG publication *Termination of Pregnancy for Fetal Abnormality in England, Wales and Scotland* (1996) – note that this is currently in the process of being updated.

Given this guidance, would a diagnosis of a cleft lip and palate satisfy the test and be classed as sufficiently serious an abnormality to make it possible to legally terminate the pregnancy? That was the question asked of the court in the *Jepson* case.

KEY CASE

R (On the application of Jepson) v *Chief Constable of West Mercia* [2003] EWHC 3318

Joanna Jepson learned that, in her area, a woman had obtained an abortion at 24 weeks' gestation because a scan identified that the foetus had a bilateral cleft lip and palate. Having had a similar condition at birth herself and undergone relatively simple treatments to correct the problem, Ms Jepson felt that the terms of the 1967 Act had not been complied with in that a cleft lip could not be held to be a serious enough abnormality to satisfy section 1(1)(d). She sought judicial review of the decision of the Crown Prosecution Service (CPS) not to prosecute the doctors involved and was successful in persuading the court that the CPS should revisit the decision. However, after that further investigation was carried out, the same decision was reached on the basis that there was no evidence that the doctors had not determined in good faith that there was a likelihood of serious disability. As in most judicial review cases,[20] the court refused to get into a detailed discussion of whether the decision was right or wrong and purely looked at whether the decision-making process had been flawed. While to the casual observer, the doctor's interpretation of section 1(1)(d) may seem erroneous, it was not sufficiently unreasonable to render the CPS decision not to prosecute unsound.

Procedural issues

Registered medical practitioners

Section 1 of the Abortion Act 1967 requires the abortion to be carried out by a registered medical practitioner, i.e. a doctor. As time went on, concerns began to surface among nursing staff that often it was the nurse who was effectively carrying out most parts of the process rather than the doctor and it was not at all clear that this was legal. Thus, the Royal College of Nursing brought a test case asking the court to clarify this point. The court confirmed that it would consider the abortion carried out be registered medical practitioner if the termination was 'prescribed and initiated by a medical practitioner who remains in charge of it and is carried out in accordance with his instructions by qualified nursing staff'.[21] While this has clarified

---

[20] See, for example, *Cambridge Health Authority ex parte B* (1995) 25 BMLR 5 and *Rogers* v *Swindon Health Authority* [2006] 1 WLR 2649.

[21] *Royal College of Nursing of the United Kingdom* v *Department of Health and Social Security* [1981] AC 800.

how the court would ideally like the process to be carried out, it is difficult to imagine that in a busy ward with doctors stretched sometimes between several wards at a time, women are not from time to time left in the sole care of nursing staff without the oversight or supervision of a doctor. Campaign groups have argue that this is no bad thing and succeeded in getting a provision into the draft HFE Bill to remove the need for a medical practitioner and allow nursing staff to carry out abortions, but again, this amendment did not find its way into the resulting Act.

Conscientious objection

Section 4(1) of the Abortion Act states that a person who has conscientious objections to participating in an abortion should not be required to take part.

> (1) Subject to subsection (2) of this section, no person shall be under any duty, whether by contract or by any statutory or other legal requirement, to participate in any treatment authorised by this Act to which he has a conscientious objection: Provided that in any legal proceedings the burden of proof of conscientious objection shall rest on the person claiming to rely on it.

However, there has been some debate about the meaning of 'participate' in this context – exactly how much involvement is required? In its guidance on personal beliefs and medical practice, the GMC states: 'Participate should have its ordinary and natural meaning' and that the phrase in the Act 'referred to actually taking part in treatment administered in a hospital or other approved place . . . for the purpose of terminating a pregnancy'.[22] In *Janaway* v *Salford*, a secretary who was a practising Roman Catholic refused to type a letter to a consultant referring a patient for a possible abortion. She was dismissed by the health authority for not carrying out the necessary duties associated with the post and sought judicial review of that decision, relying on section 4. The case went to the House of Lords where it was held that section 4 only applies to 'actually taking part in the treatment'.[23] While this is helpful in interpreting section 4, it by no means resolves all the uncertainty. In *Janaway*, the secretary was completely removed from the process and was not being asked to have any contact with the patient. What about a porter who is required to transport a woman to theatre for an abortion, or a student nurse required to check her pulse and blood pressure afterwards? It is by no means clear whether either would be able to rely on the conscientious objection clause.

---

[22] See GMC publication 'Personal Beliefs and Medical Practice', March 2008 available at http://www.gmc-uk.org/guidance/ethical_guidance/personal_beliefs.asp.
[23] *Janaway* v *Salford Area Health Authority* [1989] AC 537 HL.

Summary

So should abortion be permitted at all and, if so, how should it be regulated? If we are to follow through with the notion that patient autonomy is at the core of medical law in this country and that every person has a right to choose what happens to her body, the logical conclusion is that abortion should be freely available to all women in all circumstances, subject to the normal rules on consent. However, society is prevented from going too far in that direction by the enduring notion that a foetus constitutes a human life and that it is inherently deserving of protection. This resonates with basic instincts to protect the next generation and is one of the few things that can unite those on both sides of the debate. The question is really about whose rights interests should take precedence – those of the mother or those of the child? Resolving such fundamental ethical dilemmas has never been a particular strength of the law in this country and neither should it be – that is not the function of law. Rather, it is to regulate conduct according to the generally accepted view in that particular society about what is and is not acceptable. The lack of a generally accepted view is what causes the difficulty in this area of law.

As stated at the beginning of this chapter, it is unlikely that legislation could ever be put in place to please everyone on all sides of the abortion debate. Rather than go down the more extreme routes taken by other countries, such as Ireland where abortion is not permitted unless the mother's life is at risk, the choice in England and Wales has been to retain the criminal offence of procuring a miscarriage but to also provide numerous statutory defences to the offence, so that, in limited circumstances, abortion may be legally carried out for other reasons. However, there are several problems with the law taking this hands-off approach to the ethical debate. First, in a society with an increasing tendency towards affording abortion social acceptability and a decreasing religious presence, the reality is that the Act can be interpreted and applied in a very liberal manner so as to effectively provide abortion on demand, especially under section 1(1)(a). Whether you view this as a positive thing will depend on your ethical views on abortion itself, but one element of this situation which is widely recognised as a problem is that it risks promoting a lack of respect for the law, which is seen as out of touch, not reflecting reality and something that can be circumvented where necessary. The other major problem is that while the grounds are drafted in such a way as to effectively permit abortions on demand, because the Act is trying not overtly to encourage the practice, it also provides a set of complex procedural requirements that can sometimes hinder a woman's access to abortion. If the ethical decision has been taken to permit the practice, surely then procedural obstacles should be removed to make the process as smooth and simple as possible. Alternatively, if abortion is something that the law wishes to restrict, the Act should be amended to tighten up the grounds on which it may be legally carried out. Given the extremes of public opinion at both ends of the debate, neither option is likely to be taken by any government in the near future.

Self-test questions

1 Give two arguments for and two arguments against permitting legal abortions to be carried out.

2 There are four grounds on which an abortion may legally be carried out. One important fact distinguishes one ground from the others – what is it?

3 Can a medical practitioner refuse to participate in an abortion?

4 Give two examples of proposed reforms in the HFE Bill. Should they have been incorporated into the Act? Why or why not?

Practice essay question

'The current UK law on abortion represents the achievement of a morally sensitive compromise which should be left undisturbed'.

Critically evaluate this statement.

Practice problem question

Jane, who is 33 years old, had for about six months been in a relationship with Peter, who is 20 years older than she. She recently ended the relationship because Peter wanted to have a family and Jane was unwilling to do this as she was at a crucial point in her career and considered that it would jeopardise her prospects for promotion. On one occasion when their contraception failed she took the morning-after pill. Peter discovered this and was very angry that she had taken the pill when he so wanted a child. It was this episode that finally led Jane to end their relationship. However, the row with Peter upset her so much that she took the second pill later than she should have done in order to guarantee its effectiveness. A couple of weeks after ending the relationship she realised that she was, in fact, pregnant and so she decided to consult her general practitioner, Dr Waters, about having an abortion. After the consultation, Dr Waters contacted a gynaecologist, Dr Roberts, who had been a friend of hers at medical school to discuss Jane's request for a termination and referred Jane to him at the Bluegrove NHS Trust hospital.

On the day of the termination, Dr Roberts initiated the abortion process but was then called away to an emergency admission and left Nurse Morse to continue the procedure. It transpired that following the emergency admission, Dr Roberts had had to leave the hospital as a domestic crisis had arisen and he needed to see one of his children urgently. In his absence, Nurse Morse sought the guidance of a junior doctor, Dr Gray, who was on duty on the ward at the time. However, Dr Gray said that he had conscientious objections to abortion and would exercise his right not to participate in the procedure. Nurse Morse was left on her own to complete the procedure.

Peter seeks advice on whether:

- Jane committed a criminal offence when she took the morning-after pill.
- There was a contravention of the Abortion Act 1967 in allowing Jane to have an abortion in the circumstances and/or in the way the abortion was carried out.
- Had he known that Jane was pregnant, he would have had any rights under the Human Rights Act 1998 to prevent the abortion and whether his position would have been any different had he been married to Jane.

11 End of life I: euthanasia

In a way similar to the issues raised in Chapters 8, 9 and 10, the end of life raises a number of questions about how we view the intrinsic value of human life and just how important autonomy over our bodies is to us. Apart from the fascinating abstract ethical arguments, which essentially pit autonomy against sanctity of life, there are also very real practical questions that present themselves and to which there are no easy answers. For example, who should ultimately decide if and when a life should be brought to an end? Should it be the patient herself, even where she may be in a degree of pain or be influenced by concerns over the burden she is placing on family members? Should it be the doctor who understands the medical condition thoroughly, has insight into the kind of death that will come if the illness runs its course and knows if and when the treatments being offered can achieve no further improvement? Should other interested parties such as family members have a say? What, if any, role should the court play in such decisions? According to Ward LJ: 'Deciding disputed matters of life and death is surely and pre-eminently a matter for a court of law to judge'.[1]

The following three chapters will look at end-of-life decisions from three distinct angles. First, the focus will be euthanasia, looking at the law that applies in England and Wales and how that law has been applied in cases before the courts, specifically since the introduction of the Human Rights Act 1998 (HRA). Second, the particular type of euthanasia known as neonaticide will be examined and the law and ethics of allowing a newborn infant to die will be analysed, with particular reference to the ways in which some of the issues differ from euthanasia relating to adult patients. Third, we look further down the line at the contentious issue of organ donation and the impact of the Human Tissue Act 2004 on this area of law. Overall, the aim of these chapters is to allow the reader to develop an understanding of the complex legal and ethical path that must be trodden by a medical professional when she faces a situation in which medicine cannot cure the patient of their life-threatening condition and the manner and timing of that patient's death must be dealt with.

---

[1] *Re A (Conjoined Twins)* [2001] Fam 147.

Introduction

Let us start with a deceptively simple question – are you in favour of euthanasia or against it? A person's answer to this question will be influenced by many factors, which may include religious views, family circumstances, any previous experience of the death of a loved one and to some extent the degree of his medical knowledge and understanding. The aims of this chapter are to explain and examine the following issues:

- what is actually meant by the term 'euthanasia' and the various different types that exist
- the various ethical arguments both for and against various forms of euthanasia
- the legal status of such practices in England and Wales, including how the HRA has influenced this area of law in recent years
- whether the law is in need of reform and, if so, the likelihood of various reform proposals being implemented.

What is euthanasia?

The word 'euthanasia' comes from the Greek words *eu* (meaning 'good') and *thanos* (meaning 'death') and is variously translated as 'easeful death' or 'gentle and easy death'.[2] In England and Wales, the word has become something of a generic term for various related but different practices and it is important to clarify the various types of euthanasia that exist and some of the terminology surrounding it (see Table 11.1 for a summary).

Table 11.1 Types of euthanasia

Term	Meaning
Mercy killing	Situation in which a person who is suffering from a terminal illness, and is often in great pain or distress, is killed, usually by a family member or someone close to the patient who decides it is in the patient's best interests, rather than a medical professional
Assisted suicide	This is where a patient suffering from a terminal illness expresses a wish to bring his life to an end but because of the nature of his illness or disability, he requires assistance from a family member or another person in order to carry out the suicide
Physician assisted suicide (PAD)	As above but where it is a medical professional who assists the person to take their own life
Active or passive euthanasia	Where the patient may not be able to express his views or ask for assistance to commit suicide so the medical professionals treating him and the family members must decide between them whether steps should be taken to end the patient's life (active, e.g. administering a lethal dose of painkiller) or whether certain treatments should be withdrawn, resulting in the patient's death (passive, e.g. turning off a life-support machine)

[2] See *Oxford Concise English Dictionary*.

It is important to clarify the distinctions between the various forms of euthanasia that exist because there are differing legal rules relating to each of them and different legal consequences for those involved.

Ethical issues

Before looking at the ethical arguments surrounding euthanasia in detail, it is important to understand that informing these arguments are some different inter-pretations of the nature and timing of death. As observed by Goff LJ in the seminal case of *Bland*:

> Anthony is still alive. It is true that his condition is such that it can be described as a living death, but he is nevertheless still alive. This is because, as a result of developments in modern medical technology, doctors no longer associate death exclusively with breathing and heartbeat, and it has come to be accepted that death occurs when the brain, and in particular the brain stem, has been destroyed.[3]

As discussed in more detail in Chapter 2, there is a school of thought known as vitalism that takes the view that all life should be preserved at all costs and that it is never acceptable to end a life, even where the person will die in the near future anyway and there is no hope of cure. Much of vitalism is rooted in religious teach-ing of one sort or another, but those holding a vitalist perspective are not exclusively those who would place themselves in a particular religious group. The idea is that the continuation of the human species is all about survival and it is that instinct that must be nurtured and protected.[4] Vitalists do not make distinctions to do with the quality or otherwise of a person's life – rather, they recognise an inherent quality in the mere fact of being alive that justifies all steps being taken to avoid the loss of that life. While admirable in abstract, this school of ethical thought struggles when faced with the reality of a patient in extreme pain and distress that may go on for days or weeks if the illness is left to take its natural course. Vitalists must ask them-selves whether the survival instinct should be overridden by the equally powerful human instinct to end suffering.

At the other end of the ethical spectrum sits the idea that quality of life is more important that the inherent nature of life itself and that life should only be pre-served where there is quality in it. Of course, this inevitably leads to questions about who should decide where to draw the lines. What one person deems as a life of little or no quality may actually have sufficient quality for another person to want to stay alive. A life of paralysis, lack of speech and a reliance on round-the-clock care by others for every physical need may sound to some like a life of such little quality that it is not worth preserving, but consider the position of professor Sir Stephen Hawking

[3] *Airedale NHS Trust v Bland* [1993] AC 789 HL.
[4] See Keown, J., 'Restoring Moral and Ethical Shape to the Law after Bland', *LQR* 1997, 113 (Jul), 482–503.

who has led a life of great worth and made substantial contributions to the world in which he lives, despite his profound disabilities. There is danger with the quality of life argument that it runs rather close to the line where euthanasia meets eugenics. Is there a danger that we start deciding that only lives of a particular type or lives free of physical or mental abnormality have quality and are therefore worth preserving?

Sitting somewhere in between these two extremes is the principle of sanctity of life. In the west we tend to think of this as a largely Christian philosophy but most religions around the world have some notion of life being a gift from whichever God or deity they happen to worship and that humans do not have the right to take away life that has been bestowed in such a way. However, while those who believe in the sanctity of life recognise this inherent value in a human life, worth prolonging and protecting as a blessing from a god, this ethical school of thought also recognises notions of mercy towards those in great pain or who are enduring unbearable suffering. It does not require life to be preserved at all costs and in all situations. Rather, it starts from the notion that life is precious and should be preserved but allows some form of euthanasia where the life of the person has become unbearable.[5,6]

These ethical arguments will become clearer once the law is fully understood and some real-life cases have been discussed. The reader should bear these issues in mind as the chapter progresses. As with other chapters in which there have been contentious ethical issues involved, it is worth coming back to the question of whether you are in favour of euthanasia or against it after the law has been examined to see whether that knowledge influences your ethical stance.

The legal framework

Voluntary or involuntary?

As we saw in Table 11.1, the common law distinguishes between active and passive euthanasia, between voluntary and involuntary euthanasia and between euthanasia and assisted suicide. Voluntary euthanasia involves a mentally competent patient asking the doctor to end their life, whereas involuntary euthanasia refers to a situation where the patient either lacks mental capacity or lacks the physical ability to communicate his wishes due to severe disability or lack of consciousness. Both types can, in some circumstances, be legal (remember in Chapter 6 it was clear from cases such as *Re C* that an adult of sound mind can refuse medical treatment even where that choice will inevitably lead to his death) but there clearly need to be extra safeguards in place where the patient is not able to decide for themselves.

---

[5] See Keown, J., *Legal Studies*, vol. 26, no. 1.

[6] For an excellent review of how the law approaches such ethical issues, see Coggon, J., 'Assisted Dying and the Context of Debate: Medical Law v End of Life Law', *Med L Rev*, 2010, 18(4), 541–563.

Active or passive?

Active euthanasia involves a deliberate act intended to kill, such as a doctor injecting a patient with a lethal dose of painkillers aiming to bring about the death of the patient. This is illegal in England and Wales because it satisfies the definition of 'unlawful killing' and will therefore be either murder or manslaughter depending on the mens rea (that is, the state of mind) of the doctor at the time. He is likely to face criminal prosecution, regardless of whether the patient and/or the family requested or consented to it.[7] By contrast, passive euthanasia involves the withholding or withdrawing of treatment from the patient, i.e. an omission rather than an act, and, in certain circumstances, this can be legal.[8] Consider this for a moment: an injection of painkillers is a positive act and if the intention is to end the patient's life, this will be illegal, but the withdrawing of treatment, such as walking across a room and switching off a life support machine or physically removing a feeding tube administering artificial nutrition and hydration (ANH), is classed as an omission. As such, even if the intention is to end the patient's life, this may be legal. There are those who argue that this is rather an arbitrary distinction and one of legal convenience rather than justifiable ethical substance.[9]

The doctrine of double effect

Another important preliminary principle to understand is the doctrine of double effect. This is a longstanding protection for medical professionals who act in accordance with their Hippocratic Oath to care for their patient and prevent further suffering in terminal situations. The doctrine states that a doctor may lawfully administer a high dose of painkilling medication where the main purpose of the drug is to ease pain, even where they are aware that the medication may also, incidentally, hasten the death of the patient. The act will have a double effect of easing pain and hastening death but is legal as long as the primary intent was to use it in a painkilling capacity.[10] The origins of this doctrine stem from a time when there was great reverence for the medical profession among the general public and among judges and a reluctance to treat doctors who ended their patients' suffering as criminals. For example, in *R v Moor*,[11] the doctor in question was accused of murdering an 85-year-old patient who had been suffering from terminal bowel cancer. The jury had the doctrine of double effect explained to them and were then addressed by the judge, who pointed out the character of the doctor, the fact that he had taken time out on

---

[7] See *R v Cox* [1992] 12 BMLR.
[8] See *Bland* (n. 3 above) and *B v NHS Hospital Trust*.
[9] See for example Mason et al, 'Law and Medical Ethics', 8th ed, 2011 OUP, ch. 18.
[10] See *Aizedale NHS Trust v Bland* discussed in detail, p. 206.
[11] Newcastle Crown Court, 11 May 1999.

his day off to tend to a dying patient and the general inappropriateness of the charge he was facing. The jury took less than one hour to acquit him. However, in order to attract the protection of this doctrine, the doctor must be careful to ensure that it can be shown that the main aim of his actions was to end pain, rather than to kill. In *R v Cox*,[12] the terminally ill patient had been injected with potassium chloride by the doctor, which is a drug that is guaranteed to kill (whereas with high-dose pain-killers there is merely a risk that it may hasten death) and has no painkilling properties. It is perhaps unsurprising then that, in this case, the doctor was convicted. Devlin J perhaps summed up the legal distinction best in the case of *R v Adams*:[13]

> If the first purpose of medicine – the restoration of health – could no longer be achieved, there was still much for the doctor to do and he was entitled to do all that was proper and necessary to relieve pain and suffering even if the measures he took might incidentally shorten life by hours or perhaps even longer . . . Dr Adams' defence was that the treatment was designed to promote comfort and if it was the right and proper treatment, the fact that it shortened life did not convict him of murder.

The doctrine of double effect is a highly controversial one, not least because it is perceived as setting a different standard in the law for a doctor who ends a patient's life as opposed to a relative who hastens the end of a loved one who has a terminal illness and is in great pain. It also raises questions of proof. How do you establish beyond reasonable doubt that the doctor's intention was to end pain rather than to kill? The doctrine was part of the reason that Harold Shipman was able to get away with murdering patients in his care for so long before suspicions were aroused.[14] The courts have always countered that medical professionals have no vested interest, given that they do not stand to inherit and are not burdened with day-to-day care of the patient and that therefore the risk of benevolent intent, especially given their chosen profession, is relatively small, but this complacency was severely criticised in the report into the *Shipman* case. There is also an argument that if palliative care were properly funded and organised, there would be less need for doctors to find themselves in such situations at all.

Passive involuntary euthanasia

It is this type of euthanasia that attracts the most controversy in England and Wales, because it is legal in certain circumstances and involves a patient who cannot make her wishes known to those caring for her or to the court. The seminal case on this is that of Anthony *Bland*.

---

[12] (1992) 12 BMLR 38.
[13] [1957] Crim LR 773.
[14] See the Shipman Inquiry, Fifth Report – 'Safeguarding Patients: Lessons from the Past, Proposals for the Future', published 9 December 2004, Command Paper Cm 6394.

KEY CASE

Airedale NHS Trust v *Bland* [1993]

Anthony Bland had been a spectator at the Hillsborough football ground disaster on 15 April 1989 and suffered catastrophic injuries. He was diagnosed as being in persistent vegetative state (PVS), so he was not brain stem dead and had some respiratory function and a heartbeat but was in a deep coma, was not aware of his surroundings as far as medical staff could be aware and was kept alive by artificial nutrition and hydration (ANH). After two years with no signs of improvement in his condition, doctors applied (with the consent of the family) for a declaration from the court that it would be lawful for them to withdraw the ANH from Anthony and allow him to die. The Lords unanimously granted the declaration. They held that to withdraw the nasogastric feeding tube was an omission, a withdrawal of treatment rather than a positive act intended to kill. With this established and with Anthony unable to express his own wishes, the court was left with the task of deciding whether it was in his best interests to continue treatment. If not, then that treatment could lawfully be withdrawn. Lord Mustill in particular had difficulty with the assessment of best interests in the case of an effectively insensate patient and stated: 'The distressing truth, which must not be shirked, is that the proposed conduct is not in the best interests of Anthony Bland, for he has no interests of any kind.' However, his colleagues rationalised the assessment, pointing out that the focus should not be on whether it was in his best interests to die, but whether it was in his best interests to continue providing the treatment (the ANH). If it was not, then there was no duty to continue providing it. Approaching it in this way, the inevitable conclusion was that it was lawful to withdraw treatment, as being in PVS and judged to be insensate, it is difficult to argue that it is in his best interests or serving him any purpose to continue the treatment.

At the time that the case was decided, the best medical knowledge was that PVS patients were completely insensate and unaware of the world around them, a fact that no doubt allowed the Lords to make the decision they made to allow Anthony to have nutrition withdrawn and to die in this manner. However, in recent years, new research has shown that patients in PVS can be sensate and aware and simply be 'locked in' and unable to communicate.[15] This raises new and very frightening possibilities about the level of suffering that Anthony may have endured as a result of that court declaration (i.e. dying slowly through starvation and dehydration) and a reminder that in all these things we are heavily reliant on the state of scientific knowledge at the time, which may later prove to have been woefully inadequate.

---

[15] See for example Bruno et al, 'from unresponsive wakefulness to minimally conscious PLUS and functional locked in syndromes: recent advances in our understanding of disorder of consciousness', *Journal of Neurology*, May 2011, Springer.

ETHICS QUESTION

The Lords stated that there was no distinction in law between withholding and withdrawing treatment – do you agree? Do you think withdrawing treatment should be considered to be 'active'?

It was always envisaged in *Bland* and subsequent cases such as *Frenchay*[16] that, initially, doctors would make applications to court for a declaration in PVS cases, but that as the law became clarified and medical professionals gained confidence in dealing with such cases, the need to seek such declarations would diminish. This reducing need has not materialised, primarily because the law has not been at all clear in cases since *Bland*. For example, in *Re D*[17] and *Re H*,[18] patients who were comatose but did not fit the PVS diagnostic guidelines drawn up by the Royal College of Physicians (in other words, there was debate about whether or not they were actually in PVS) were nevertheless the subject of court declarations authorising withdrawal of ANH. Going one step further, such an injunction was also granted in *Re G*,[19] where the only medical expert in the case was adamant that the patient was not in PVS. This rather worrying extension of the *Bland* principles to cover patients who were not so clearly PVS was criticised and departed from in the 2004 case of *W Healthcare Trust* v *H*,[20] but the uncertainty has left doctors wary of relying on their own understanding of the law and cautious about proceeding without a declaration from the court. Mason et al. have argued that instead of talking of concepts such as PVS or 'intolerability' of life, we should be honest and admit that what we are allowing doctors to do by withdrawing treatment in such circumstances is indistinguishable from active euthanasia.[21]

Assisted suicide

It is no longer an offence in this country for a person to commit suicide. Under the principle of autonomy, a person is free to choose to take whatever action he likes with his own body, even if that ultimately results in his death. However, it is an offence to assist someone to commit suicide and the law has changed in this area recently to try to clarify the offences that apply.

---

[16] *Frenchay NHS Trust* v *S* [1994] 2 All ER where the feeding tube of a patient in PVS became dislodged and an application was made to the court for a declaration that it would not be unlawful if doctors failed to replace it.

[17] [1997] 38 BMLR 1.

[18] [1997] 38 BMLR 11.

[19] [2001] 65 BMLR.

[20] [2004] EWCA.

[21] Mason et al., *Law and Medical Ethics*, 8th edn, 2009, Oxford University Press, p. 594.

Before February 2010, the legal situation regarding suicide was governed by the Suicide Act 1961. Section 2 of that Act stated that it was an offence to 'aid, abet, counsel or procure' a suicide, but this would only apply if the person who had been so assisted actually went on to take his own life, or attempt to do so, thus there would be no liability merely for doing the aiding or abetting. This provision was supplemented by the Criminal Attempts Act 1981, which made a person liable for aiding, abetting, counselling or procuring a suicide or a suicide attempt, and this was so even if there were no ultimate attempt on a person's life. In fact, the assistance did not even have to be aimed at a particular person or group. This was partly an effort to counter organised groups that campaigned for assisted suicide to be legalised and provided materials explaining how to carry out various forms of suicide. These different legal provisions were far from clear and further complicated by the fact that even where it appeared an offence had been committed under one of these Acts, it was still necessary to get the consent of the Director of Public Prosecutions (DPP) in order to prosecute. Criticisms were levied (in very high-profile cases such as Diane Pretty and Debbie Purdy – see later for full discussion of these cases) that it was impossible for a person (medical professional or relative) to know whether they were likely to be prosecuted or not if they helped a terminally ill patient to end his life.

Since 2010, the situation has been governed by section 59 of the Coroners and Justice Act 2009 (CJA), which aims to clarify the whole area and bring the law on suicide up to date, particularly in light of various websites and other resources that have appeared in recent years in support of assisted suicide. It means there is now one statute and one offence, that of encouraging or assisting suicide, but the provision has largely the same effect as the old law had. Section 2 of the CJA states that a person commits an offence if:

- He does an act capable of encouraging or assisting the suicide or attempted suicide of another person.
- And it was his intention to encourage or assist the suicide or attempted suicide.

A person will be liable under the Act whether he aimed the assistance at a specific person or group or not, whether the person was known to him or not and whether or not an actual suicide attempt materialises as a result of his actions. Crucially, it still requires the DPP consent to prosecute and it is this that has caused great controversy in the courts, because it was argued that the exact circumstances in which someone would be prosecuted were not clear.

Human rights arguments – Diane Pretty and Debbie Purdy

Does the uncertainty regarding the situations in which the DPP will choose to prosecute someone for assisting a person to commit suicide infringe the patient's human rights? This was a question raised in two very high-profile cases in recent years.

R (Pretty) v DPP [2002] 1 All ER 1 HL

Diane Pretty was a 42-year-old woman who was suffering from motor neurone disease. She was terminally ill and rather than allow her condition to further deteriorate slowly over time, she wished to end her life immediately. However, she was handicapped physically by her condition and this meant that she was not able to take her own life – she would need the assistance of another person in order to carry out the suicide. Her husband was prepared to help her, but not if he would be prosecuted under the Suicide Act 1961 (the legislation governing suicide at the time) so Mrs Pretty sought assurances from the DPP that in the circumstances, he would not prosecute her husband for helping her. The DPP refused to give her such assurance.

Mrs Pretty challenged the Suicide Act on the basis that it breached her human rights. In particular, she alleged breach of Article 2 (the right to life) and Article 3 (freedom from torture and inhumane treatment). Her argument that Article 2 naturally included the right to choose how to end your life was unanimously rejected by the court (and by the European Court of Human Rights on appeal the following year), as was her argument that she was being subjected to inhumane treatment by being forced to suffer the full development of her illness. In relation to Article 8 (right to a private life), the court recognised that this right had been interfered with because she was unable to make the choice to avoid what she considered would be an undignified death, but the interference was deemed to be justified and proportionate. The alternative would be to compel states to allow assisted suicide and this was something the court was not prepared to entertain – although Mrs Pretty was in possession of her full mental faculties and was a strong woman making a reasoned and independent decision, it was not unreasonable for a country to ban assisted suicide in order to protect more vulnerable patients.

The *Pretty* case focused mostly on whether there was a right to die or to avoid what some would view as inhumane situations and the court was very clear that there was no such right. Debbie Purdy focused more on Article 8 when she challenged the laws on assisted suicide in 2009.

Purdy v DPP [2009] UKHL 45

Debbie Purdy's dilemma was similar to that of Diane Pretty in that she was suffering from a terminal illness and wanted to end her life as she saw fit when the time came that she felt it no longer had sufficient quality and meaning. She was suffering from multiple sclerosis (MS) and accepted the fact that physician assisted suicide was not available in the UK, so planned to travel to the Dignitas clinic in

Switzerland[22] to end her life at a time of her own choosing. The problem was that because of the nature of her condition, she was not able to travel to Switzerland alone; she would require the help of her husband to book flights, organise packing and transport and to physically board the aircraft. Like Diane Pretty, she wanted to know in advance if her husband was likely to be prosecuted under domestic legislation for assisting her with her suicide. All the DPP would say was that a prosecution would only be brought if it were in the public interest to do so, but Mrs Purdy argued that the policy was not transparent enough and it was not made clear in what circumstances it would be in the public interest to prosecute. This, she argued, breached her Article 8 rights to plan and organise her private life in the way she wanted to.

The Lords agreed with her and ordered the DPP to provide clearer guidance on how he would assess whether it was in the public interest to prosecute and the factors that would be taken into consideration.

It is important to note that although Debbie Purdy saw this as a successful outcome and the media gave the story a lot of coverage, it did absolutely nothing to change the law and the DPP was not compelled to guarantee that he would not prosecute Mrs Purdy's husband if he helped her to travel to Switzerland. When the guidance required by the court was published, it did no more than confirm the sort of factors that would be considered and these had been well known beforehand, such as whether the person who assisted stood to gain from the death and whether the patient had capacity to decide to end their own life.[23]

The passing of the HRA also required the courts to revisit the issue in *Bland* regarding withdrawal of treatment from patients in PVS. This was challenged in *NHS Trust A* v *M*,[24] where the court looked at whether such a withdrawal might be a breach of Article 2 or Article 3. It found that Article 2 did not compel doctors to keep a patient alive in all circumstances, especially where there was no hope of cure, and also that a patient in PVS could not be aware of any degrading treatment because they were insensate, so there was no breach of Article 3.

ETHICS QUESTIONS

Article 2 provides citizens with what it calls a 'right to life'. The courts have ruled that this does not mean doctors have to keep a patient alive in all circumstances. Is this not exactly what it should mean?

In relation to Article 3, simply because a patient is insensate and therefore unaware of how they are being treated, does that mean that they have not been subjected to inhumane or degrading treatment? Does it require mental awareness on the part of the victim or should it only require the knowledge/awareness of the perpetrator?

---

[22] A clinic near Zurich, Switzerland where assisted suicide has been legal since 1940.
[23] The DPP policy is available at http://www.cps.gov.uk/publications/prosecution/assisted_suicide.html.
[24] [2001] Fam 348.

If further human rights argument that has been raised in the courts is whether a patient can do the opposite of what Diane Pretty and Debbie Purdy wanted to do – can a patient insist beforehand that doctors keep him alive and/or provide a certain type of treatment once the patient becomes too ill to ask for it? That is what Leslie Burke wanted to do.[25] He suffered from a degenerative neurological condition that would eventually leave him unable to speak, see or swallow but with full mental faculties, at which point he would need to rely on ANH to keep him alive. However, the GMC guidance to doctors available at the time suggested that once a patient was unable to communicate his wishes, it was then possible to discontinue treatment (including ANH) using the principles laid down in the *Bland* case. Mr Burke argued that this breached his right to life under Article 2 and would subject him potentially to the inhumane and degrading experience of dying slowly from starvation and dehydration. The court held that his position was protected while he was competent and able to express his wishes, as any doctor withdrawing treatment in such circumstances against the patient's wishes would be acting unlawfully. However, the Court of Appeal was absolutely clear (and was backed up by the Lords and then the ECHR) that no doctor could be compelled to provide treatment to a patient lacking capacity if the doctor felt was it was futile or not in the patient's best interests. Margaret Brazier has described the decision in *Burke* as 'a blow to patient autonomy and a victory for medical paternalism'.[26]

It is therefore clear that the introduction of the HRA *should* have had a profound impact on this area of law, given that it implements Articles of a convention protecting a right to life, a right to freedom from torture and inhuman treatment and a right to conduct our private lives in any way we choose. However, this expected impact has not materialised. This may be partly due to the fact that the courts are reluctant to compel any medical practitioner to provide treatment where the doctor feels that it is not in the patient's best interests to do so – the ghost of *Bolam* rears its head again. Another possible reason for its limited impact is the issue of limited NHS resources. Whether it is right to take costs into account or not, the fact is that keeping a patient on a life support system or in a high-dependency bed receiving ANH is extremely expensive in terms of equipment and staffing and it may well be that this unstated consideration impacts on the court's approach to such applications.

Reform

One of the more convincing arguments for reform of the law to openly allow active forms of euthanasia and/or assisted suicide is that, currently, we allow some methods

---

[25] *Burke* v *UK* [2006] App 19807/06.
[26] Brazier, M. and Cave, E., *Medicine, Patients and the Law*, 4th edn, 2007, Penguin, p. 504.

of ending a patient's life, such as withdrawing ANH or giving life-threatening doses of painkillers, but we do not allow lethal injection. What is the justification for this distinction, especially when, as Emily Jackson has pointed out, lethal injection may offer a quicker and more painless death?[27] Various private members' bills and committees have proposed changes, including limited legalisation of euthanasia, over the years,[28] but all have failed to achieve sufficient support in Parliament and among the general public to become law. Most recently, MSP Margo MacDonald introduced her End of Life Assistance (Scotland) Bill to the Scottish Parliament in January 2010, but it was defeated (82.5% against to 15.5% in favour) in December of that year. It was reported in May 2011 that she intends to redraft the bill and reintroduce it in the near future. What all this demonstrates is that there is still reluctance among elected MPs and the general public to go down the road of legalising euthanasia and assisted suicide.

Summary

While there is never going to be a consensus among those with strong ethical or moral views on euthanasia, it appears to be more practical concerns that prevent Parliament from passing legislation to legalise the practice. Issues such as how to police a legal euthanasia and prevent its being carried out where relatives stand to gain from the death or where doctors are motivated largely by space, staffing or resources issues mean that firm steps towards legalisation are unlikely. Even the professional body advising doctors on such ethical issues, the BMA, has struggled to decide where it stands on this issue and, after adopting a neutral stance on legalisation of euthanasia and assisted suicide back in 2005, has since reconsidered and 'again opposes all forms of assisted dying'.[29] At the heart of the concerns is really an instinctive awareness of the intrinsic value of human life and an urge to protect it in most circumstances. However, those values may be further tested as society faces the issue of an ageing population and a developing science that can physically keep a person's body alive long after they would otherwise have died. Yet again, what is medically possible and what society considers ethically acceptable may have become rather out of step, leaving the law to tread a difficult and undesirable middle path.

---

[27] See Jackson, E., 'Whose Death Is It Anyway? Euthanasia and the Medical Profession', 2004, 57 CLP 415–42.
[28] See, for example, House of Lords Select Committee (Walton Committee) Report (HL Paper No. 21 1994, London), the Patient (Assisted Dying) Bill 2003 introduced by Lord Joffe and the House of Lords Select Committee (Mackay Committee) Report 2005.
[29] 'End of Life Decisions: Views of the BMA', August 2009, p. 4.

Self-test questions

1 What is the difference between 'euthanasia' and 'assisted suicide'?

2 In what circumstances may a doctor withdraw life-prolonging treatment from a patient who lacks capacity?

3 What was the legal effect of the decision in *Purdy* v *DPP*?

4 Does the practice of euthanasia infringe a person's human rights under the Convention?

5 What criminal charge will a person face if they assist somebody to commit suicide?

6 What is meant by the doctrine of double effect?

Practice essay question

McCall-Smith has said 'the current state of the law (on euthanasia) can be defended as the embodiment of a moral compromise which satisfies the needs of a delicately nuanced problem.' Discuss the extent to which you agree or disagree with this statement.

Practice problem question

Charlie, aged 58, lives with his mother Grace, aged 84. Grace is disabled and suffers from rheumatoid arthritis, for which she takes strong painkilling tablets. She is increasingly in pain, however, and her general health is poor. She has become increasingly depressed and both Grace and Charlie beg their GP, Dr Lucas, to 'do something'. Dr Lucas prescribes a higher than usual dose of painkiller and leaves the tablets with Charlie and Grace with instructions that since this is a much higher dose only one tablet should be taken a day, since an overdose could be fatal.

Two days later Grace is rushed to hospital unconscious, having had an overdose of the painkillers. She is treated and put on a ventilator, since she remains unconscious and unable to breathe unaided. She requires a nasogastric tube to fed and hydrate her. The prognosis is uncertain. Charlie is adamant that the ventilator be turned off since Grace would not have wanted to live like this. The care team accedes to his wishes and turns off the ventilator.

In fact, Grace starts to breathe on her own but remains unconscious and in a vegetative state. She continues to require a nasogastric tube in order to feed and hydrate her. Charlie continues to be adamant that Grace would not have wanted to live like this and that all treatment should cease.

Discuss the legal and ethical issues arising from this scenario.

12 End of life II: neonaticide

Introduction

Neonaticide is a form of euthanasia that relates to the practice of letting newborn babies die by not treating their ailments. It occurs mainly in two situations. The first is where a baby is born extremely prematurely and a decision needs to be made whether or not to attempt resuscitation given the very small chance of long-term survival. The other is where a baby is born with severe health problems that are incompatible with life. Here, a decision is made as to whether the child should be kept alive artificially and have numerous medical interventions with very little hope of improving her condition. Strictly speaking, neonatal death is a term used in the medical profession to describe babies who die within 28 days of birth, although various dictionary definitions restrict it to the first 24 hours. This chapter is not too concerned about time limits but rather with the highly emotive issue of allowing babies to die, and in the course of exploring some of the law and ethics surrounding the practice, we will look at case law where such decisions have been made about older babies and children, as well as newborns.

Clearly, as well as the traditional ethical concerns over euthanasia in general, euthanasia that relates to babies and young children raises even more profound questions. These are arguably the most vulnerable members of society and those whom we, as adults, naturally feel strongly responsible for. Issues such as the rights of the parents, the role of the courts and statutory protection for children[1] make this a difficult area for medical practitioners and judges to navigate. As Morris has observed: 'The dilemmas raised by these babies encompass the limits of medical technology, professional ethics, parental responsibility and the role of the law in setting standards for society.'[2]

The aims of this chapter are:

- to recap the general legal rules relating to euthanasia
- to highlight the specific considerations when applying those legal rules to babies and young children

---

[1] Such as the Children Acts 1989 and 2004.
[2] Morris, A., 'Selective Treatment of Irreversibly Impaired Infants: Decision Making at the Threshold', Med L Rev, 2009, 17(3), 347–376 at 348.

- to examine the case law to try to identify coherent threads and principles by which the law is applied

- to explore some of the ethical arguments surrounding neonaticide.

General legal rules

As we saw in Chapter 11, in which euthanasia in relation to adults was discussed, a deliberate act to kill will be a criminal offence, whether committed by a relative or a medical professional.[3] As before, this is subject to the doctrine of double effect (see p. 204), and intent (i.e. the fact that the person is motivated by compassion) will be irrelevant.

An omission to act will only be unlawful if the person has a duty to act. In other words, if a doctor is breaching his duty of care by failing to act, this can be unlawful, but if it is deemed to be in the patient's best interests for treatment to be withheld or withdrawn, then there is no breach of duty.[4] This is known as passive involuntary euthanasia and it is this form that will be discussed in relation to babies during the rest of this chapter. Remember, too, that the rules make no distinction between 'withholding' and 'withdrawing', but as discussed in Chapter 11, the practice of withdrawing treatment very often involves some form of a positive act such as turning off a life support machine or removing a feeding tube and the lines between active and passive euthanasia become extremely blurred. The Royal College of Paediatricians states in its guidance to doctors that 'ethically the withholding and the withdrawal of life sustaining treatment are equivalent but emotionally they are sometimes poles apart'.[5]

The key to applying the law will be the concept of best interests, but this is at best an ill-defined and inexact legal test, made all the more difficult in the case of children owing to the fact that there can be many other stakeholders in the decision.

Specific issues in neonaticide

Consider the following quotation from a judge giving directions to a jury in a neonaticide case in 1981:

> Where a child gets pneumonia and is a child with an irreversible handicap whose mother has rejected him, if the doctor says I am not going to give it antibiotics and by a merciful dispensation of providence he dies . . . it would be very unlikely . . . that you would say that the doctor was committing murder.[6]

[3] *R v Cox* (1992) 12 BMLR 38.
[4] *Airedale NHS Trust v Bland* [1993] AC 789.
[5] *Withdrawing or Withholding Life-sustaining Treatment in Children: A Framework for Practice*, 2nd edn, 2004, Royal College of Paediatrics and Child Health, at p. 13.
[6] *R v Arthur* (1981) 12 BMLR 1.

What this quotation demonstrates very clearly is the close relationship between the assessment of what is in a child's best interests (i.e. when should a doctor be under a duty to treat the child) and society's current view regarding the particular condition of the child. Thirty years ago, a child born with Down's syndrome (as was the case in R v *Arthur*) was considered to be facing an extremely difficult life and the kind of facilities, support and assistance for families that have become the norm today were simply not available. It was against that backdrop of social intolerance and practical difficulty that the decision was made. Many commentators, such as Emily Jackson, have argued forcefully that R v *Arthur* is consigned to the history books and is of no value as a precedent[7] and they are probably correct, but it nevertheless raises interesting questions about the interplay between the views of wider society and the decisions that are made in the courtroom.

ETHICS QUESTION

Should the views of society play a part in the decision-making process, either expressly or impliedly? On the one hand, it could be argued that judges are applying the law on behalf of us all and are often criticised for being out of touch and not representative of society, so they should take into account the views of the average person in these issues. On the other hand, public opinion is notoriously fickle and, one could argue, uninformed. It can be swayed by many things, such as personal experience, politics, economic concerns, media exposure etc. and the courtroom is supposed to be a place in which an issue can be examined away from all those other influences in an objective way.

Before examining further case law in detail, it should be noted that the specific issues relating to the withdrawal or withholding of treatment from children have been addressed in a very influential guidance document issued by the Royal College of Paediatrics and Child Health in 2004.[8] The introduction to this guidance sums up the problems facing doctors in these cases very well by observing that: 'Sometimes it is necessary to come to the conclusion that for an individual child . . . the more humane path is one of palliation rather than a continuation of life saving treatment. To so resolve is profoundly difficult, challenging the doctor and all members of the healthcare team with issues of conscience and internal conflicts. Nevertheless, our professional responsibilities do not allow us to walk away from such difficulties.'

It is true that while books such as this can endlessly debate the rights and wrongs of neonaticide and the suitability of the various legal rules that apply, it is doctors

---

[7] For example see Jackson, E., *Medical Law*, 2nd edn, 2010, Oxford University Press, at p. 974 and Pattinson, S.D., *Medical Law and Ethics*, 2nd edn, 2009, Sweet & Maxwell, p. 544.

[8] See n. 5 above.

Table 12.1 Situations in which it may be possible to withdraw/withhold treatment

Scenario	Explanation
The brain dead child	Here the child is medically termed to be brain dead, meaning there is no detectable brain stem function. Such a situation is wholly incompatible with life and there is no hope of recovery
The PVS child	A child who is in persistent vegetative state (PVS) will have some brain stem function in that breathing and circulatory function may continue to be present, but he is not considered to have any form of consciousness and the likelihood of recovery is very slim
The no-chance situation	This is explained in the guidance as a child who is so ill that treatment 'simply delays death without significant alleviation of suffering. Such treatment is inappropriate'
The no-purpose situation	In this case, treatment may actually keep the child alive but the degree of impairment if he does survive would be so great that it is unreasonable to expect the child to bear it
The unbearable situation	Here a child has a progressive and irreversible illness. Further treatment is more than can be borne, even if it may be of some benefit.

and other health professionals who have to face the situation directly and make decisions one way or another. In recognition of this, the guidance sets out five situations in which it may be permissible to withdraw or withhold life-saving treatment (see Table 12.1).

These scenarios are aimed at clarifying for doctors the sorts of situation in which it may be permissible to withhold or withdraw treatment but they are not without criticism. As Morris notes: 'The guidelines are to be commended for striving for transparency and certainty but they do not represent a complete solution.'[9] For example, in 2004 when the guidelines were drawn up, doctors were very sure that where they diagnosed PVS in a patient that patient had no conscious awareness. However, recent studies have alarmingly found that patients diagnosed for many years with PVS were, in some instances, able to communicate in basic ways with the researchers, such as activating particular parts of their brain when asked to imagine themselves playing tennis. It has been estimated that in up 40% of cases, PVS may actually be a misdiagnosis and this leads to huge concerns about authorising withdrawal of treatment.[10] The final two situations also pose significant questions. They talk about its being 'unreasonable' to expect the child to bear the treatment or the disabilities that will be present afterwards and its being 'more than can be borne', but who should decide that this is so? These are very individual concepts and what is unbearable to one person may well be tolerable to another. Also, the guidance provides that parents may refuse treatment 'irrespective of medical opinion that it may be of some benefit'. This may be the recommendation in the guidance but it does not, of course, represent the legal situation. If doctors feel that the parents are

[9] See n. 2 above at p. 351.
[10] For a good overview of these developments, see http://www.timesonline.co.uk/tol/life_and_style/health/article6930589.ece.

Table 12.2 Nuffield Council on Bioethics guidance

Gestation at birth	Recommendation
25 weeks and over	Intensive care should be provided unless the baby is affected by a 'severe abnormality incompatible with any significant period of survival'
Between 24 and 25 weeks	Intensive care should normally be provided unless doctors and parents agree that it is not appropriate in light of the baby's condition or likely condition
Between 23 and 24 weeks	Here the guidance recommends that precedence be given to the wishes of the parents but make it clear that doctors are not under a duty to provide intensive care where they judge it would be futile
Between 22 and 23 weeks	Resuscitation should only be carried out where parents request and doctors feel it is an exceptional case where it is in the child's best interests
Before 22 weeks	No baby should be resuscitated unless as part of a clinical research study approved by an appropriate research ethics committee

not acting in the best interests of the child, they can seek a declaration from the court allowing them to carry out the proposed treatment. Many of the cases we will look at later in the chapter arise out of such situations. For now, it is sufficient to note that there are key concerns about professional guidance giving doctors advice that does not represent the legal situation. The last thing needed in this already fraught legal and ethical issue is confusion among the profession about what they are and are not allowed to do.

Similarly, in relation to the resuscitation or otherwise of extremely premature infants, guidance has been produced by the Nuffield Council on Bioethics[11] to try to establish clear principles and transparent practices in this area. The guidance provides that certain approaches should be taken in relation to infants of a certain gestational age (see Table 12.2).

Again, these guidelines are to be welcomed as an attempt to provide transparent advice and general principles, but do not in any way solve individual dilemmas for doctors or parents. For example, they provide that parents may decline intensive care for their baby, but may not insist on it. Is this fair? Is it ethical?

ETHICS QUESTION

Should a baby born after 24 weeks (the point at which they are defined as viable and at which abortion on the 'social' ground is prohibited) have treatment withheld or withdrawn because they are 'likely' to have a particular condition or disability if they survive? Should this not have to be proved before treatment is withdrawn? What if the diagnosis is not accurate? What if it is accurate? Does that person have less right to life under Article 2 than a healthy infant? Are we practising eugenics?

---

[11] 'Critical Care Decisions in Fetal and Neonatal Medicine: Ethical Issues', 2006, available at http://www.nuffieldbioethics.org/neonatal-medicine.

These guidelines also talk about treatment being 'futile'. This can mean that no amount of treatment or resuscitation is going to allow the child to survive (physiological futility) and this would be the case in the first situation in the RCPCH guidance as well. However, it can also mean that the life of the child can be saved but that the level of disability or damage that the child would have to live with makes it futile to treat (qualitative futility), which is a very different concept involving quality judgments about the value to be placed on the life of the child. Morris sums up the problem of parental involvement in such decisions by stating: 'An opinion on qualitative futility is arguably a matter on which, in the case of an infant, properly informed parents have equal or even greater claim in decision making.'[12] Nevertheless, as far as the law is concerned, parents can be overruled by the doctors and the court.

Case law

We mentioned the case of *Re Arthur* earlier,[13] where a child with Down's syndrome had been prescribed nursing care only by Dr Arthur and he was acquitted of charges of murder. Although this was accused of being a case specific to its time, it should be noted that there was another case in the same year, *Re B*, where a baby born with Down's syndrome developed an intestinal blockage and doctors had to decide whether to operate.[14] With treatment, his life expectancy was 20–30 years but the parents did not want treatment to be provided. At the High Court, it was held that if the parents wished the child to be allowed to die and his quality of life was going to be very poor, it was in his best interests to be allowed to die. The High Court decision very much reflects the attitudes demonstrated in *R v Arthur*. However, in *Re B*, the decision was overturned by the Court of Appeal. In consideration of the assessment of 'best interests', Lord Templeman reminded the court that the focus must be on the best interests of the child, not the parents, and urged doctors to focus on whether the life of the child was 'demonstrably going to be so awful that in effect the child must be condemned to die?'.[15] So was this to be the test for best interests? Whether the question formulated by Lord Templeman was a formulation of the best interests test or simply another question to consider in such cases was debated for years after the case was decided. However, it was not substantially addressed again until the important case of *Re J*.

---

[12] See n. 2 above at p. 358.
[13] See n. 6 above.
[14] *Re B* [1981] 1 WLR 1421.
[15] See n. 13 above at 22.

KEY CASE

Re J [1991] Fam 33 AC

J was a severely premature infant with multiple serious health problems, including severe brain damage. He was not expected to survive very long regardless of what treatment was offered and was likely to become spastic quadriplegic, without sight, hearing, or speech before he died. If he stopped breathing or had some sort of turn for the worse, doctors did not want to be obliged to provide intensive care or resuscitation, but the parents wanted everything possible done to keep him alive. Doctors therefore sought a declaration from the court that it would be lawful for them not to provide such treatment.

The court ultimately decided that the doctors were right and it was not in J's best interests to have invasive and aggressive resuscitation treatment. Taylor J took the opportunity to clarify the law as he understood it, setting out three key principles:

1 The court's prime and paramount consideration must be the best interests of the child.

2 The court's high respect for the sanctity of human life imposes a strong presumption in favour of taking all steps capable of preserving it save in exceptional circumstances.

3 The court never sanctions steps to terminate life. That would be unlawful.

He went on to state that in relation to deciding what is in the child's best interests: 'The test must be whether to that child in question . . . life would be intolerable.'

This is a helpful clarification as it makes it clear that the test of intolerability is individual to each child. However, it is arguable that there was a big gulf between the rhetoric in this case and the actual decision as J was largely unaware of his condition and had never known anything else. Can it really be said that to him, his life was intolerable? We will never know.

One of the issues raised by the case of *Re J* is that of how wide the concept of best interests is. If it is merely a matter of medical best interests, then clearly doctors will usually be best placed to make that assessment. However, if it is broader and individual to the child, encompassing issues such as family relationships, home circumstances, level of awareness, pleasure experienced in things etc., it is arguable that others are equally well placed to make that assessment. As Kennedy has noted: 'Just because a doctor says it, does not make it a "medical" opinion which cannot be challenged'.[16]

The question of how far the courts will take into account the views of the parents and indeed, how far they should take them into account was highlighted in the case

[16] Kennedy, I., *The Unmasking of Medicine*, 1981, Allen & Unwin.

of Charlotte Wyatt, who was born very prematurely at 26 weeks' gestation.[17] She had never left hospital and was suffering from profound brain damage which left her blind, deaf and incapable of movement. She also had chronic respiratory and kidney problems. Doctors were fairly sure that she experienced pain but were doubtful whether she experienced any pleasure. However, the parents were convinced that she did experience pleasure and recounted that she responded to them and to various stimulation. They wanted all steps taken to keep her alive in all circumstances, partly because of this perceived pleasure that they felt she experienced and partly because of their deeply held religious views that God would provide a miracle. Doctors argued that to ventilate her should she experience respiratory failure would result in 'increased suffering for no commensurate benefit'. The case is interesting because it addressed the issue of the best interests test. Hedley J made it clear that: 'It is in my view essential that the concept of intolerable to that child should not be seen as a gloss on, much less a supplementary test to, best interests. It is a valuable guide in the search for best interests in this kind of case.'[18] This was confirmed in the Court of Appeal, where the ruling in *Re J* was affirmed. A declaration was granted that if Charlotte experienced respiratory failure, it would be lawful for doctors not to resuscitate her.

By way of context, there were numerous cases in this litigation as various appeals and counter appeals were brought before the court and the situation was kept under review in light of Charlotte's fluctuating health status. In one of the later appeals, the court made it clear that these declarations were permissive but not prescriptive and: 'At the moment the decision arises to be taken the medical authorities are required to use their best judgment in Charlotte's best interests as to whether they desist (intubation or ventilation).'[19]

Although this case was useful in terms of clarifying the court's view of the best interests test, subsequent events make the inherent dangers in making these sorts of judgments all too clear. By 2007 Charlotte had improved sufficiently to be released from hospital, was learning to walk and talk and had begun to attend nursery. Although still severely disabled, she went on to have a life of some significant value. Had she been unfortunate enough to have experienced respiratory failure during 2004 or 2005, her life would have been assessed as not worth saving. I would imagine that Charlotte and her family would today take issue with that.

All the case law we have discussed so far has tried to elucidate the concept of best interests and the idea of intolerability in a coherent fashion. However, it was a powerful House of Lords judgment in *Re A*, the Siamese twins case, that really addressed these issues and refused to allow them to be fudged.

[17] [2005] EWCA Civ 1181.
[18] [2004] EWHC 2247.
[19] [2006] EWHC 319.

KEY CASE

Re A (Children) (Conjoined Twins: Surgical Separation) [2001] Fam 147

Jodie and Mary were conjoined twins born to a Maltese couple in a Manchester hospital on 8 August 2000. The parents had travelled to the UK for the birth after scans revealed the problem with the twins. The degree and nature of their condition is demonstrated in Figure 12.1. Effectively, they shared many vital organs, with Jodie, the stronger twin, breathing for both of them. Her heart was providing oxygenated blood to both her and Mary. Their spines were fused. Jodie was mentally alert to the same degree as any newborn. Mary's mental state was difficult to assess. She was reported to have opened one eye and moved her limbs. Doctors wished to perform a surgical separation as they believed Jodie had a strong chance of surviving once she no longer had the strain of supporting Mary. However, the operation would be carried out on both twins and once they were separated, Mary would immediately die as she had no way of existing independently from her sister. The medical prognosis was that if they were not separated, they would both die as Jodie's system would not be able to support them both as they grew. The parents refused to consent.

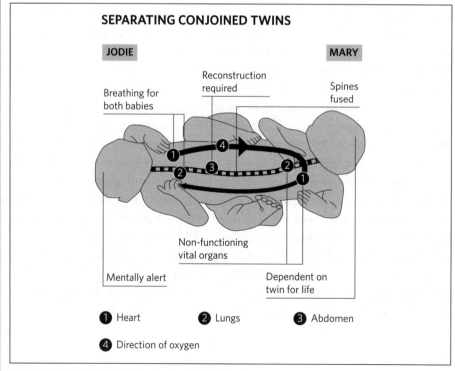

Figure 12.1 Conjoined twins in *Re A (Children)*

The Court of Appeal granted a declaration that the doctors would not be acting unlawfully if they operated without the parents' consent as to do so was in the best interests of the children. Their reasoning in relation to Jodie was fairly clear as she had a good chance of survival with a good quality of life after the operation but it was less clear how they had reached the conclusion that separation was in Mary's best interests. Had they applied the tolerability test? What they said in the judgment was that they felt it was in Mary's best interests because she would die anyway, even without the surgery, but that she would suffer more pain as Jodie became stronger and began to move around.

The case was appealed to the House of Lords. While upholding the decision and granting the declaration, the Lords roundly condemned the reasoning of the Court of Appeal in relation to Mary and her best interests, with Ward LJ asking at the outset: 'Persuade me I can kill Mary.' The Lords made it clear that this would be an act, rather than an omission, and there was clearly no issue of double effect regarding Mary, as the primary intent was not to alleviate her suffering. However, it would not be an offence because the primary intention was not to kill Mary but to save Jodie. Crucially, they made it quite clear that the separation was not in the best interests of both twins, it was only in the best interests of Jodie. The Court of Appeal had been wrong to conclude that it was in Mary's best interests to die and the Lords insisted that they needed to look at the conflicting interests and weigh up which should take precedence. They held that Jodie's best interests outweighed Mary's because Jodie had a chance of survival. Ward LJ described the conclusion of the court as 'the lesser of two evils' and as 'the least detrimental choice'.[20] The twins were separated not long after the judgment. As expected Mary died almost immediately but Jodie went on to make a good recovery and returned to Malta a short time later with her parents.

The case raises profound legal and ethical issues. Leaving Jodie aside, the court in this case permitted doctors to carry out a positive act that it expressly recognised was not in Mary's best interests, against the wishes of the parents. This departs from all the previous case law on this issue. It also questions the very heart of our value for human life and our right to end what we perceive to be a life of less value. As Archbishop Cormac Murphy-O'Connor, head of the Catholic Church in England and Wales at the time, stated: 'There is a fundamental moral principle at stake. No one can commit a wrong action that good will come of it.' However, the question must be asked, had they chosen to side with the parents and ruled that the separation would be unlawful, leading to the death of both Mary and Jodie, would that have been ethical? As Ward LJ remarked in the case, it would have been equally legitimate to do nothing.

[20] *Re A (Children) (Conjoined Twins: Surgical Separation)* [2001] Fam 147 at 203.

Summary

This chapter has looked at some profound ethical and moral issues, as well as a legal framework that, at best, lacks coherence and consistency. Many have been very critical of the law, especially the *Re A* case, asserting that effectively judges are making up this area of law as they go along and departing from established principles in order to come to the conclusion they feel is appropriate.[21] However, to be fair to judges, it may well be that this is an area in which it is simply not possible to have hard and fast legal rules dictating when and if acts or omissions are justified. The *Re A* case has been described by some as 'unique' in an attempt to justify the creative reasoning adopted by the court, but surely each of the cases referred to in this chapter could be so described. Each child, family, medical prognosis and development of disease or disability is unique. Each judge who has to decide the issue will come to the case with a predetermined set of beliefs and values that will shape her approach to the case. No prognosis is 100% accurate and doctors, being human, will continue to sometimes get things wrong, as, of course, will judges. However, the fascinating thing about medical law is that these are the people to whom the decisions ultimately fall, for better or worse. Perhaps the best we can hope for is an open, honest and accessible judgment in each case, achieving an outcome that can legitimately be described as being in the best interests of the child.

Self-test questions

1 To what does the term 'neonaticide' refer?
2 To what extent do the normal rules on euthanasia apply to babies and young children?
3 What is the significance today of the *R v Arthur* case?
4 What arguments would a utilitarian stance on the ethics of neonaticide put forward?
5 Should there be different legal considerations when dealing with euthanasia in relation to adults and children?
6 Explain the difference between the Court of Appeal reasoning and the House of Lords reasoning in the *Re A* case.

Practice essay question

'While some parents will want doctors to do everything possible to keep their baby alive, others who discover at birth that their baby is severely disabled may be perplexed by suggestions that their newborn baby must now be subjected to aggressive measures to keep him alive' (Brazier, M., *Medicine, Patients and the Law*, 4th edn, Penguin, at p. 377).

---

[21] For example, see Pattinson, S. D., *Medical Law and Ethics*, 2nd edn, 2009, Sweet & Maxwell, pp. 548–550.

Critically assess this statement with reference to the rights of parents and medical professionals to make decisions about withdrawing treatment from a newborn child that will result in the child's death.

Practice problem question

Victoria and James have just had their first baby, Laura, who has been born very premature with brain damage. Although this is likely to cause her severe physical and mental disabilities, the full extent of the impact of these disabilities will not become clear for some months, as the full impact on Laura's development can be assessed. Victoria and James are very upset. In particular, Victoria says that they would never have had a baby had they known that the baby was going to be handicapped. Both Victoria and James have demanding jobs and both planned to work full time as soon as possible after Laura's birth. They are now concerned that they will simply not be able to cope with Laura.

Laura becomes very poorly with an infection that affects her ability to breathe and she has to be ventilated. Victoria and James tell the care team that they do not want 'invasive measures' taken to keep Laura alive and that they want the ventilator turned off.

Advise the care team of the legal and ethical considerations involved in continuing to treat Laura.

13 End of life III: organ donation

Introduction

In this chapter, we will move on to look at the law relating to use of body parts after a person is deceased, although we also touch on the issue of living organ donation. One may assume that once the patient is dead, the legal and ethical issues become simpler and more clear cut, but in fact, the opposite is true. While issues such as euthanasia, affecting those who are still alive but either approaching or requesting death, dominate the political agenda, relatively little attention has traditionally been paid to post mortem issues such as organ donation. What focus it has received in recent years is due in large part to scandals during the 1990s where organs were found to have been retained from deceased patients (often children) without appropriate consent.[1] This lack of attention has resulted in a very complex and confusing area of law, with even basic questions such as whether there is property in a dead body, and if so, who owns that property, yet to be definitively resolved. Issues of consent have also been poorly addressed. The Human Tissue Act 2004, rushed through in an attempt to calm the storm over the organ retention scandals of the 1990s, is a hastily drafted and inexact piece of legislation. It contains vague wording that leaves medical professionals and researchers unsure of the legal position and having to fill in the gaps in order to deal with patients and bereaved relatives sensitively, while maximising the use that can be made of donated tissues and organs. Of course, behind the legal debate rage numerous ethical dilemmas. Should people be forced to donate their organs because of the good that can be done with them? Should religious objections be valid? Should the state own your body after death? Is it ethical to bury or burn organs that could save lives? Should each person have the right to dictate what happens to his body, even after death? As Brazier and McGuinness have observed:

> In the hyper-medicalized west, death, like many other life events, has become a medical event, more so when it occurs in a busy hospital setting. Death is feared and medically heroic efforts may be taken to avoid it. Thus the use of bodies of the recently dead, through organ or tissue donation, represents a point of collision between life and death.[2]

---

[1] Ref Alder Hey and Bristol reports.
[2] McGuinness, S. and Brazier, M., 'Respecting the Living means Respecting the Dead too', *O J L S*, 2008, 28(2), 297–316 at p. 306.

The aims of this chapter are:

- to look at the background facts and statistics in relation to organ donation
- to examine the legal framework relating to living and deceased donation
- to discuss the ethical implications of the current system and other proposed systems.

Facts and statistics

Organs can be harvested from either living donors or deceased donors and the rules governing the process differ depending on the type of donor. Organs from living and healthy donors are generally more successful and are usually directed to a specific person. Often if someone wishes to donate an organ, such as a kidney to a loved one, but they are not a tissue match, they enter into what is known as a 'pooled' or 'paired' transplant. This involves patients being matched up with another patient who has a relative willing to donate and who is a tissue match. With deceased donors, organs will either come from a non-heart-beating donor (NHBD) or a heart-beating donor, where brain stem death has been diagnosed but mechanical ventilation is still ongoing. Organs from heart-beating donors are usually in better condition, but there has been controversy over the practice of beginning or continuing ventilation for the benefit of the organs where there is no hope of the patient recovering (see later for further discussion).

It has been estimated that while 70% of the general public are in favour of organ donation after death, only around 30% carry a donor card.[3] This illustrates the key problem. A general acceptance of donation as the 'right thing to do' needs to translate into positive steps to give consent to the use of organs after death and this is a step that far too many people do not take. There is evidence that donor numbers are slowly increasing, especially with the launch of the organ donor register, but the disparity between the number of donors and the number of people on the waiting list is still vast. In 2010–2011, there were 1010 deceased donors from whom organs were taken and 1034 living donors. That resulted in 3733 transplant operations, which at first glance seems positive, but contrast this with the transplant waiting list figures which indicated that, at the end of March 2011, there were 7797 people on the list awaiting transplants.[4]

There are various reasons for the steady increase in the need for transplants, such as:

---

[3] Jackson p. 694.
[4] See http://www.uktransplant.org.uk/ukt/statistics/downloads/stats_170611.pdf.

- *Improving transplant techniques* – it is becoming a more advantageous option for more patients as the science and the techniques improve. Around 90% of kidneys transplanted into patients are still functioning well one year after the surgery.[5]

- *Costs benefits* – to keep a patient on kidney dialysis for one year costs over £30,000. For around £17,000 that patient could be provided with a transplant and all the associated drugs and that new kidney could last many years. It is estimated that if every patient on the waiting list for a new kidney actually received one, it would save the NHS over £150 million.

- *Ageing population* – as people live longer the chance of one or more organs wearing out and needing to be replaced are increased.

- *Lifespan of transplanted material* – as people live longer and as transplants are more effective, more patients are living longer than the lifespan of their transplanted organ, necessitating a further transplant years after the original operation.

The stark reality is that while the need for organs is at an all time high, the supply continues to fail to meet that demand and at least one person dies each day waiting for a transplant. Reasons for the shortage include:

- There are fewer organs available from cadavers due to the fact that there are fewer accidental deaths – for example, the introduction of compulsory seatbelts dramatically reduced the number of deaths in car accidents.

- There is a shortage of appropriately trained and skilled surgeons in the UK – this is a somewhat circular problem as the small numbers of transplants that are carried out here lead to those with an interest in such surgery often travelling elsewhere to work.

- Issues of consent – either a lack of clarity about what consent is valid, whether the donor had previously consented at all or a conflict with the wishes of the family.

- Failure in the use of timely brain stem testing – if this were done earlier, a determination of brain death could be made when the organs are still viable.

Some of these issues will be picked up in more detail later in the chapter when the legal provisions are discussed. Because of this great disparity between supply and demand, the focus of law reform in this area continues to be focused on increasing the number of organs available for transplant. However, as Pattinson points out: 'The scarcity of human organs is causing preventable death and suffering. Every year many are buried or cremated when their organs could save lives. Every year, many suffer or die on waiting lists. This invites moral concern, but so do the alternatives.'[6]

---

[5] http://www.organdonation.nhs.uk/ukt/about_transplants/success_rates/success_rates.jsp.
[6] Pattinson, S. D., *Medical Law and Ethics*, 2nd edn, 2009, Sweet & Maxwell, p. 418.

The legal framework

◼ Introduction to the Human Tissue Act

The Human Tissue Act 2004 (the 'Act') came into force in September 2006 and replaced the 1961 Act of the same name and the Human Organs and Transplants Act 1989. It created the Human Tissue Authority (HTA) to oversee both living and deceased organ donation, to issue licences, inspect licensed facilities and issue statutory codes of practice and other guidance.[7]

The Act covers the *retention* and *use* of body parts, organs and tissues from both living and deceased donors. It also covers the *removal* of such materials from a deceased donor. However, strangely it does not cover the removal of such materials from a living donor, so that continues to be governed by common law principles (which will be discussed in more detail later). It also specifically excludes certain materials such as cell lines, hair and nails from the living (those from the deceased will be covered) and live gametes and embryos (because they are governed by the Human Fertilisation and Embryology Act 2008 – see Chapter 8).

◼ Consent

Consent is the fundamental principle around which the Act is framed. As discussed already, its primary focus is to reassure the public that no organs or tissues can now be retained or used without appropriate consent. Indeed, the Code of Practice clearly states that 'obtaining consent is the first mandatory step'.[8]

Dealing first with consent in relation to organ donation from deceased patients, the Act essentially requires consent to have been obtained from either:

- the deceased patient before death
- a nominated representative
- a qualifying relative.[9]

When a medical professional is faced with a recently deceased patient who is a potential organ donor, the most important issue she will have to address is whether or not that person has consented or refused to donate. Such a decision must have been in force immediately before he died. If such a decision can be shown to have been made, for example, by the fact that he carried a donor card, was on the donor register or by the fact that his wishes were written into a will or other document, then that decision is binding. If the person consented, doctors may lawfully proceed

---

[7] Human Tissue Act 2004 section 2.
[8] HTA Code of Practice 1 – Consent, 2009, p. 15.
[9] Sections 2–4 Human Tissue Act 2004.

to harvest his organs, whereas if he refused, then to proceed would be unlawful.[10] Of course, any such consent is subject to the normal legal rules covered in detail in Chapter 5. The patient must have had full mental capacity to make the decision at the time that it was made, as assessed using the test set out in the MCA 2005, and must not have been coerced.

If the deceased has not made a decision one way or the other prior to death, then the doctor must find out whether the patient ever appointed a nominated person to consent or refuse on his behalf. This cannot simply be someone appointed under an ordinary LPA or a court deputy who is looking after their affairs while they are alive. Rather, there must have been an express appointment of them as a nominated person for the purpose of the act to make a decision in relation to organ and tissue donation.[11] The problem with this provision is lack of awareness. How many people reading this chapter will have previously known that such a provision existed or thought about appointing a person to make organ donation decisions after their death? It is argued that this will be of very limited use. Arguably the only situation in which it could prove useful is where a person knows that his family members have very different views from him on the subject of organ donation and wants to make sure that someone else has the legal power to make the decision.

Finally, if there is no nominated person, the doctor must fall back on trying to obtain consent from someone in a qualifying relationship with the deceased. Section 27 of the Act sets out the list of qualifying relatives in order of priority. They are:

- spouse/partner
- parent/child
- brother/sister
- grandparent
- nephew/niece
- stepparent
- half-sibling
- friend of long standing.

Several problems with this list are immediately evident. First, what happens if there are two relatives on the same level: for example, a brother and a sister, or, more awkwardly, a spouse from whom the patient is separated but not divorced and a new partner and they disagree over whether or not to give consent? The HTA has said that consent from anyone on that level will suffice, but on a practical level, if doctors are faced with a situation where a bereaved relative of equal rank has strong

---

[10] See section 3(6)(a).
[11] See section 3(6)(b) and section 4.

objections, are they really going to proceed and take the organ? In actual fact, the concept of 'partner' is not defined in the Act. How long does someone have to have been in a relationship before they can be a 'partner'? Second, while grandparents rank fairly high up the list, apparently a grandchild can never give consent to their grandparent's organs being used as they are not on the list at all. Yet surely it is going to more frequently be the case that an elderly person is in a position to be a donor and an adult grandchild may well be the next of kin? No explanation for the omission has been put forward.

Don is seriously injured in a road traffic accident and dies. His kidneys and liver can be transplanted. He leaves a wife, Jane, two adult daughters, Meg and Carol, and a mother, Mary. From whom should the doctors obtain consent?

There will be several options.

1 If Don is on the organ donor register or carries a donor card then doctors can legally proceed to harvest the organs regardless of any objections raised by any of the relatives. Of course, there is a question mark as to whether doctors actually do proceed in the face of extreme objections from the family.

2 If there is no legal consent in place from Don immediately prior to death, is anyone appointed as a nominated person?

3 If not, then the first person on the list of qualifying relatives would be Jane.

4 If Jane could not make the decision for some reason, for example she lacked the necessary mental capacity, then consent could be sought from either Meg, Carol or Mary as they are all on the same level in the list. If one or more of them objected, then legally doctors could proceed with consent from any one of them, but again, realistically, while objections cannot invalidate a consent, in practice, it may be enough to prevent the organs from being harvested.

In relation to a deceased child, the consent provisions are similar, subject to the normal legal rules governing consent in relation to children. The child may consent if they have capacity to do so (either by being *Gillick* competent if under 16 or by passing the tests in the MCA if aged 16 or 17 – see Chapter 6). If not, then they could not have appointed a nominated person, so instead, the second category relates to persons who have parental responsibility (PR) for the child. This is usually the parents although not always: for example, where a child is in care, PR will rest with the local authority. Finally, in the unlikely event that consent cannot be obtained from someone with PR, perhaps because the parents cannot be contacted or do not have capacity, then it can be sought from someone in the list of qualifying relatives.

With living donors, similar consent provisions apply, but with the additional requirement that a panel of at least three members of the HTA approve the donation.[12] There is also the proviso that where someone else is making the decision, for example a person with PR for a child or a donee of an LPA where an adult lacks capacity, the decision that is made must be in the patient's best interests.[13] Thus, an adult of full capacity can decide to donate a kidney or some bone marrow, even though it is risky for them, purely for the benefit of someone else, but a child or a person lacking capacity can only donate if it is in their best interests to do so. Clearly it will almost never be in their medical best interests to undergo unnecessary surgery, but the court has made it clear in many cases that the concept of best interests extends beyond medical issues to social and emotional considerations. For example, in *Re Y*,[14] a young woman lacking mental capacity was a tissue match for her terminally ill sister who required a bone marrow transplant. The court held that because Y relied very heavily on her relationship with her mother and because her mother would be devastated if the sister died, this would have a negative impact on Y. As such, the court ruled that it was in her best interests to donate her bone marrow to her sister.

In addition to the consent requirements detailed earlier, the following requirements must be met in relation to *capable* donors:

- the donor's consultant must refer the matter to the HTA
- an independent assessor must meet the donor and the recipient
- the assessor must produce a report confirming whether the requirements are met
- the HTA must approve the transplant
- the transplant must take place within six months of the HTA approval, otherwise the whole process must be gone through again
- the transplant must be reported to the Department of Health.

Where the donor is *incapable*, not only must the HTA approve the transplant but a court order must also be obtained.[15]

Payment

Currently, no payment may be offered or received for the donation of organs or tissues.[16] However, this is not the case worldwide and many desperate patients have resorted to travelling abroad to buy organs. Between 1997 and 2002, organs worth over £19.4 million were trafficked in India alone.[17] In 1999, an eBay advertisement for a kidney attracted a bid of $5.7 million. Deaths as a result of transplants carried

---

[12] See section 33 HT Act 2004.
[13] See *Re A* in relation to children and MCA sections 4 and 5 in relation to over-16s.
[14] Ref case.
[15] See HT Act 2004 (Persons Who Lack Capacity to Consent and Transplants) Regulations 2006, regs 9–12.
[16] Section 32 HT Act 2004.
[17] CMO report 2006.

out in countries where payment is the norm are common and the Chief Medical Officer, in his 2006 report into organ donation, drew attention to the fact that when someone travels abroad and then suffers adverse consequences, it is often our NHS that picks up the pieces, at huge cost.

ETHICS QUESTIONS

Should we have a regulated system to allow payment to living organ donors and/or to the estates of deceased donors? Ethical concerns about exploitation and people taking unnecessary risks with their health due to financial strains are certainly valid. However, we allow women to donate their eggs for IVF treatment in another couple or for research and offer them half-price fertility treatment in return.[18] Is this not effectively paying a woman around £1500 for her eggs? The law allows several thousand pounds worth of 'expenses' to be paid to a surrogate for using her egg to create an embryo and then donating the resulting child to the commissioning couple. Is this not significantly more ethically concerning? Could it be argued that there is more of a moral imperative to save a life than to 'cure' infertility?

Conditional donation

Conditional donation relates to a situation where a person consents to the donation of their organ but directs that it must go to a particular person or type of person. It has always been a fundamental principle of the organ donation system that a donor may not direct where their organs may go after their death. While live donations are often directed, for example, to a relative or friend who is a tissue match, if a person carries a donor card or puts his name on the register, the organ will go into the system and will be allocated on the basis of greatest clinical need. However, there is nothing in the Act that specifies that this must be the case and there are many who argue that not only is conditional or directed donation legally permitted, it is desirable because it would increase the numbers of donors.

The concerns over conditional donation have been highlighted in two key situations. The first was in Sheffield during the 1990s, when a white male was fatally injured in a car crash and the relatives agreed to the use of his organs, but only on condition that they went to a white person.[19] The dilemma for the hospital was clear – should they accept the organ because of the drastic shortage and the fact that it would at least save someone, or should they refuse the organ on the basis of the fundamental principle of equality of access and difficulties in drawing the line? In the event, the hospital accepted the organ and used it to treat a white patient but could show that the recipient was the person in most clinical need and therefore

---

[18] See Chapter 6 for a detailed discussion.
[19] See http://news.bbc.co.uk/1/hi/health/387817.stm.

would have got the organ anyway. The question remains as to what would have happened had the person in most clinical need not been white. Arguably, they would not have had valid consent to use the organ.

A more recent example is that of Laura Ashworth. Her mother, Rachel Leake, needed a kidney transplant and Laura wished to donate one of her kidneys. However, Laura died in 2008 before she could begin the process of becoming a living donor. She carried a donor card and after her death, several organs, including her kidneys, were removed for transplant, but because she was a deceased donor, the organs had to go to the person in greatest clinical need. There was a great deal of press interest in the story and much criticism of the system for not allowing Laura's dying wish to help her mother to be fulfilled, but the HTA was adamant that the consent had been unconditional and that it was not ethical to allow conditional or directed donation. Rachel Leake died in 2009, while still on the waiting list for a kidney transplant.

In 2010 the government issued a policy document setting out the position in relation to deceased donor organs.[20] While generally reiterating the traditional position that donations must be unconditional and all patients on the waiting list must be treated equitably, it does acknowledge that there may be some limited situations where a request for specific allocation may be considered. One of those situations is where, as in the Rachel Leake case, the deceased donor was intending to be a living donor.

ETHICS QUESTIONS

Should conditional or directed donation be allowed? In the Rachel Leake case, it is easy to see why she felt it would be justified to have her daughter's kidney allocated to her, but it is also easy to see why many are concerned about going down a slippery slope to a situation such as the Sheffield case. If you allow deceased donors to include conditions in their consent, where is the line to be drawn? Will organs end up being wasted because there is no recipient who matches the donor's criteria? Would it be ethical to specify that your liver is not to be transplanted into an alcoholic or that your organs are not to be used to treat someone who is obese because there is less chance of the transplant being successful?

Elective ventilation

Where a patient is suspected to be brain dead or is in PVS and a decision has been taken that there is no hope of recovery, can ventilation be started or continued in order to maximise the quality of the organs in the event that consent is available for

---

[20] 'Requested Allocation of Deceased Donor Organs', available at http://www.dh.gov.uk/en/ Publicationsandstatistics/Publications/PublicationsPolicyAndGuidance/DH_114800.

donation? The legal rules on treatment of such patients while they are alive is discussed in detail elsewhere. In brief, any treatment that is carried out where the patient cannot consent for himself must be done in the patient's best interests. Clearly, in this situation, it may not be in the patient's best interests to continue to ventilate and doctors will be carrying out a battery if they proceed.[21] Thus, it is important with such patients to discuss organ donation with the family in a sensitive but timely fashion so that there is as short a time as possible between ceasing ventilation and harvesting the organs. With a patient who is actually brain dead, it is not necessary to act in their best interests, but then the issue arises as to who owns the body? Can anyone consent to continued ventilation of a body for the purposes of organ donation? Common law has long been clear that there is no property in a corpse unless some skill has been exercised over the body part or tissue (i.e. if a biopsy has been taken and fixed onto a slide it can constitute property) and even then, this caveat only applied for the purposes of theft.[22] Clearly, such skill has not been exercised on a body recently diagnosed as brain dead. The law has also not been keen to attribute interests to a dead person until very recently. For example, it was always the case that, although recommended by professional bodies as good practice, it was never a legal requirement to keep medical information about a deceased person confidential – there was no legal person to whom a duty of confidentiality could be owed. Doubt has been cast on that position, however, in the recent case of *Bluck*,[23] which raised the possibility of the legal duty continuing after death. Could a similar principle extend to best interests of a deceased person? A recent House of Lords report seems to indicate that this is a possibility.[24] It states that if a person has clearly stated their desire to donate organs, it should be recognised legally that it is in their best interests to facilitate donation through appropriate use of their organs prior to and immediately after death.[25]

ETHICS QUESTION

To put this into context, we return to the *Bland* case, where the court decided that artificial nutrition and hydration could be withdrawn as it was not in Anthony's best interests to continue treatment. He was in PVS but his heart was still beating and he was still breathing on his own. If he had expressed an interest previously to be an organ donor, the question would be whether artificial ventilation could be started just prior to or just after death in order to maximise the chances of the organs being successfully transplanted. Before death, on a strict reading of the case law, the answer would be ➡

[21] See *Airedale NHS Trust* v *Bland* [1993].
[22] *R* v *Kelly and Lindsey* [1999] QB 621.
[23] *Bluck* v *IC* (2007) 98 BMLR 1.
[24] House of Lords Select Committee Report of the European Union Committee, 'Increasing the Supply of Donor Organs Within the European Union', volume 1: HL Paper 123–1, 17th report of session 2007–08.
[25] Ibid. at paras 262 and 440.

no. If it was unlawful to continue to provide ANH, then surely it would be unlawful to ventilate? After death, there would be no property in the body and it would be unclear whether steps over and above those necessary to the removal of the organs could be taken. However, in light of the *Bluck* case and the House of Lords report, it seems that an assessment of best interests can sometimes include taking whatever steps may be necessary to fulfil the patient's desire to be an organ donor. Do you agree with this approach? Would it extend to cases where consent is given by a nominated person or a qualifying relative, rather than the deceased themselves? Arguably not.

One final thought – if we are going to respect the wishes of a person after death and even their confidentiality, should we also be respecting their autonomy after death and not ventilating unless there is specific consent for that? Can we pick and choose some rights to continue after death and others that do not?

It should be noted that certain countries, such as France, Spain and Sweden, do not permit non-heart-beating donors to be used because of the ethico-legal problems of ensuring sufficient oxygen supply to the organs after the heart stops beating.[26]

Summary

Organ donation is an unusual area of law in that there is little in the way of case law to guide us through the statutory rules and ethical dilemmas. This leaves many questions unexplored and leaves both the public and those working in the healthcare system very unclear about the legal requirements. It is also clear that because the drafting of the main statute in the area is sloppy and inexact, putting the legal provisions into practice requires loose interpretation and common sense adjustments. None of this makes for a coherent or consistent system and the way the law moves forward in the future will depend on whether, as a country, the decision is to take a more consequentialist approach that requires organs to be used for the greatest good, or whether we continue to hold autonomy to be the key principle in healthcare law.

Self-test questions

1 What is the HTA and what is its remit?
2 List all the people who can potentially consent to the removal of organs from a deceased adult.

---

[26] See Price, D., 'End of Life Treatment of Potential Organ Donors: Paradigm Shifts in Intensive and Emergency Care', *Med L Rev* 2011, 19(1), pp. 86–116.

3 Can organ transplants be carried out using child donors?

4 Can you donate organs to a specific person?

5 In what circumstances can a patient be ventilated in order to preserve the organs for transplant?

Practice essay question

Critically analyse the extent to which the law adequately protects the rights of family members to decide what should happen with the organs of their deceased relative.

Practice problem question

Jack, a publican aged 35 and in good health, was seriously injured in an accident at work, sustaining fractures and abdominal injuries. At the hospital it was decided that he needed immediate surgery. He survived the operation but died 48 hours later.

Advise the trust as to the legal and ethical issues involved in the following alternative scenarios:

1 Conscious and rational, Jack had told the ward sister that if 'anything happened to him' he wanted his kidneys to be used for the benefit of another patient. His partner of three months, Sue, objects to the transplant. She is a Jehovah's Witness and claims that Jack was baptised as a witness the week before his death. Witnesses require the burial of the body intact.

2 Jack said nothing about the donation of his organs before his death. Elise, Jack's stepdaughter, arrives at the hospital and states that Jack told her she was to act for him on his death and that Jack wanted his organs donated.

3 Jack again said nothing about what was to happen on his death. The trust has ascertained that Jack did not appoint a nominated representative. The following people have since made representations to the trust:

- Eve, Jack's estranged wife. Eve says she will consent to donate all Jack's organs on condition his heart is offered to her brother, Marcus, who is dying of cardiac disease. Should Jack's heart not be a tissue match for Marcus she insists that Marcus be given priority on the heart transplant waiting list.

- Sue, Jack's partner of three months. Sue objects to the transplant. She is a Jehovah's Witness and claims that Jack was baptised as a witness.

- Jack's daughters, Jess and Jodie. They want Jack's organs to be given to as many recipients as possible.

14 Medical research

Introduction

The conducting of medical research on human subjects is essential to the development of safe and effective treatments. Treatments that we now consider commonplace were once experimental and often controversial. Consider how big a leap of faith was necessary to carry out the first heart transplant.[1] Prior to 1978, how many people really believed that doctors could fertilise an egg in a test tube, implant it into a woman and have her deliver a live, healthy baby nine months later?[2] Many of the drugs that we now take routinely will once have been the subject of various types of medical research in order to ascertain, first, whether they actually have an effect against the complaint they are designed to treat and, second, whether and in what quantities they are safe for human beings to take. Despite the necessity of such research, it is inevitable that there will be side effects, inconveniences and sometimes pain, damage and distress caused by the application of experimental treatments. Does this mean that research should not be carried out on humans unless it is of therapeutic benefit to them as individuals? Should people be allowed to participate in such research purely for the benefit of others? How much information do they need before their consent to involvement can be considered valid and informed? Given the large-scale benefits to society as a whole of the research being carried out, is there a moral obligation to take part? Crucially, is research in the UK adequately regulated to protect the interests of individual participants whilst allowing and encouraging innovative research to be carried out? These are all complex legal and ethical questions and are ones that it could be argued that the UK has been slow to tackle head on. Regulation has almost crept in via European and international obligations, often resisted by scientists and medical researchers who were hitherto being governed by and answerable to their professional bodies (often made up of similarly qualified and like-minded individuals and generally supportive of research). Legal regulation has been seen among the scientific community as something of a threat and a potential restriction, but has in recent years been accepted as necessary. There is an acknowledged need to regain public confidence in

---

[1] The world's first human heart transplant was carried out by Christaan Barnard on a patient named Louis Washkansky in 1967.

[2] The first testtube baby, Louise Brown, was born on 25 July 1978 in Oldham, Greater Manchester.

the medical profession as a whole after scandals such as Alder Hey, Bristol Royal Infirmary[3] and Shipman,[4] but also because of high-profile difficulties with medical research, the most notable being the thalidomide tragedy in the 1960s and 1970s[5] and the more recent Northwick Park Hospital clinical trial which left six men fighting for their lives.

The aims of this chapter are:

- to explain and define the various types of medical research carried out in the UK
- to examine the system of regulation currently in place and link that with the various ethical arguments for and against carrying out medical research on human subjects
- to consider whether the current regulatory regime is being properly enforced and the sanctions available in the event of a breach.

It should be noted that this chapter assumes the reader is familiar with the concept of consent (set out in Chapter 6) and confidentiality of medical information (set out in Chapter 7). In addition, this chapter will not focus on research involving embryos as this has already been discussed in Chapter 8.

Types of medical research

One of the key distinctions made in the debate about the regulation of medical research is between therapeutic and non-therapeutic research. Broadly, therapeutic research is research that offers some therapeutic benefit to the person participating in the study, e.g. the testing of a new drug treatment for multiple sclerosis on a patient suffering from that disease who is likely to receive a health benefit by taking part in the research. This position can be contrasted with non-therapeutic research, where the drug or treatment being tested will be of no benefit to the person participating in the research. This author would argue that the name 'non-therapeutic research' is misleading as it suggests such research is somehow of less value. In fact, the research may well have huge benefits for persons other than those participating in the study, perhaps some time after the initial study is carried out. However, the terminology remains, not least because of concerns over what is known as the 'therapeutic mis-conception'. This is a phenomenon whereby patients often assume or convince themselves that participation in a research project will have a therapeutic benefit and this can induce them to consent. As Hewlett has observed:

---

[3] The retention of organs from babies and of other samples without appropriate consent was examined and investigated in the Report of the Royal Liverpool Children's Hospital Inquiry 2001 (the Redfern Report) and 'Learning from Bristol: the Report of the Public Inquiry into Children's Heart Surgery at the Bristol Royal Infirmary 1984–1995', Command Paper: CM 5207.

[4] Dr Harold Shipman was confirmed as having killed 218 of his patients over his career – for a full analysis, see the Inquiry's six reports, available at http://www.shipman-inquiry.org.uk/reports.asp.

[5] Thalidomide was regularly prescribed to pregnant women to combat morning sickness – only after many babies had been born disabled was it discovered that the drug caused developmental abnormalities to foetuses.

So strong is the trust in doctors that patients may agree to anything the doctor suggests and even the invitation to participate may be viewed as a recommendation rather than a request. Patients may feel flattered by the request and under an obligation to help because of past care received . . . patients may view clinical research as a means of access to care . . . and may also equate the frequent safety visits with improved care.[6]

As will be seen when the detail of the regulation is discussed, this distinction matters because different rules about consent to participate may apply to different patient groups depending on whether or not there will be a direct benefit to that participant.

Another crucial distinction between types of research when considering how they are regulated is that between clinical trials and other forms of research. A clinical trial is defined as 'any interventional trial on a human participant that is designed with the object of ascertaining the safety or efficacy of medicinal products'.[7] Therefore, research falling within the definition of a clinical trial will include things like testing a new drug treatment for a particular condition, testing a previously licensed drug for a use other than that for which it is licensed or testing a device used to administer a treatment. It will not cover methods of treatment such as new surgical procedures. This is important because a clinical trial will be regulated by the Clinical Trials Regulations 2004, whereas other forms of research that do not fall within the definition of a clinical trial will be governed by common law principles.

ETHICS QUESTIONS

Is it right for different rules to apply to different types of research on human participants? The testing of a new surgical procedure may be just as risky, invasive and potentially damaging to a patient as a new drug, yet those participating in research into the former have no statutory protection in the UK – can you think of a justification for that?

Also, do we have a right or a duty to participate in medical research? If we have a right to participate, then many commentators, such as Hellman and Hellman, have noted that stringent protections regarding consent are absolutely fundamental.[8] Conversely if we follow the reasoning of duty-based ethicists such as Kant and say we have a duty to take part because of the wider benefits to society, then as Pattinson points out: 'Obtaining consent for such a project can only be a procedural safeguard rather than a principled requirement.'[9] Others such as John Harris agree. He likens the requirement to participate in medical research to the requirement to undertake jury service – people should inconvenience themselves in the wider interests of benefiting society.[10]

Do you take a utilitarian, duty-based position or would you agree more with rights-based theorists such as Hellman and Hellman?

---

[6] Hewlett, S., 'Consent to Clinical Research – Adequately Voluntary or Substantially Influenced', 1996, *Journal of Medical Ethics*, 22, 232.

[7] Reg. 2 Clinical Trials Regulations 2004.

[8] Hellman, S. and Hellman, D. S., 'Of Mice but not Men – Problems of the Randomised Clinical Trial', 1991, *New England Journal of Medicine*, 30, 1585–1589.

[9] Pattinson, S. D., *Medical Law and Ethics*, 3rd edn, 2011, Sweet & Maxwell at p. 387.

[10] Harris, J., 'Scientific Research is a Moral Duty', 2005, *Journal of Medical Ethics*, 31, pp. 242–248.

Yet another definitional distinction should be drawn between medical research where the participant knows what the trial treatment is, when they are getting it and how much they are getting and has given full free consent (see later for further discussion of valid consent) to receiving such treatment and those situations where the patient agrees to take part in a randomised controlled trial (RCT). This is where some of the participants will get the new treatment or drug and others will receive a placebo (a non-active substance, such as sterile water) in order that the researchers have a control group against which the effects of the new treatment can be measured. RCTs can be either blind (where the patient does not know whether they are in the treatment group or the placebo group) or double blind where neither the patient nor the researcher knows which group the patient is in. The scientific value of blind and double blind RCTs is clear. They allow high-quality data to be gathered about the efficacy of a new treatment without the possibility of patient or researcher bias skewing the results. However, they also raise interesting legal and ethical questions about exactly what the patient has consented to. For example, does the patient fully understand that if they are placed in the placebo group, their condition is effectively going untreated and may very well advance at a faster rate as a result (as very often in order to make the research results valid, other treatments have to be stopped). If they have not fully grasped this, they may well not have given valid consent. Such research projects also present ethical dilemmas for the researchers. Many will be working in the speciality involved in the trial and may know the individual patients and be regularly involved in their care. When the patient is trusting that doctor to take care of them and is clearly hoping that this (often last hope) new treatment will either cure or improve their condition, is it ethical for that researcher to knowingly (in a blind trial) administer the placebo? Could it even be argued that it contravenes the Hippocratic Oath and the doctor's duty to do the best for his patient? This is one of the reasons that, often, doctors prefer the double blind RCT. It is also why it is considered good practice to separate clinical treatment from research and have different people treating the patients and conducting the trials. However, the counter argument is that clinicians are better placed to select participants and evaluate results because of their better level of knowledge about individual patients.

The regulatory system

The reality is that this area has been governed over the years by a complex and multi-layered web of legal, ethical and professional guidance that has been variously amended, updated, overturned, misinterpreted, misquoted and ignored. For this reason, at first glance it can seem rather daunting. As such, Table 14.1 attempts to explain what the various bodies are that will be referred to in the rest of this chapter

Table 14.1 Key organisations and documents

Organisation	Known as	Remit
Medicines and Healthcare Products Regulatory Authority	MHRA	Responsible for regulating clinical trials, as well as post-research marketing and use of medical treatments and devices
Gene Therapy Advisory Committee	GTAC	National ethics committee for gene therapy – approval is needed before any trial involving gene therapy may take place (as well as MHRA approval)
Research ethics committees	RECs	Responsible for assessing whether a proposed research project is ethical and giving approval on that basis. RECs do not confirm the legality of the project, just whether or not it is ethically acceptable
Medical Research Council	MRC	Body overseeing medical research and producing non-legal guidance to researchers on regulation and ethics
General Medical Council	GMC	Advises its doctor members on various professional matters including carrying out research, obtaining consent and dealing with vulnerable patient groups
		The guidance is not legally binding but breaches may give rise to professional sanctions

Table 14.2 Key legislation and other documentation

Document	What is it?
Nuremberg Code 1947	Ethical guidelines relating to medical research that came out of the Nuremberg trials of Nazi doctors accused of carrying out experiments on prisoners
Helsinki Declaration 1964	A declaration by the World Medical Association giving advice to researchers on the ethical issues associated with research
	There have been several updates, most recently in 2008
Clinical Trials Regulations 2004	The main piece of domestic legislation regulating clinical trials of medicinal products
Human Rights Act	While not specifically related to medical research, any breach of consent provisions or inappropriate disclosure of information about a participant is likely to breach section 6 of the Act. Similarly anything that constitutes inhuman or degrading treatment or restriction of liberty
Human Tissue Act 2004	Limited application but does create an offence of holding bodily material intending to analyse the DNA in it without appropriate consent

and broadly what their remit is. I then set out the various key pieces of legislation and associated documentation before going on to explain in detail what they contain and how they apply.

Table 14.2 contains a list of key pieces of legislation and other documents that will be referred to in the forthcoming discussion on regulation of research.

There are other documents that have been produced by various professional bodies, such as the MRC,[11] which are not legally binding but that researchers tend to treat as authoritative. There is also a Council of Europe Convention on Human Rights and Biomedicine 2005 but the UK has not signed up to this.

The regulations

The Medicines for Human Use (Clinical Trials) Regulations 2004[12] were passed to implement the European Clinical Trials Directive.[13] They specifically reference the Helsinki Declaration and require compliance with it but, interestingly given the date of the Regulations, they specify compliance with the 1996 version of the Declaration, rather than the 2000 version. This may be because in some areas the 1996 version is more robust, as noted by Pattinson who points out that the 2000 version states that rights and interests of the individual *should* prevail over the interests of society, whereas the 1996 version stated that individual interests *must always* take precedence.

The regulations apply to research involving clinical trials.[14] They nominate the MHRA as the body responsible for overseeing the implementation of the Regulations and require researchers to obtain 'clinical trial authorisation' from the MHRA in order to proceed with a trial.[15] Breach of this requirement is a criminal offence. The regulations also require researchers to comply with what it calls 'good clinical practice' and goes on to set out what this is in Schedule 2. Effectively it takes the principles set out in the Helsinki Declaration and other pieces of professional guidance on good practice and incorporates them into the legislation. Clearly, the aim of this is to protect the rights of individual participants. However, the regulations are not perfect and many researchers feel that they have hindered scientific progress. For example, the issue of the use of placebos was discussed earlier. The 2008 version of the Helsinki Declaration cautioned researchers to be careful about their use and required clear justification, but recognised that there were some circumstances in which their use was legitimate. This included not only situations where no current proven intervention exists, but also where there were compelling scientific reasons for using it and there was no risk of serious or irreversible harm. However, the 1996 version had been more restrictive, only allowing their use where there was no other proven intervention available to the patient and this is the version that the regulations require researchers to follow.

---

[11] 'Guidelines for Good Clinical Practice in Clinical Trials' 1998.
[12] 2004/1031.
[13] 2001/20/EC.
[14] Reg. 2.
[15] Reg. 12.

One of the key requirements imposed by the regulations is that the proposed trial must be approved by a research ethics committee (REC). Lots of these committees had operated for many years on a non-statutory basis, some being part of the NHS and others being set up by private healthcare providers and other medical and research organisations. The regulations require REC approval for clinical trials,[16] but RECs also consider applications regarding non-clinical trial research such as projects looking at empirical data and new surgical techniques etc. RECS are governed by the National Research Ethics Service (NRES), which issues standard operating procedures that all NHS RECs must adhere to. The latest version of these[17] makes it very clear that the stringent requirements imposed by the regulations relating to clinical trials should be applied to all research projects that come before a REC. As such, over the last 12 months or so, there has been a general tightening up of REC scrutiny of all research projects. This may lend some weight to the recent assertion by the Academy of Medical Sciences that the introduction of the Regulations has: 'increased the administrative burden and cost of clinical trials for both non-commercial and commercial sponsors with no discernible improvements to patient safety or to the ethical basis of clinical trials.'[18]

When we are talking about scrutiny carried out by RECs, it should be remembered that this is scrutiny of the ethics of the proposed research project, not the legality of it. Indeed, at least one-third of the membership of the REC is required to be laypersons, with the rest being medical and research professionals. It is very unlikely that there will be anyone with an expert knowledge of the law present when the project is discussed. The issue of whether the project should automatically be rejected if potential illegality is spotted has been hotly debated for the last few years. NRES takes the view that the REC has a duty to point out the potential illegality to the researchers involved but that it is the responsibility of those researchers to seek proper legal advice and not the place of the REC to offer such advice. Therefore, as far as NRES is concerned, the REC can approve the project, even where a potential illegality has been found.[19] This is extremely controversial and potentially gives rise to some complex legal issues. For example, judicial review of decisions regarding treatment was considered in Chapter 4. This is a mechanism by which a person who feels a decision of a public body was illegal (or irrational or procedurally inappropriate) can challenge the validity of that decision before the court. Given the broad definition of a public body as any organisation exercising public functions, it seems clear that an REC would be open to judicial review claims and if it gave approval for a project that contravened the Human Tissue Act or the Data Protection

---

[16] Reg. 49.
[17] Dated May 2010.
[18] 'A New Pathway for the Regulation and Governance of Health Research', AMS, January 2011.
[19] See Standard Operating Procedures for Research Ethics Committees, May 2010, para. 11.9.

Act (or the Human Rights Act for that matter), this would seem on the surface to be a classic case of illegality. This remains to be tested since the introduction of the HRA and the Clinical Trials Regulations, but previously in 1988, a hospital ethics committee was the subject of a judicial review claim when a woman challenged the decision to refuse her fertility treatment as being irrational on the grounds that she had once, 20 years previous to her application, been convicted of prostitution-related offences.[20] Ultimately, the position taken by the RECs on the issue of legality has been criticised by many commentators. Roy-Toole has stated: 'There is no value in an ethics committee unless it can and does protect the research subject from the illegality of research and especially if the legal rights of the subject are violated by it.'[21]

Consent

This is the underpinning principle of the whole system and is a non-negotiable requirement for an adult of sound mind entering into a clinical trial. Given that RECs are now applying similar standards to non-clinical trial research projects, it is likely that all medical research is effectively subject to the consent requirements set out in the regulations. That said, the regulations themselves are rather vague about what valid consent is, merely requiring it to be freely given and adding little to the common law position discussed in detail in Chapter 6. This, it will be recalled, allows an adult of sound mind to consent or refuse medical treatment and to do whatever he chooses with his own body, even if that decision appears unwise to observers and even where harm will be caused to that person. The regulations do go on to require that sufficient detail and information is given to the participant about the nature, significance, implications and risks of the research being carried out and failure to do so can lead to criminal liability.[22] However, they are not required to divulge any conflicts of interest or institutional affiliations as they would be under the 2008 version of the Helsinki Declaration. The regulations appear to be trying very hard to strike a balance between protection of participants and progression and encouragement of research. Ultimately, they uphold the common law principle of patient autonomy and the free will of a person to choose to take risks with his safety and health.

Children

Non-clinical trial research
Imagine a couple are getting divorced. They have a 5-year-old son and during the course of the divorce proceedings there is a dispute about the paternity of the child.

---

[20] *R v Ethical Committee of St Mary's Hospital ex parte Harriott* [1988] 1 FLR 512.
[21] Roy-Toole, C., 'Illegality in the research protocol: the duty of research ethics committees under the 2001 Clinical Trials Directive', 2008, *Research Ethics Review*, 4(3), pp. 111–116.
[22] Sch. 1 pt 3.

Should that child be subjected to a paternity test (involving blood being taken from his arm and analysed) in order to facilitate the divorce settlement and the issue of child support? He clearly cannot consent himself. The *Gillick* case established that a child who is sufficiently mature to understand the nature of the medical procedure and the consequences of consenting to it may give valid consent but it is very unlikely that a 5-year-old would satisfy those criteria. This was the situation in *S v S*.[23] While in general, the courts take the view that any intervention must be in the child's best interests (as variously defined), here the House of Lords felt that the tests could be lawful as long as they were not 'against the interests' of the child. It must be said that this case very much goes against the grain of most other judgments in relation to medical treatment and children, and its status as an authority for the fact that research may be carried out on children with parental consent as long as it is not against their interests is debatable.[24]

Indeed, even with older children, the situation is complicated because the *Gillick* case does not mention medical research, and as far as this author is concerned, it is rather a big leap to say that the concept of *Gillick* competence applies to such research – it does not seem that this is what the judges intended. Certainly, they do not specifically include participation in medical research in the judgment. Similarly, Section 8 of the Family Law Reform Act which declares children over the age of 16 as capable of giving valid consent to treatment mentions nothing about research. Thus, it is highly doubtful that a child under 18 can ever give valid consent to participate in a clinical trial or other medical research project.

ETHICS QUESTIONS

If a child can consent validly and legally to a heart transplant, should they not also be able to consent to participating in a trial of a new drug aimed at curing their heart condition? Is such a restriction justified? Is the aim of protecting children from being exploited in the course of medical research worth the risk of restricting access to children for clinical trials and thus making new treatments for children more difficult to develop? Will it ultimately result in poorer standards of treatment for children?

One of the few relevant cases on research or experimental treatment in potentially competent children is the case of *Simms*.

---

[23] [1972] AC 24.
[24] Although the MRC and other professional bodies treat it very much as authority for that point.

KEY CASE

Simms v Simms[25]

This involved the devastating illness, Creutzfeldt-Jakob Disease (otherwise known as 'mad cow disease' or CJD). Material from infected animals had been used in the manufacture of a treatment for growth retardation that had been given to many young people prior to discovery of the problem in the 1980s. In the *Simms* case, a 16-year-old and an 18-year-old sufferer wanted to consent to the use of a drug that, while long used and tested in the treatment of other conditions, was very experimental in the treatment of CJD – indeed, it had only ever been tried on rodents. This was a golden opportunity for the court to clarify the position regarding young people and their ability to consent to participation in medical research, but, unfortunately for our purposes, the court decided to classify the proposed course of action as experimental treatment, rather than therapeutic research. Thus it approached the consent issue as it would with any risky treatment that a young person was consenting to. As both were over 16, the FLR Act stated that they should be assumed competent to consent. The court also looked at the fact that the experimental use of the drug was in the patients' best interests because there was no other known treatment that would cure or improve their condition, so it was really their only chance. This last point is important because had it not been deemed to be in their best interests (for example, because they were refusing another, more proven treatment in order to try this experimental approach), the court could have overturned the decision of the young patients.[26]

There has been much comment on the *Simms* case, with some trying to extrapolate principles that might apply in the context of children and consent to medical research. For example, Pattinson states that: 'It displays a willingness on the part of the courts to apply the best interests test flexibly.'[27] In the view of this author, it displays the opposite. The court applied the best interests test as it would in any treatment situation (which is what it classified this case as) and overtly left the issue of children consenting to research unresolved. While in other cases the court has been prepared to widen the definition of best interests beyond medical interests and to look at social and psychological factors alongside that,[28] it has been conspicuously silent on the issue of children consenting to research projects and for that reason, caution should be exercised when taking principles from cases such as *Simms* and *Re Y* and trying to make them fit a research situation. In a US case, *Curran*

---

[25] [2002] EWHC 2734.
[26] See Chapter 5 and cases such as *Re W* [1993] Fam 64.
[27] n. 8 at 415.
[28] For example, see *Re Y* [1997] Fam 110 where an incapacitated adult was subjected to painful and invasive removal of bone marrow because saving her sister would strengthen her relationship with her family.

v *Bosze*, it was stated that altruism on the part of the child, i.e. wanting to help others suffering from similar conditions or wanting to contribute to medical knowledge, was not enough to classify an experimental treatment as in the child's best interests, although the court did restrict its assertion to non-therapeutic research and, clearly, its persuasiveness in the UK is debatable. Effectively then, consent will need to be sought from those with parental responsibility and, perhaps in some cases, a declaration from the court may be required before the project proceeds. Of course, we are talking here about non-clinical trial projects, i.e. those that fall outside the Clinical Trials Regulations (which are discussed in relation to vulnerable groups later).

Mentally incapacitated adults

The Mental Capacity Act 2005 (MCA) applies to all those aged 16 years and over and states that they are assumed to have capacity to consent unless there is evidence to the contrary.[29] It sets out tests for capacity and a checklist to help the assessment of what is in the patient's best interests.[30] However, unlike the position relating to children, it has a specific section dealing with the participation of those lacking capacity in medical research. It makes clear that it does not apply to those projects covered by the Clinical Trials Regulations, but otherwise provides that intrusive research that would be illegal to carry out on a competent adult without consent must not be carried out on such patients unless it is done within a specified framework approved by an REC.[31] The MCA also specifies that both therapeutic and non-therapeutic research can potentially be carried out on incapacitated patients if it meets the criteria set out in the Act. However, if the research is non-therapeutic (i.e. it will not provide a direct health benefit to the participant), then it must:

- be intended to provide knowledge that will benefit those affected by the same or a similar condition

- pose a negligible risk to the participant

- not significantly interfere with the participant's freedom or privacy or be unduly invasive or restrictive.[32]

The Act provides further protection in that if the participant shows any sign of unwillingness to cooperate they must be withdrawn. It also requires that any third party such as those appointed under an LPA and giving consent on their behalf must confirm that the patient would want to participate in such a project, taking into account previously known views.[33]

---

[29] Section 1.
[30] Sections 2, 3 and 4.
[31] Section 30.
[32] Section 31(5)(b)(6).
[33] Section 32.

Clinical trials and vulnerable groups

If a research project is classified as a clinical trial and the regulations apply to it, the rules on consent in relation to children and incapacitated adults may differ from those outlined earlier. In relation to mentally incapacitated adults, there is no provision for non-therapeutic clinical trials to be carried out on them unless the researcher can say there are absolutely no risks to the patient. As such, the option that is open to researchers carrying out research into a new surgical technique will not be open to a researcher looking to develop a new drug treatment. There is no immediately obvious rationale for this distinction. With therapeutic research, consent will need to be obtained from someone who has been appointed under an LPA or another person close to the patient who can act as a legal representative.[34] Similarly in relation to children, the regulations make it very clear that they cannot consent to participation in a clinical trial. Thus while academics and doctors argue about the validity of a child's consent to other types of research, there is never an option of a child giving valid consent to a clinical trial. Consent must be sought from someone with parental responsibility.

Enforcement

Where the research involved is a clinical trial under the regulations, the MHRA will have certain powers of enforcement. The trial can be suspended if there is any concern about the safety or the scientific validity of the project and infringement notices can be served on researchers if they breach any of their duties, such as failure to report any adverse events or to comply with the terms of their licence. Breach of some of these is actually a criminal offence under the regulations but it should be noted that liability can be avoided if the researcher can show that all reasonable precautions were taken and due diligence exercised.[35]

If the patient is taking part in any research project within the NHS and that has been cleared by a REC, there is always the theoretical possibility of a negligence

[34] Sch. 1 pt 5.
[35] Reg. 51.

claim if any adverse consequences ensue for the patient. However, negligence is notoriously difficult to prove,[36] especially where you might be dealing with a drug or treatment where little is known about its effect on the body and the patient is already in poor health or suffering from a serious condition. How do you prove that participation in the research actually caused the harm they suffer? Does the REC even owe a duty of care to the participants? Generally, English law does not recognise duties to third parties where those third parties are not identifiable, on the basis that you cannot owe a duty to the wider world.[37] There are no cases on record of an REC or indeed an NHS trust being successfully sued in such a situation. The only situation where a negligence claim is potentially stronger is where the researcher is carrying out a project that falls under the Clinical Trials Regulations, which require indemnity insurance as a pre-requisite to approval to proceed with the project. However, the strength of a negligence claim against the individual researcher remains largely untested in English law because common practice is to automatically award compensation for any adverse event suffered by the patient as a result of the research without their having to resort to litigation.[38]

A claim that sufficient information was negligently not given to the participant, thus rendering the consent invalid, may stand a better chance, especially in light of recent cases in negligence that have attributed great importance to patient information. For example, in *Chester* v *Afshar*,[39] the patient alleged that she had not been warned about the small risk of long-term effects of the spinal surgery that was being proposed. Even though she admitted that she would still have gone ahead with the operation, albeit perhaps on a different day, and that the surgery was carried out perfectly proficiently, her negligence claim was upheld – the negligent failure to inform her of that small risk was deemed to have caused the ultimate damage that she suffered. While some judges admitted very openly in the judgment that the decision was influenced by 'policy reasons', it does indicate that there may be some flexibility in the application of the negligence rules when it comes to failure to give adequate information to patients, and if a research participant's claim is couched in those terms, they may arguably have a better chance of a successful outcome.

One final offence should be noted. Section 45 of the Human Tissue Act 2004 makes it illegal to hold human material intending to analyse its DNA without appropriate qualifying consent, unless the intention is to treat that particular patient. This is a rather strangely drafted provision and reflects the preoccupation of the government of the day when it was passed to reassure the public that nothing would be done with any tissue sample without explicit consent. The Act is discussed in Chapter 13 in relation to organ donation and holding of human tissue generally.

---

[36] See Chapter 3.
[37] See *Palmer* v *Tees Health Authority* [2000] 2 LGLR 69.
[38] See Association of the British Pharmaceutical Industry, 'Clinical Trial Compensation Guidelines', 1991.
[39] Discussed in detail in Chapter 3.

Summary

Medical research is a complex process and is thus complex to regulate. However, science is moving fast and the regulation must keep up in order to adequately protect the interests of participants while avoiding the so called 'brain drain' of scientists moving to other, more permissive jurisdictions in order to carry out their work. Clearly, as far as the Academy of Medical Sciences is concerned, regulation is already hampering the scientific community too much. However, we return to arguments rehearsed throughout this book about inequality of bargaining power between doctors and patients and in particular here to the concept of 'therapeutic misconception'. Laypeople do not understand the science of high-level research in the same way that doctors do. They do not always completely comprehend what it is they are consenting to and they often mistakenly perceive that participation in research will bring a benefit that never materialises. Therefore, we must be very careful to ensure that we maintain a very tight control on the types of research that can be carried out and on how patients are protected while participating in such research. Adverse events and tragedies can never be completely prevented but we have a responsibility, particularly in relation to vulnerable patient groups, to ensure that they are minimised.

Self-test questions

1 What is a randomised controlled trial (RCT)?

2 What is the difference between therapeutic and non-therapeutic research?

3 Define a clinical trial.

4 Explain a duty-based ethical theorist's view on participation in medical research.

5 Can a child consent to participate in medical research?

6 Can a clinical trial be carried out on a mentally incapacitated patient?

7 Does a research ethics committee owe a duty of care to participants in the research it approves?

8 Can a research project that contains illegal elements receive ethical approval from an REC?

Practice essay question

The regulation of medical research may very well stifle innovation that might result in positive medical advances, but that is a price worth paying for ensuring people's rights are adequately protected.

Critically assess the extent to which you agree or disagree with this statement in relation to the regulation of medical research in England and Wales.

Practice problem question

Amelia is 17 years old and has suffered from anorexia nervosa for several years. This is a psychiatric condition that causes sufferers to restrict their intake of food, ultimately causing many to starve to death or suffer heart failure and other complications due to malnutrition and dehydration. Dr Roberts is a clinician and researcher at Amelia's local hospital and is testing a new anti-depressant drug that he believes may alleviate some of the effects of anorexia in young people by correcting a chemical imbalance in the brain. At one of Amelia's regular hospital visits, he asks if she would be interested in participating in the study. Amelia refuses on the grounds that, if he corrects the imbalance, she might start putting on weight and she does not want that to happen. She understands that other treatments have failed, that she is dangerously underweight and that her life is in danger but still refuses to consent. Her father becomes very angry at her refusal and tells her that while she is still a minor, he will decide what is best for her, and he signs the consent form allowing the experimental drug to be given to her.

Amelia agrees to give it a try, albeit reluctantly, and goes to a treatment room with a nurse. The nurse begins to explain what the drug is and some possible side-effects but Amelia replies that she doesn't care, she is just taking it to keep her dad happy and she doesn't want to know anything about it. She takes the tablet and then returns home. Some hours later she complains that she feels very tired and nauseated. Her father, still angry and upset, tells her she must expect that when she has not eaten all day. He goes to bed at around 11 p.m. When he goes to wake Amelia for college in the morning he finds her unconscious in bed. An ambulance is called and the crew attempt resuscitation but Amelia dies in the ambulance on the way to hospital. It later becomes clear that one of the ingredients in the experimental drug can speed up a patient's heart rate, and as Amelia's heart was already very weakened, it was not able to pump blood around her body at the rate required and could not withstand the strain.

Discuss any possible liability arising out of Amelia's death.

Index